Robert Pinget

Twayne's World Authors Series
French Literature

David O'Connell, Editor
Georgia State University

TWAS 842

ROBERT PINGET
Courtesy A.P.P.M. Agence photographique, Paris.

Robert Pinget

Léonard A. Rosmarin

Brock University

Twayne Publishers
An Imprint of Simon & Schuster Macmillan
New York

Prentice Hall International
London Mexico City New Delhi Singapore Sydney Toronto

Robert Pinget
Léonard A. Rosmarin

Twayne Publishers
An Imprint of Simon & Schuster Macmillan
866 Third Avenue
New York, New York 10022

Library of Congress Cataloging-in-Publication Data

Rosmarin, Léonard A.
    Robert Pinget / Léonard A. Rosmarin.
        p.   cm. — (Twayne's world authors series ; TWAS 842)
    Includes bibliographical references and index.
    ISBN 0–8057–4537–8
    1. Pinget, Robert—Criticism and interpretation.   I. Title.
    II. Series.
    PQ2631.I638Z86   1995
843'.914—dc20   94–24098
                                                                                      CIP

10 9 8 7 6 5 4 3 2 1

Printed in the United States of America.

Contents

Acknowledgments

I wish to thank Professor Jean-Claude Liéber for sharing with me his wealth of knowledge of the French New Novel in general and of Robert Pinget's works in particular. I would also like to thank my wife, Beatrice, for the unfailing patience with which she read the various drafts of my manuscript, and the equally unfailing support she gave me while the book was being written. I wish to express my gratitude to Professor Alexandre Amprimoz for his encouragement and advice. Finally, my heartfelt thanks go to the subject of this book, Robert Pinget, who graciously granted me several interviews and inspired me with renewed enthusiasm for his works.

Chronology

1919	Robert André John Pinget, first child of Blanche Montant and Emile Pinget, is born in Geneva on 19 July.
1920–1925	Births of his sisters Josette and Blanche-Marie and his brother Jacques.
1931–1938	Pursues classical secondary studies (literature, Greek, Latin) at the Collège de Genève. Plays the cello and writes poems.
1938–1941	Studies law at the Université de Genève.
1942–1944	Receives practical training as a lawyer.
1944	Is called to the bar.
1944–1945	Practices law in Geneva.
1946	Moves to Paris. Enrolls in the Ecole des Beaux-Arts to study painting.
1946–1949	Travels to Spain, Morocco, and Tunisia (1946); Greece (1947); Yugoslavia (1948), where he participates in the construction of a railroad; and Israel, (1949), where he works on a kibbutz.
1950	Exhibit of his paintings in a gallery in Saint-Germain-des-Prés. Very soon he gives up painting to devote himself to literature.
1950–1953	Performs literary odd jobs to make ends meet (for Maurice Nadeau, *Jours de France*, the Bompiani-Laffont dictionary).
1951	*Entre Fantoine et Agapa* is published by Editions de Feu in Jarnac (picked up by Editions de Minuit in 1956).
1952	*Mahu, ou le matériau* is published without much success (picked up by Editions de Minuit in 1956).
1953	Meets Albert Camus, who agrees to publish *Le Renard et la boussole* for Gallimard. Raymond Queneau refuses the manuscript of *Graal Flibuste*, which bears the title of *Forêt de Grance*.

1955   Meets Samuel Beckett, who will become one of his closest friends. Spends nine months in London. Accepts all kinds of temporary jobs to feed himself, including messenger and tutor. Returns to Paris.

1955   *Graal Flibuste* is published by Editions de Minuit, where Alain Robbe-Grillet is a reader. Henceforth this same publishing house will put out all of Pinget's works.

1958   *Baga* is published by Editions de Minuit.

1959   Publishes a novel, *Le Fiston*, as well as a play, *Lettre morte*, from which a film will be made in 1988. He appears with Alain Robbe-Grillet, Claude Simon, Claude Mauriac, Samuel Beckett, Nathalie Sarraute, Claude Ollier, and their editor, Jérôme Lindon, in the famous photo taken on Lindon's initiative in front of Editions de Minuit, rue Bernard-Palissy. This photo "officializes" the *Nouveau Roman*.

1960   Pinget retrieves his French citizenship, which his maternal grandfather and paternal great-grandfather had given up. Keeps his Swiss citizenship. Spends two months in the United States and Mexico. Attends the production of *Lettre morte* in New York by the Théâtre Récamier, then directed by Jean Vilar. Publishes the play *La Manivelle*, which Samuel Beckett translates as *The Old Tune*.

1961   Publishes *Clope au dossier* and the plays *Ici ou ailleurs, L'Hypothèse*, and *Architruc*.

1962   At the request of Jérôme Lindon, publishes a lengthy novel of 511 pages, *L'Inquisitoire*, which renews the aesthetic of the contemporary novel. He wins the Prix des Critiques for this work after narrowly missing the Prix Fémina.

1964   Takes up residence in Touraine. Spends his time between Paris and the country.

1965   Receives the Prix Fémina for *Quelqu'un*. Publishes the series of dramatic dialogues *Autour de Mortin*.

1965–1970   Travels to the United States, Finland, Holland, England, and Italy.

1968   Publishes *Le Libera*.

1969   Publishes *Passacaille*. Becomes a corresponding member of the Academy of Mainz (Germany).

1970   Father dies.

1970–1971   Publishes *Identité*. *Abel et Bela* is produced by the Théâtre de l'Absidiole. One evening the author replaces one of the actors. He joins the company on a tour of most of the Eastern European countries. Publishes *Fable, Paralchimie*, and *Abel et Bela*. Participates in the Colloque de Cerisy on the *Nouveau Roman*. *Architruc* is performed by the Comédie-Française.

1973   Publishes *Nuit*.

1975   Publishes *Cette voix* and *L'Apocryphe*.

1982   Publishes *Monsieur Songe*. On 30 September and 1 and 2 October participates in the Colloquium on the Nouveau Roman in New York, along with Robbe-Grillet, Claude Simon, and Nathalie Sarraute. Receives the Legion of Honor. Red Dust Editions in New York undertakes the translation and publication of his works.

1983–1986   Travels to South Korea, Japan, and Mauritius.

1984   Publishes *Le Harnais*.

1985   Publishes *Charrue*.

1986   Publishes *Un Testament bizarre*. Public readings of his works in London.

1987   Is one of the featured authors at the Avignon Festival. *Lettre morte* and *La Manivelle* are successfully mounted. *L'Hypothèse* is a triumph. The author is finally making some money. Publishes *L'Ennemi*. In December, receives the Grand Prix National des Lettres.

1988   In February five of Pinget's plays are performed at the Ubu Repertory Theater in New York City. The author engages in discussions with the audience after performances of *Abel et Bela*, *Architruc*, *L'Hypothèse*, *Lettre morte*, and *La Manivelle*. On 18 July French television networks FR3 and La Sept profile Pinget in the program "Océaniques."

1989   Receives the Ordre du Mérite. *Monsieur Songe* is adapt-
       ed for the stage by Anne-Brigitte Kern and Pinget and
       is staged at the Théâtre de Poche-Montparnasse in
       Paris. Mother dies in July; Beckett dies in December.
       Presents readings from his works in London. Is inter-
       viewed by the BBC World Service French Section.

1990   Publishes *Du nerf*. Receives the Grand Prix National
       des Lettres for the whole of his literary production.
       Receives in Geneva the Grand Prix de la Création.

1991   *A Tribute to Robert Pinget* is staged in London at the
       Théâtre Artaud of the Institut Français on 12, 13, and
       14 February. Pinget performs his play *De rien* with
       Peter Gale in a bilingual version, in Barbara Wright's
       English translation. In October publishes *Théo, ou le
       temps neuf*.

1992   Stage adaptation of his novel *L'Inquisitoire* in Lausanne.
       The play triumphs in Paris at the Théâtre de la Bastille.
       On 18 June reads excerpts from his works at the
       Centre Pompidou in Paris. On 16 October in Limoges
       gives a reading of his most recent novel, *Théo, ou le temps
       neuf*, under the auspices of "Fureur de Lire."

1993   Makes slow recovery after an automobile accident.

Chapter One

A Voice of Many Tones

Biography and Portrait

Unlike many writers who enjoy baring their souls to the media and seek
the status of *monstre sacré*, Robert Pinget remains impenetrably discreet
about his private life. Ever since he acquired a certain celebrity in the literary world, he has managed to keep sensation-hungry reporters at bay.
Back in 1965 during an interview with L. A. Zbinden of the *Gazette de
Lausanne*, Pinget made it abundantly clear that questions of a personal
nature were irrelevant:

> It seems to me that when one is drawn to a writer it is not his biography
> which is interesting. I am always astonished that people approach a writer
> with questions which have nothing, or very little to do with his works. I
> have no life other than my writing. My existence is in my books. [. . .] A
> Writer's life reveals itself in what he writes. If you read *Quelqu'un*, you
> will know who I am.[1]

On another occasion he stated flatly, "I don't like pouring my heart
out." And in 1990, when asked by Madeleine Renouard whether a
writer's life should have any importance for critics, he replied, "None, as
far as I'm concerned."[2] The same year I was to discover for myself how
tenaciously Robert Pinget still clings to his privacy. He very graciously
granted me an interview in his somewhat spartan yet whimsically fur-
nished apartment on the Left Bank of Paris. The moment I tried to
direct our conversation toward personal matters, his kindly face took on
an expression of dismay and weariness as though to say, "Must we go
through this again?" I promised then and there that I would no longer
try to hound him into a corner, and the rest of the interview went
beautifully.

Because it is not possible to provide a full account of Robert Pinget's
life, we must make do with whatever biographical material is available.[3]
I will supplement this information, however, by sketching his psychological and artistic portrait.

1

Born in Geneva in 1919, Pinget enjoyed an immensely satisfying childhood, surrounded by a large, affectionate family, which he still loves and frequently visits. His mother was perhaps his closest friend. It was she who advised him to go to Paris in order to realize his creative potential. As a child, he revealed considerable talents for drawing, music, and poetry. He also became such a voracious reader that his mother once asked him whether any gifts other than books interested him. He obtained a law degree but soon discovered that the legal profession did not suit his temperament. He did, though, acquire from his experience as a lawyer rigor and precision in his use of language. In 1946 he decided to study painting at the Ecole des Beaux-Arts in Paris and even produced an exhibit of his works that earned critical plaudits. But several years later he gave up a promising artistic career just as easily as he had abandoned law. In a conversation with Jean Roudaut, he explained that he had never stopped writing, and it eventually occurred to him that he was probably more authentic and less influenced by other people's styles as a writer than as a painter.[4] Before making a complete commitment to the art of writing, however, he did try out various other lines of work, including journalism and interior decorating, where his sensitivity to detail must have been quite an asset. He traveled to Yugoslavia and Israel, where he spent some time on a kibbutz. He even taught various subjects in a secondary school near London, all the while attempting to master the English language in order to keep up with his students.

During this transitional period the swirling configurations of his imaginary world were beginning to take shape. His first book, *Entre Fantoine et Agapa*, a collection of short stories fairly bristling with surrealistic pranks, was accepted for publication in 1951 by the obscure provincial firm Editions de Feu. He had to underwrite the cost of the enterprise himself, but at least this way he had the satisfaction of seeing his work in print. His second text, the novel *Mahu, ou le matériau*, published by Robert Laffont, barely caused a ripple.

The author's third work, the novel *Le Renard et la boussole* (*The Fox and the Compass*), had better luck. It found a champion in no less a literary luminary than Albert Camus, who urged his publisher, Gallimard, to submit it for an important award given out annually in France. Fortune looked upon him even more favorably in 1956 when his next novel, *Graal Flibuste*, was accepted by Jérôme Lindon of Editions de Minuit on the recommendation of Alain Robbe-Grillet, perhaps the most influential of the avant-garde writers at the time. Robbe-Grillet would become a good friend. Thus began a remarkable partnership between Pinget and a publishing house unafraid of innovation and risk-taking. Having served as an underground press during the Resistance against the Nazi occupation, it was perfectly natural and indeed appropriate for Editions de Minuit to further the careers of the most unorthodox French authors of the postwar period. Lindon demanded that some passages of *Graal Flibuste* be removed as a condition for the text being published. Pinget agreed to these changes only when it became obvious to him that the alternative would be even worse: not getting the book printed at all. Eventually Lindon saw the wisdom of reprinting the novel in its original version and even reissued Pinget's first three texts under the aegis of his publishing firm. He has since then handled all of the writer's production, which, as of 1992, totaled 30 novels, short narratives, plays, and *carnets* (notebooks).

No doubt because of the very innovative nature of his talent, recognition was long in coming to the author. The average French reader was caught off guard by the ambiguous atmosphere of narratives that seemed to lure him on with the promise of a "normal," linear plot, only to pull the rug from under his feet less than half-way through and send him somersaulting into a realm of pure fantasy. Surprisingly enough, during the first stages of his career, Pinget enjoyed far more popularity abroad, especially in Great Britain, Germany, and the United States, where the Ford Foundation sponsored one of his visits. The British Broadcasting Corporation (BBC) and Radio Stuttgart were eager to put on his radio plays. He was understandably hurt by the contrast between this enthusiastic reception in other countries and the indifference his texts suffered at home. It seemed incongruous to him that the bold experiments of the French New Novelists could be hailed by critics in London and greeted with derision by their counterparts in Paris.

The tide began to turn in 1960. On the advice of Samuel Beckett, who would become a very dear friend, Pinget at the age of 40 tried his hand at writing plays. Aroused by his percussive, extremely witty dialogues, his countrymen finally took notice. Then came more official recognition. In 1963 his longest novel, *L'Inquisitoire* (*The Inquisitory*), received the Prix des Critiques, and in 1965 *Quelqu'un* (*Someone*), perhaps his most representative work, was awarded the Prix Fémina. The French government bestowed another honor on him in 1975 through the Centre National de Lettres by granting him a one-year sabbatical income, which only a handful of French writers are fortunate enough to receive in any given year. He was thus able to pursue his creative activity without being plagued by financial anxieties.

As time went on, Pinget's stature as a novelist and playwright continued to grow. Prominent critics both in France and abroad devoted perceptive articles to his work. The Comédie-Française, one of the country's most venerable institutions, began performing his dramatic texts. In 1987 his reputation reached new heights. The prestigious Avignon Festival arranged its program around his plays, enlisting the talents of some of the finest French actors to bring them to life. (Pinget could remark facetiously that he was at last earning enough money from his writing to be able to pay income tax.) By 1990 the author had become one of the glories of French letters. Signs advertising his latest play, *Monsieur Songe*, could be seen on local Paris buses, French television had presented many of his dramatic works, theses on his books were being defended at universities all over the world, radio and television programs were being devoted to him, and France honored him with a special award in recognition of his outstanding artistic attainments.

All this acclaim has not altered his exceptional modesty and open-mindedness. A man of strong convictions, Pinget is nevertheless willing to reassess them if his opponent can bring forward convincing arguments to the contrary. He revealed this admirable trait during the lengthy and sometimes heated discussions he had with two friends, the stage director Jacques Seiler and Seiler's wife, Anne-Brigitte Kern, about adapting *Monsieur Songe* for the theater. He seemed adamant in his refusal to allow his personage—a crotchety, self-deluding, would-be writer—to be split into two characters for greater dramatic effectiveness. He insisted that the idea would never work. Yet after an evening of apparently fruitless discussions with them, he continued mulling the possibility, and at three o'clock the next morning he phoned them to say that he agreed, albeit reluctantly, to let them try the experiment. The rest was history. Pinget's receptiveness to new concepts resulted in a smash hit not only with the critics but with theatergoers.

The acclaim he has been enjoying in recent years and of which *Monsieur Songe* is an example can be viewed retrospectively as a vindication of the courage he has always shown in pursuing his artistic ideals. There were many times during his long career when he was barely able to make ends meet. Nevertheless, penury never deterred him from following a course he firmly believed the right one—indeed, the only one—for him. Rather than compromise to curry the favor of his public, he waited patiently until the public was ready to meet him on his own terms.

The unswerving commitment to his particular conception of literature does not entail any dogmatism on his part. He may prefer to write novels which, shunning reality, unfold like musical compositions. But he is far too enlightened a person to insist that his way is either the best or the only one available to the creative writer. In fact, he readily acknowledges that the younger generation of readers is swinging back to the more traditional literary forms, and he does not hesitate to recognize talent in authors like Jean-Paul Sartre and Albert Camus, whose objectives were radically different from his own.

Although Pinget may turn his back on the "real" world when conjuring up his literary vision, his life is not hermetically sealed. For him, art belongs to one realm and daily living to another. Besides, however far removed his novels may be from reality, he readily acknowledges that he draws his raw material from it. The keen interest he takes in contemporary events was in evidence during the crisis that followed the desecration of the Jewish cemetery in Carpentras in 1990. He not only expressed sympathy for the Jewish community in France but admiration of the chief rabbi, Joseph Sitruk, who in a televised address found just the right words to calm inflamed passions and reassure his fellow Jews that the vast majority of their countrymen, regardless of their particular religious affiliations, shared their sorrow and sense of outrage.

Pinget extends this same receptiveness and sensitivity to his various personal relationships. Being extremely discreet, he is loath to pour out his soul on this or any other matter. But it is obvious that he views friendship as one of the few necessary luxuries. It represents a long-standing commitment to other human beings, bringing with it joy and solace. In a book of conversations entitled *Robert Pinget à la lettre*,[5] the author confides to his interviewer, Madeleine Renouard, that he could never have survived, emotionally and artistically, without the support of friends. Love may be a more pleasurable experience, but it will not last, according to Pinget, unless it deepens into the kind of tenderness only friendship can offer.

Undoubtedly Samuel Beckett was for him the ideal friend. The author of *En attendant Godot* (*Waiting for Godot*) was a man of exceptional generosity and kindness. These moral qualities were enhanced by a profound intelligence, a lively wit, and sense of humor. Finally, "Sam," as Pinget affectionately called him, served as a model of professionalism to emulate. While Beckett did not influence his younger friend's artistic vision, the uncompromising integrity and striving for perfection he showed in pursuing his career as a writer would leave a lasting impression on Pinget. Given Pinget's horror of death, it is understandable that he was devastated when Beckett died. The poverty and solitude in which

Sam's life ebbed away bore a heartbreaking resemblance to the plight of Beckett's characters.

At such terrible moments the author's devotion to his art has brought him not only solace but a reason to go on living. Indeed, writing is a vital necessity for Pinget because through it he plumbs his subconscious depths in a never-ending quest for the secret of his identity, and yet at the same time this quest links him, through time and space, to all of his fellow creatures, past and present. "My work is my safeguard in this lowly world," he told Jean Roudaut (Roudaut, 97). Creating, then, is as necessary to Pinget as breathing. "The carrot makes the donkey move forward," he remarked half-jokingly, "the secret to be discovered keeps me alive" (Roudaut, 96).

The author candidly admitted to me, however, that this creative process has become increasingly painful with age simply because he has become far more demanding on himself. Up to five rewrites of a given manuscript are not uncommon. He also readily acknowledged a feeling of strangeness toward novels that he produced several decades ago, as though the person who created them at that time and the one rereading them many years later were very different. Added to these difficulties is the awareness that the writer, elaborating as he does his artistic visions in solitude, may represent a dissonance in the world of his fellow man. As Pinget explained to Roudaut, to be a false note in human society may cause suffering for any artist who lacks the ability to adapt to it. He may feel disinherited in that respect. Nevertheless, artists are certainly not false notes within the context of the universe, since they alone possess the talent to exalt it.[6]

Robert Pinget is obviously endowed with such a talent. Although he probes the mysteries of our human condition in an intensely personal manner, he has been influenced, directly or indirectly, by other creative minds. Aside from Virgil, some of whose verses found their way into his novel *L'Apocryphe*, and Rabelais, whose snowballing verbal effects he imitated in *Graal Flibuste*, the most venerable source of inspiration has been Cervantes. His *Don Quixote* is for Pinget the most beautiful book in Western literature. The greatness of the Spanish writer consists in having made his dying hero realize the madness of his attempts to institute justice in the world. Among twentieth-century authors, Pinget has a special affinity for Max Jacob and James Joyce. He admires in the former's works the elements of the irrational, the fantastic, and the unexpected, all fused into an impish sense of humor. In the latter's he relishes the diversity of tones and styles of writing, ranging from the archaic to the journalistic. He also appreciates the oral qualities of Louis-Ferdinand Céline's syntax, which is not at all surprising since Pinget himself possesses the gift of suggesting the ebb and flow of conversation in his novels.

Among nonfiction writers, the two who have made the strongest impression are Mircea Eliade and Carl Jung. Eliade's understanding of myths, symbols, and archetypes Pinget finds stupefying. But it is with the great psychoanalyst that our writer feels a special affinity. He plunges into the subconscious to rediscover Jung's *homo religiosus* (the religious man) we all carry within us. He seeks out achronic time, inseparably linked to that part of our being containing the universal myths that chronological time cannot ravage. Like Jung, he views creative activity as an interplay between the vital Dionysian forces of imagination and sensitivity welling from the subconscious on the one hand, and the Apollonian agent, reason, on the other, which monitors their outpouring while recording it.

Robert Pinget and the *Nouveau Roman*

Pinget's fascination with the subconscious explains in part at least his attraction to the *Nouveau Roman*. This label, however—used to designate a body of literary works that began appearing in the 1950s—is rather vague and unoriginal. Although analogies between these texts undoubtedly exist, the artistic visions they represent vary considerably from one writer to another. Nearly all French critics during the 1950s vied with one another to coin a catchy expression for this new conception of the novel. It was called simultaneously or successively *Ecole du Regard* (School of the Eye), *Chapelle de Minuit* (The "Minuit" Chapel), *Romans de la table rase* (Tabula Rasa Novels), *Romans blancs* (White Novels), and *Anti-roman* (The Anti-Novel). Only the term *Nouveau Roman* has stuck, even though it is probably the least evocative of them all.

Setting aside for a moment the profound differences between the various authors who nevertheless consider themselves to be *Nouveaux Romanciers*, what, then, are they referring to when they use it? With the passing of time we can stand back and draw out certain traits that define this remodeled genre. In general, the New Novel implies a break with the novelistic tradition of the nineteenth century as exemplified in the works of Balzac and Flaubert. This is not to say that writers such as Alain Robbe-Grillet or Michel Butor rejected or minimized the contributions of those outstanding creators of the past. They simply expressed the firmly held conviction that if the French novel was to avoid sclerosis, if it was to express adequately the reality of their particular era, then it would have to change radically. By radical change they meant eschewing the conventions of the traditional novel. They meant doing away with linear plot development, debunking anecdotes, and abolishing the notion of believable characters whose personalities unfold as the story progresses. They justified their systematic rejection by asserting that nineteenth-century novelists and their twentieth-century followers had arbitrarily selected certain aspects of reality that they then passed off as the very reflection—indeed, the only conceivable one—of that reality.

The New Novelists readily admitted that their works, however subversive, were also based on conventions and arbitrary processes. But at least they never tried to foist on their reader the illusion that by exploiting these artistic devices they were actually giving him or her a definitive interpretation of life. Their various techniques of novel writing were part of an elaborate game in which the reader was invited to become an active participant. In fact, the act of writing was no longer viewed as a means to an end but as an end in itself—an opportunity to explore the very functioning of language as it is applied to narrative form. To quote a phrase of which the novelist Jean Ricardou is particularly fond, fiction is no longer the "written account of an adventure but the adventure of a written account."[7] Writers in the past would never have thought of dissociating signifiers from their references to reality. The New Novelists considered it perfectly legitimate to explore the relationships between signifiers within the verbal context itself, with all of the disquieting permutations and combinations this experimenting implies.

Yet despite their commonly held belief that radical changes were necessary, none of the writers answering to the name of *Nouveaux Romanciers* have ever been part of a concerted effort to revolutionize literature. Indeed, they were unanimous in denouncing as a fallacy the view that they had banded together for the purpose of launching a literary movement that would illustrate their theories. Nathalie Sarraute declared that the very idea of writing a novel with a specific theory in mind would be enough to paralyze her creative process. Even the unofficial spokesman of the New Novelists, Alain Robbe-Grillet, has admitted that although he may have naively intended at the outset to abolish conformity to traditional novelistic modes, no such revolution ever occurred.[8] What may have given credence to the myth that a well-coordinated movement was underfoot was a group photo taken in 1959 in front of the building housing Editions de Minuit. It included many of the most prominent New Novelists of the time: Alain Robbe-Grillet, Claude Simon, Claude

Mauriac, Samuel Beckett, Nathalie Sarraute, Robert Pinget, and Claude Ollier, along with their editor, Jérôme Lindon.

From the early 1950s to the late 1960s, writers considering themselves to be New Novelists seemed primarily intent on freeing the reader from the perceptual positivism inherited from the nineteenth century. In the late 1960s and 1970s the anti-referential motif came into play, and some novelists such as Jean Ricardou strove to remove the narrative from any perceptual links with the outside world. By the end of the 1970s and in the early 1980s, the preoccupation with structure gave way to interest in the different modes through which the author makes his/her presence felt within his/her text. Language was increasingly viewed as the writer's vehicle for expressing his/her distinctive "voice." By 1990 the most famous of the *Nouveaux Romanciers* could no longer be considered avant-garde. People like Robbe-Grillet, Beckett, Simon, Sarraute, and Pinget have become modern classics, studied in high schools and universities alike. As for the aesthetic of the New Novel itself, it seems to have run out of momentum. An important sign of the times, which Pinget has readily acknowledged, is the young French reading public's renewed interest in traditional narrative forms.

Profound dissatisfaction with the traditional novel can be traced back to the 1950s, when a number of young French writers began questioning the validity of the metaphysical and political themes expounded so often by their elders. During the 1930s and 1940s renowned literary figures like André Malraux, Georges Bernanos, Antoine de Saint-Exupéry, and Jean Giono, followed by Sartre, Camus, and Simone de Beauvoir, fervently believed that the purpose of the novelist was to grapple with the problem of conferring fullness and significance to individual lives. They saw themselves as creators of new codes of ethical values—indeed, as guides for readers who had lost faith in human existence and were floundering. But the succeeding generation of authors would no longer accept their tutelage, having measured the abyss that often separates idealism from reality. Terms like *heroism, revolt, lucid will*, and *solidarity* began to have a hollow ring or even fall on deaf ears. The virulent satires of Marcel Aymé and Jean-Louis Curtis mirrored this new frame of mind.

Perhaps more than any other texts of the period, Samuel Beckett's trilogy—*Molloy* (1951), *Malone meurt* (*Malone Dies* [1951]), and *L'Innommable* (*The Unnamable* [1953])—spell the death of the metaphysical novel. In these disquieting allegories the characters are embodiments of abject human misery. They appear spiritually as well as physically destitute, in a state of semi-paralysis and semi-death. Relegated to the status of pariahs, they stagger around the fringe of a forbidding universe. They keep searching compulsively for something but are hard-pressed to define the object of their search. They get bogged down in interminable monologues during which they give voice to the sense of powerlessness felt by human creatures forever trapped within themselves. In all of Beckett's novels existence is deemed to be the fundamental evil, and his characters wish only to shrivel up into nonbeing in a vain attempt to exorcise this curse of being alive.

There is yet another explanation for the rejection of the traditional novel: younger writers refused to accept as valid the notion of man as a solid, immutable substance and its corollary, the concept of an "inner" human being whose existence remains unaffected by external circumstances. As Laurent Lesage has pointed out, this calling into question of the idea that the human personality is fixed can be traced back to David Hume and his *Treatise on Human Nature*.[9] But with the advent of psychoanalysis, Marcel Proust's monumental novel *A la recherche du temps perdu*, and stream-of-consciousness writers such as James Joyce and William Faulkner, it could no longer be defended. And the German philosopher Edmund Husserl administered the coup de grace when he propounded his interpretation of man's relationship to reality called "phenomenology."[10] According to his study on human perception, consciousness cannot exist within a rational, imperturbable vacuum. It derives its very activity from its place *within* the world. It targets the various objects of its experience with the intention of conferring meaning on them. At the very moment it illuminates the elements of reality by focusing on them, however, it illuminates its own functioning as well. Self-understanding and understanding of one's surroundings are thus inseparable. No wonder Jean-Paul Sartre, who studied with Husserl in the 1930s in Berlin, praised the philosopher for having freed man from interiority by developing the concept of the intentional consciousness.

Like Beckett, other French writers endorsed this new perception of reality, expressing it in divergent ways. Robbe-Grillet was among the first to take up Sartre's triumphant cry that the self-contained, interior consciousness was abolished. He has persistently rejected all psychological analysis in the classical sense as well as any reference to metaphysics. He has eschewed all theories about the "social function" of objects, preferring to reveal them in their utter strangeness. He has refused to present reality from the point of view of an omniscient observer "à la Balzac." He has adopted, rather, the narrow, subjective vision of a consciousness enmeshed in the inextricable labyrinth of experience. In such Robbe-Grillet works as *Le Voyeur, La Jalousie,* and *Dans le labyrinthe,* a one-dimensional per-spective thus replaces the multidimensional thrust so characteristic of the nineteenth-century novel. Jealousy, as Robbe-Grillet depicts it, does not undergo the standard analysis based on principles inherited from a venerable Western tradition of psychological analysis; rather, the novel-ist makes its presence tangible through a succession of obsessive images. He, too, shows how the "intentional" consciousness operates by project-ing itself on the objects that surround it.

Like their colleague, Michel Butor and Claude Simon also practiced a form of phenomenological realism. The former translated A. Gurwitsch's *Théorie du champs de la conscience* and declared openly that the novel was the domaine par excellence of phenomenology. The latter had the honor of seeing his novel *La Route des Flandres* (*The Flanders Road* [1960]) used by the philosopher Maurice Merleau-Ponty in advanced courses at the Collège de France. Simon's colleague would quote from the work to illustrate his own reflections on the nature of experience. When perusing the texts of these two novelists, one realizes just how strong is this affili-ation with the phenomenological method. The lengthy descriptions one finds in Butor's *La Modification* (*A Change of Heart* [1957]) and Simon's *La Route des Flandres* do not break the narrative sequence. They give tan-gible form to an incessant flow of mental images. The reduplication with multiple variations of characters, actions, and places is not the result of a gratuitous whim, a bias or a deliberate attempt to confuse the reader. It represents the authors' determination to explore a given object in all its possible facets.

In her own inimitable way, Nathalie Sarraute also jettisons the novel-istic conventions of the past. She denounces the illusions perpetrated by the traditional language of psychological analysis. For her, language is a mask; its definitions serve as a haven for hypocrisy and disguise in their reassuring verbal tatters a human reality that is dizzyingly complex and often quite terrifying. Once their masks are removed, people in her nov-els react toward one another like beasts of prey and their victims. Sentiments appearing harmless or kindly hide unconfessible appetites beneath their surface. Novels such as *Le Planétarium* (*The Planetarium* [1959]), *Les Fruits d'or* (*The Golden Fruit* [1963]), and *Entre la vie et la mort* (*Between Life and Death* [1968]) compel the reader to realize that behind the facade of conventional language and attitudes, social groups, whether families or literary circles, reveal themselves as human jungles.

Like these *Nouveaux Romanciers,* Robert Pinget conjures up a fictional world where traditional landmarks of language, psychology, and linear structure disappear, leaving his reader at first bewildered, then intrigued. Owing to his artistry as a writer, however, this world cannot be confused with any other. A special "voice" always emerges from Pinget's texts regardless of the different "tones" through which it manifests itself—a voice startlingly original and consequently unmistakable.

In 1982 Pinget presented a lecture at the City University of New York within the framework of a colloquium on the *Nouveau Roman*. It was later published by the *Nouvelle Revue Française* with the title "Propos de New York."[11] This document constitutes perhaps the author's most significant and complete statement on the nature of his art. He begins by reproaching the nonreferentialist critics. Being a man of exquisite politeness, Pinget couches his remarks in very diplomatic terms. He even emphasizes the contribution this school of criticism has made to the understanding of the ways in which language works within his texts. His attack is no less devastating for being understated, however. In their commitment to study a text solely as an exercise in the functioning of language, nonreferentialist critics have missed the point. It is dangerous, declares the author, to view a literary work simply as a field where signifiers interact. If this were indeed the case, then just about any text would be equally suitable for linguistic analysis. They could all be considered as productions emanating from the same universal mechanism—the language process—whose operations it would be the task of the critic to comprehend. Moreover, if advocates of the purely semiotic or structuralist approach took their ideas to their logical conclusions, they would refrain from signing their names as the authors of their own studies inasmuch as they are simply instruments through which the intellectual machine manifests its activity. As Pinget mischievously remarks, however, these critics continue signing their names.

For Pinget, a literary text cannot be reduced to an interplay of purely material signs. These signs refer to something infinitely more significant than themselves. They convey vital information about a writer's creative faculty, his imagination, emotions, sensations, and memory. In other words, they capture the resonances welling spontaneously from his subjectivity, which is to a large extent irrational, and from a realm lying beyond the irrational—his subconscious. As though to justify his conception of what literature is all about, Pinget cites two outstanding nineteenth-century French writers, Stéphane Mallarmé and Charles Baudelaire. For many, the former's poetry epitomizes the triumph of the cerebral, the quest for pure formal beauty. Yet, as Pinget mentions, the symbolist poet, referring to his *Hérodiade* (1871), affirmed that a text reflects the temperament of its author, and so can be an instrument of self-knowledge. The latter's views on the art of Edgar Allan Poe corroborates those of Mallarmé on the subject of poetic inspiration. According to Baudelaire, the American writer of fantastic tales struck a perfect balance between spontaneity and rigor.

This is precisely what Pinget strives to achieve in his own creative works. Lucid control is a means to an end, with the end being the in-depth exploration of the unfathomable riches hidden within the subconscious. Because the subconscious contains an infinite variety of possibilities to explore, Pinget has always found it necessary to devise a special tone for each novel he embarked on. Fortunately, as he informs us,

> It matters little how hard I try, my readers seems to be of the opinion that they can recognize the same voice in whichever book of mine they happen to pick up. And I say fortunately indeed because in the long run, the essential for me, through these experiences which it is my duty to transmit, is to explore and shed light on what my intimate being conceals, and this is possible only by continuous experimentation. ("Propos de New York," 100–101)

By mining his subconscious depths, Pinget gains access to the time-less realm of the collective subconscious. He enters the realms of legend and myth and the world of childhood. Thanks to the weightless power of words, he returns to the very beginnings, thus transcending chronological time. In his remarkable ground-breaking study on Pinget, Robert Henkels, Jr., described this descent into the realm of timelessness as a "quest." While the choice of this term is certainly legitimate, I would prefer using another one, since a quest generally implies a precise object or goal to be reached. As I interpret them, each one of Pinget's novels complemented by his plays and even narratives represents successive stages in an inner voyage of exploration. As he probes deeper and deeper into his imaginary universe, its confines seem to expand, opening up innumerable perspectives, bringing forth all kinds of disquieting paradoxes. The reader, in turn, becomes increasingly fascinated by the same voice that, expressing itself in an astonishingly varied array of tones, invites him to participate in a meditation on the meaning of life and death.

Chapter Two
Between Fun and Seriousness

In the concluding paragraphs of his "Propos de New York," Robert Pinget speaks of passing over to "the other shore"—that is, of penetrating into the kingdom of legends where time never flows away, where what was expressed in the beginning remains forever. To successfully complete this voyage, declares the author, it is necessary to travel light. In fact, the baggage must be of a very special nature. It must be alive and humming with words. It is any anthology of literary texts resurrecting the *homo religiosus* inside of us, to which we can refer at any moment of our existences.[1] Yet, however original or even revolutionary this adventure may be, Pinget, at the outset, must still deal with the problem of the vehicle to be used in order to embark on it. Like all outstanding writers, he must at first feel his way. He must question the existing structures before getting rid of them. Since originality never emerges ex nihilo, Pinget begins to define his literary vision by revolting against the conventions of the past. Being endowed with a marvelous sense of humor, the demolition job he does is a gleeful one. And he has recourse to the many discoveries of the surrealist movement to ensure that the job is indeed well done.

Surrealism was officially launched in 1924 by the French poet André Breton in the incendiary text *Le Manifeste surréalise*. In the aftermath of World War I many French poets, including Breton, Philipe Soupault, Paul Eluard, and Louis Aragon, were determined to undermine the whole edifice of social, moral, and artistic ideas built up by previous centuries. As disillusioned survivors of a generation sacrificed for a senseless war, they no longer expected succor from religion or society. Their insurrection represented what they called the "superior revolt" of the individual consciousness. These adventurers of the mind were anarchists by temperament as well as by doctrine. They refused to inaugurate a "school." Even artistic and literary creation was secondary to them. What counted was their new attitude toward existence. Their immense ambition consisted in nothing less than a declaration of human rights.

Poetic activity represented for them one way among many of regaining their lost freedom, because it offered them the opportunity to travel through the nebulous regions of the consciousness that are refractory to all forms of control imposed from without and so to achieve mastery of themselves. In time, surrealism came to mean the body of creative and expressive processes using all of man's psychic forces (automatism, dreams, the unconscious) freed from reason's domination and opposed to conventional values.

Taking his cue from these poetic revolutionaries, Pinget summons up all of his verbal wizardry for a dual purpose: he turns conventional wisdom and consecrated literary precepts upside down, often with hilarious results, and simultaneously probes deeply into his imagination in an attempt to unlock its treasures. His first five books—*Entre Fantoine et Agapa* (1951), *Mahu, ou le matériau* (1952), *Le Renard et la boussole* (1953), *Graal Flibuste* (1955), and *Baga* (1958)—illustrate this initial creative period. In fact, they confirm our belief that if surrealism had not existed, Pinget would have had to invent it himself. Nevertheless, while using these works to perform acts of exploration as well as sabotage, he begins a lifelong inquiry into the nature of literary creation, perception, and self-knowledge.

Entre Fantoine et Agapa (*Between Fantoine and Agapa*)

Pinget's first book is a collection of 20 miniature tales followed by a diary in which an anonymous narrator (or is it the author himself?) relates the weird events taking place in an imaginary country. Being a work of unbridled fantasy, it could not have appeared at a worse moment to launch the career of a writer. In 1951 existentialism, with its emphasis on ethical commitment and political involvement, was in vogue. Such an attitude toward art has always been foreign to Robert Pinget's temperament. The stories in *Between Fantoine and Agapa* resemble conscious dreams that occasionally skid into nightmares. Although there is no thread linking them together, they are all characterized by a total freedom from rational constraints, from the notion of plausibility, from cause and effect perceptions. In this fictional world, anything goes. Objects behave like people; people become smitten with objects; bizarre events are described as though they were the most natural occurrences. The reader is titillated, intrigued, bewildered, jolted, and even at times revolted by what happens. Bored he is not.

In the first tale, "Vishnu se venge" ("Vishnu Takes Revenge"), an ignorant and bored curate sets an uninspiring example to his parishioners in the town of Fantoine, while the church steeple gallivants about at night. But life becomes suddenly exciting when the priest takes an interest in the Cambodian language and culture. Carried away by his newfound passion, he commits an act of sacrilege by inadvertently substituting the word "Yak" for "Christus" as he intones the Latin invocation at the consecration of the Mass. The results are devastating: "A gigantic demon rose up from the host, knocked the curate senseless, and pulverized the church. And eternal Vishnu deigned to smile at it."[2] What has happened? Was the priest punished for having blasphemed the Christian or the Hindu faith, or both? Is the author poking fun at the superstitious excesses into which religion can fall? Should the reader bother interpreting the story at all or simply enjoy it for its fancifulness?

From blaspheming curates we move on to lascivious cucumbers ("Les Concombres"). Pinget exploits with obvious gusto the resemblance between this particular vegetable's form and the male sex organ. A whole town is thrown into commotion when one very virile cucumber brazenly displays his wares on the public beach, thereby driving his female counterparts crazy: "He used to stretch his proactive peduncle with his eyes half-closed. The female cucumbers were wild about him. He had a certain way of sliding up to you, of rubbing himself. . . . If that weren't enough, he had enormous membranes. What can I tell you, he was the darling of the beach" (EFA, 23).

Soon, the whole town becomes cucumber-obsessed. The vegetables proliferate. Laws are passed to regulate their cultivation, but to no avail. A morally upright, unmarried female citizen, Mlle Solange, gets pregnant while handling one and gives birth to a whole lot of them. Girls and boys play dirty little games with them. The local priest inveighs against them. No one seems to care, least of all the sexy male cucumber who instigated all the trouble in the first place. It is very tempting to see in this cucumber craze, which no legal or religious power can stop, a symbol—albeit expressed in very jocular terms—of Eros's irresistible urge.

Although very humorous, the tone changes considerably in "Le Café du Cygne." The author seems to be satirizing two vices: snobbery in art and the old literary convention of cause-and-effect relationships. The narrator of this tale despises his wife for being unable to appreciate the style of the sculptor Dâd Surprend. Even though he himself admits that the artist's work appears shapeless and too obvious in its attempt to get its message across, he finds very appealing its stammering efforts to convey the inexpressible. Happy to be understood, Dâd Surprend takes the narrator into his confidence. He suspects the female cashier at the Café du Cygne of being responsible for a number of deaths that occurred each time she seemed to reach under the counter to touch an invisible object, either a switch or a bell. He convinces his interlocutor that the woman does indeed possess some frightening and mysterious power by asking him laconically,

"What do you think?"
  A paraphrase would have left me skeptical. Not this concision. From that very moment I understood far better the sculptor's consciously stammering art: he dreaded laying himself open to the cashier. (*EFA*, 46)

In the final story of the collection, "Firenze Delle Nevi," Pinget as narrator again plays the part of the prankster. This time he thumbs his nose at the age-old precept of historical veracity. According to history books, there exists only one Florence, the resplendent Italian city that reached its artistic zenith during the Renaissance. But Pinget imagines an even more fantastic architectural achievement—this one erected on the southern slope of Mont-Blanc by a Laurent de Médicis fed up with all the puritanical and jealous adversaries who were always stirring up revolts against him. As though to corroborate his assertion that his imaginary alpine Florence, buried under avalanches at the end of the Renaissance, actually did exist, the author quotes all kinds of supposed "facts" and "figures": it was situated at an altitude of 4,700 meters; its location was discovered by Lorenzo and a companion in 1488 during a mountain climb; marble for its magnificent buildings was dragged all the way from Tuscany; and great artists like Botticelli and Bramante contributed to the city's glory. Pinget parodies the criterion of veracity even further by accusing the media of hiding the truth:

What should one say about the silences of the Information Network? Monopolized for centuries by a gang of bribe-takers, it filters everything. They make us believe that the moon is made of green cheese. Open any encyclopedia: you'll see that in 1787 H.B. de Saussure was one of the first to climb up Mont-Blanc! This is inadmissible!
  But the Savoyards have not forgotten. It is traditional, in certain families, to call the first son Laurent. (*EFA*, 75)

In this tale Pinget gleefully exploits the ambiguous nature of words. On the one hand, they refer to specific realities, and in "Firenze Delle Nevi" they refer to specific historical realities. On the other, they enjoy a strange new life in the particular context in which the writer inserts them and which they help create. Playing as he does with words that evoke the Florence of the Renaissance, he conjures up a fanciful alpine city of Tuscan origin in whose existence he then pretends to believe. As a result, he gives his reader an idea of what can happen to all these terms we take for granted when they are cut off from their conventional moorings and allowed to float freely.

In the diary that follows these miniature stories, an observer visits an unnamed country between November of one year and September of the next (no doubt the author himself exploring the territory between Fantoine and Agapa). In disconnected segments he simulates a sociocritical analysis, relating all kinds of "details" about the citizen's customs, moral values, leisure activities, and social relations. Here, as in the first part of the book, Pinget takes off on such wild flights of fancy that the reader succumbs to their fascination even while remaining incredulous. He describes fingernails and toenails being poured down from huge silos and engaging in races watched by crowds of spectators perched several thousand meters high. He tells us of weird burial practices involving sinister female grave diggers who strip dead bodies of their flesh, which they can sink, sausagelike, into wells. He relates the scalping of women by their coiffeurs and the herds of urchins attracted to the burning odors. Then there are the people themselves, welded into a kind of universal moral conscience, so tormented by guilt and shame when any of their fellow citizens commit evil deeds that they become masses of suffering flesh. Artists in that country are recruited from among the criminal population. They are so convinced of their unworthiness that whenever anyone admires their work, they lose their reason and go on a rampage, destroying what they have created.

Some episodes are so gruesomely unreal that they become downright funny. In the 19 March entry the observer describes the decomposition of living people to the point where they are unrecognizable. The accumulation of medical terms designating organs, which fall by the wayside one after the other, acquires a weird independence from its referents. The horror we might feel initially on imagining the scene is neutralized by this dizzying piling up of nouns, adjectives, and verbs that end up parodying the technical language they constitute:

> You lose a contour, or a segment, or a whole side of your body, and the hachured surface diminishes by as much, your armpits are no longer included in it. You wander about with holes, carrying your charcoal silhouette in

a briefcase. Your cheek declares its independence. Your jaw, standing out, does not occupy its accustomed place between the neck and the glottis; the nostril's wings get covered with pharyngeal edemas; nauseating liquors ooze out along the apophyses. The truncated sphincters recede toward the nerve centers, the epigastrium subdivides itself. The briefcase ends up falling as well, your hand invaginates itself and the sketch prepared the night before is soiled with watery excrement. It's a loss of plasma. It happens frequently during hikes in the country. Several pals who go off for the day are unrecognizable when they return. (*EFA*, 94)

As was the case with the first part of *Entre Fantoine et Agapa*, the reader hesitates between interpreting the events of the diary and simply appreciating them for their sheer zaniness. There is one passage at least where the author appears to be dead serious, however. In the 5 September entry he explains briefly the purpose of his art:

Incapable of being a gentleman who walks, smokes, visits friends, my natural reaction is to invent in clay or on canvas or on paper a gait, a taste of smoke, a visit where my arteries palpitate.

Thus I am convinced today that one doesn't attempt, in a work of art, to bring forth the beautiful or the true. One has recourse to it—as to a subterfuge—for the sole purpose of continuing to breathe. (*EFA*, 105)

The reader who has perused Pinget's entire production realizes retrospectively that in his very first work he was already voicing a firmly held conviction, because this conception of art has been reiterated on many occasions since 1951.

It complements another view of the creative process expressed in the first part of the book, in a story entitled "Le Coffret." I would agree with Madeleine Renouard that "Le Coffret" represents a key to the understanding of Pinget's writing.[3] In it he declares, "One must take language for what it is. We never think more than we express. People who say nothing are ham actors. I'm suspicious of 'eloquent silences.' You think you are understood by someone who is content to take up a pensive attitude after you've spoken: ninety times out of a hundred, if you make him talk in spite of himself, you notice that he hasn't understood one word" (*EFA*, 56). Language, then, is a precious instrument for exploring one's inner world, for exorcizing silence, which is a prefiguration of death. This is another belief to which Pinget will religiously adhere throughout his spiritual voyage of discovery.

Mahu, ou le matériau (*Mahu, or the Material*)

In *Entre Fantoine et Agapa* Pinget began staking out the parameters of his imaginary world. He pursues this spiritual adventure in his next work, the novel *Mahu, ou le matériau* (1952), with one notable difference. In the collection of short stories he seemed content to thumb his nose at literary conventions. In this first novel he demonstrates through his whimsical "hero," Mahu, that these outmoded structures simply will not work any more. Of the three characters in the book who feel driven to write novels, Mahu is the only one to realize the futility of trying to encapsulate the incomprehensible complexity and ceaseless flow of life by using the norms of the past. He has the raw material for a work of literature, but he believes that welding it into a rigorous form would betray it. In fact, constructing a slick, well-organized plot with a beginning, a middle, and an end would ensure the enterprise's failure.

Well into the second part of *Mahu, ou le matériau* the narrator senses that the reality he has been trying to depict is eluding his grasp. The stories he relates go off on wilder and wilder tangents until they simply come to an abrupt stop. Far from feeling dejected by his inability to "conclude" his text according to conventional norms, he proclaims a victory of sorts:

> Between you and me, the first part is a failed novel but it doesn't matter. I used it as warm-up exercises. What is important for me is not to sing well but to hear my voice without bronchitis. You know, with bronchitis there are many little whistles.
>
> Well, there you have it. I have nothing more to say except that everything remains mine. I have won.[4]

Mahu has indeed won to the extent that he has achieved a new aesthetic awareness. He realizes that the whirling mass of reality that engulfs him can only be suggested by means of a different approach to writing. Having assessed the conventional novel in the first part of the book and found it inadequate, he experiments in the second part with all kinds of far-out hypotheses in an endeavor to shake this old form out of its lethargy. In the process he suggests the direction in which Pinget will move.

In the first part of *Mahu, ou le matériau* called "The Novelist," the town of Agapa appears to be in the throes of a novel-writing epidemic. Mahu, his friend Latirail, and a rather hare-brained old maid, Mlle Lorpailleur, are feverishly at work on their respective texts. Of the three,

Mahu is the only one engaged in literary creation to give meaning to his existence. Unlike the others, he is incapable of following a predetermined plan. In order to write, he must give free rein to his spontaneity. He has far more inventiveness than his two colleagues and far more modesty. (Being one of 14 children may have something to do with this lack of pretentiousness.) Latirail and Mlle Lorpailleur, on the other hand, are in the business of writing for purely egocentric motives. They love the power and authority the profession brings. The latter especially wallows in the admiration of her credulous female friends. Each one is racing the other to get his/her novel finished first and onto the bookstore shelves. Each one is eager to monopolize Mahu as his/her satellite. Hanging over the destinies of Latirail and Lorpailleur like some all-powerful puppeteer is the postmaster, Sinture. Although not an author himself, he manipulates their inspiration at will, fairly reveling in the knowledge that the creative freedom they think they possess is nothing more than an illusion.

Latirail and Lorpailleur are both doomed to failure as novelists because they are laboring under the delusion that it is possible to effect an all-encompassing synthesis of life's raw material. Latirail firmly believes that to encapsulate the complexity of experience it is sufficient to align words and facts. Thus he is nearly distraught when he discovers that his wife has lent his Larousse dictionary without consulting him, as though access to vocabulary in itself would enable him to elaborate an intensely personal vision. But Latirail's folly reaches comic heights in the chapter "The Shampoo." Being obsessed by a very narrow and purely arbitrary concept of realism, he insists on filling his novel with all kinds of details that will be "true to life." First, he changes the title of his text from "Les Chercheurs de poux" ("The Lice-Hunters"), an obvious allusion to the famous poem by Arthur Rimbaud, to "Les Chercheurs de clous" ("The Nail-Hunters"), convinced that the second one is far more believable from the realistic perspective. Then he tries to satisfy his writer's vanity by including the following sentences because, according to him, it is part of the "material of life": "Fifteen-year-old girls have greasy hair. They wash their hair with vinegar when they go to the ball. Their partners are nauseated. Because vinegar has a bad smell" (*M*, 36). Latirail's pride in having produced this true-life observation is short-lived, however. His wife, Ninette, deflates it by reminding him that no girls wash their hair with vinegar any more, that they go *dancing*, not "to the ball." When poor Latirail tries to salvage something from his literary wreckage by substituting the popular "Dop" shampoo for vinegar,

Ninette replies skeptically, "You think it will be interesting? I wonder. . . .
Besides, Dop shampoo, ten years from now, you know . . ." (*M*, 37).

Mlle Lorpailleur's art of writing is equally superficial and founded on
just as gratuitous assumptions. She persistently questions Mahu about
his friend, Latirail, who is to be the hero of her new novel, since she, too,
is determined to fill her text with precise details. She rejects Mahu's sug-
gestion that she interview her rival personally, since she fears the information she would receive would be less accurate. Unfortunately, she
confuses factual knowledge with profundity. Accumulating all kinds of
exterior details about Latirail would bring her no closer to understanding
his life or life in general. Mahu finally pronounces a damning judgment
on both of these misguided novelists. When Mlle Lorpailleur invokes the
criterion of *vraisemblance* (plausibility), Mahu replies, "You talk just like
Latirail. He writes things which are true, or plausible, or veritable. . . . It's
a craze" (*M*, 77).

The only character in *Mahu, ou le matériau* capable of composing a
traditionally well-constructed novel—one with a tightly woven plot,
sharply delineated characters, recognizable situations, and cause-and-
effect sequences—is Sinture the postmaster. His very name is identical in
sound to the French word *ceinture*, meaning "belt." It evokes an overarching constraint, an encircling of all events that unfold under his gaze.
In the novel he knows everything that happens in the towns of Agapa
and Fantoine. By monitoring every letter that passes through the postal
services, he acquires an omniscience similar to that of the traditional
writer. But what good would it have done to make him the hero of the
present work? If he were aware of all events before they even occurred,
how could he possibly suggest the swirling, restless flow of life?

As though to rule out any thought of the omniscient writer taking
control of the story line, Pinget begins to bewilder his reader early in the
novel by relating several different versions of the "slap" incident. Mahu
passes by the school of Petite Fiente ("Little Bird Droppings"), the
daughter of his employer, Juan Simon. In the first version, it seems as
though Mahu slapped the bratty child. Then another version appears in
which Mahu playfully pretends to hit her. In the final version Juan
Simon apologizes to his employee for his daughter's frightful behavior
when he finds out that she struck him. At this point it is no longer possible for the reader to entertain the illusion of a story unfolding along
logical lines. He has been hurtled into a world of whimsical possibilities.

Since Pinget, through his narrator, has discredited the conventional
novel, how does he propose to rebuild? The answer, however tentative, is

to be found in the second part of *Mahu, ou le matériau* called "Mahu Bafouille" ("Mahu Babbles"). Ideally, Mahu would like to reproduce the inexhaustible complexity of Life, but he knows that he possesses neither the knowledge nor the verbal power to do so. Besides, there lurks in Mahu's mind the fear that words simply cannot evoke experience in all its richness. According to him, the living presence of the narrator infuses the words he uses with a soul. When these same words are committed to paper, their soul is destroyed:

> I find that many people know how to tell a story, even everybody, when you write you ruin it, the voice is no longer there, neither are the eyes, you can't do anything about it, when you talk you are truer than what you have seen since you explain yourself, you are at the same time the ear and the mind of the person who listens to you but above all you are his eyes, you look with him, and he doesn't have to make any effort, the story is alive because I am alive next to him. Do you understand? I don't write for pleasure, but only to invent people around me who might listen to me, otherwise, what purpose would I have? I would be dead. (*M*, 187)

Not having real people around him all the time, Mahu speaks to an imaginary interlocutor in 35 disconnected monologues. Not knowing how to encompass in written form the never-ending flow of life, he tries at least to open up new perspectives of perception. He does so by asking more than 130 questions, many of which are infantile ("When you walk, do you pay attention?" "Do you think you're responsible for other people's legs?"), but some of which shake up the conventional modes of thought and expression, thereby compelling us to reflect on how our minds really function. The fourth soliloquy, "L'A peu près" ("The Approximation"), is a striking example of observations that appear absolutely preposterous at first glance but actually make sense on further reflection. Mahu maintains that when we compare a new object to one we have already experienced, this previous one really becomes the most recent, since it now occupies our mind: "When you look with your binoculars, you have a precision instrument and you see very clearly a little hut which would appear blurred without them. Right away you say, "'Well, it looks like that other one, they are just about alike.' Already you no longer see it, in your mind you are comparing it to the one which you think is *before* whereas it is *after*, the other hut. It's a queer habit" (*M*, 114).

Mahu stammers and babbles with irritating frequency in the second part of this novel. An illustration of this tendency can be found in the twenty-fourth monologue, "Donnke, Donnke, Donnke," where he goes from talking about his substitute cello teacher to his regular one, before approaching the subjects of chocolate, potato salad, coffee, and the lack of intellectual excitement in married couples—all in less than three pages. But at least he is making an honest attempt to enlarge his perception of himself and the world around him. Totally unlike his conventional novel-writing colleagues, he endeavors to assess the raw material of life without imposing artificial constraints on it—constraints that would simplify and betray it. As a result, Mahu adumbrates the vision of an endlessly proliferating reality that will emerge from Pinget's future novels.

Le Renard et la boussole (The Fox and the Compass)

Despite the overtones of anguish we perceive as Mahu tries to come to grips with the raw material of his life, his adventure "ends," however arbitrarily, on an optimistic note. He has freed his mind from worn-out conventions and has expanded it. The narrator of Le Renard et la boussole (1953), John Tintouin Porridge, already enjoys this heightened perception. His dilemma consists in finding a way to convey it adequately. During the course of the novel this dilemma becomes a veritable hang-up. His mind, like the reality around him, branches off in all directions. Yet he desperately wants to squeeze the protean mass of his inspiration into some definitive form. He knows full well that he is embarked on a foolhardy venture. Structures enclose and compress. They are inimical to the swirling configurations that refuse to stay put. Still, he doggedly pursues this elusive goal of reconciling the unreconcilable.

Compounding his anguish is his instability. John Tintouin Porridge's personality is in a mess. It needs some kind of spiritual glue to hold its fragments together. Art seems, then, at first glance, the indispensable therapy for keeping his being whole. Unfortunately, the narrator realizes that art implies order and that order, in turn, means imposing artificial arrangements and immobilizing a substance that, by its very nature, will simply not sit still.

The structure of Le Renard et la boussole mirrors the fruitful tensions between John Tintouin Porridge's explosive imagination, which balks at being contained, and his yearning to make sense of its activity by containing it within conventional, and therefore completely unsuitable, narrative forms. Since Pinget has his narrator keep a diary, he provides himself with a very convenient instrument to orchestrate these tensions on various registers and exploit the ambiguities to which they give rise.

As the novel unfolds, it seems to function on three levels. On the first level, John Tintouin Porridge addresses the reader directly. He takes the reader into his confidence through his diary as he voices his conflicting thoughts and emotions about his experiences and reflects on the creative process. On the second level, there is a voyage to Israel with its various ramifications. Sometimes the narrator appears to be recording factual events; at other times this expedition to the Holy Land acquires a bizarre momentum of its own within the work's loose framework. Finally, on the third level, the reader finds himself creating a novel of his own as he continuously assembles and reassembles the torrent of material with which Pinget provides him.

Following the narrator's tortuous intellectual trajectory is all the more challenging because his powers of invention keep rejecting the logical solutions by which he would like to govern them. It is no doubt his frustration at not knowing where to start or stop that explains his abandonment of his first project—a "semi-critical" study on the tragic Mary Stuart, Queen of Scots. Being felled by chicken pox shortly after having begun this work must have been a blessing in disguise, because it has given him a legitimate excuse to suspend his activity indefinitely. Yet, however plagued John Tintouin Porridge may be by doubts about his ability to seize control of his inspiration, he, like Mahu, views writing as a vital necessity. When he addresses an unknown interlocutor in his diary, he is in essence carrying on a dialogue with himself in the desperate hope of finding out who he is and why he persists in being a writer.

As a writer, John Tintouin Porridge knows that he should strive to remain in a heightened state of awareness, to reproduce the uninterrupted flow of life. He chatters incessantly in order not to leave out anything that crosses his consciousness, even at the risk of boring his anonymous confidant:

> What madness this uncut conversation with you is, I don't have the time to catch my breath but this is the way I wanted it, breathing is a change of air and I am more than willing to change air, for once I didn't want to have recourse to subterfuge. The subterfuge of breathing? Yes, vital, but the exercise that some people do of holding their breath makes them live more intensely, and think of divers, they wouldn't go down deep without this asceticism, careful, I'm not an ascetic, I choose my examples badly, I wish for nothing else but approximate ways of expressing myself. You should have caught on to that by now, I've been repeating it long enough, this is what I mean by what madness: since I've decided to break silence I deliberately risk boring you by this continuous navel-gazing.

Instead of keeping it to myself I generously offer it to you, there are acts
of generosity which one can surely do without, but really, why should one
do without them? An honest ideal is rather touching, perhaps one should
submit to its tiresome demonstrations.[5]

The narrator is so intent on sharing his navel-gazing with his interlocutor that all his attempts to control his hyperactive mind or discipline
his hyperfecund imagination come to naught. Art, in the traditional
sense at least, implies choice and elimination. By virtue of his temperament, John Tintouin Porridge can neither choose nor eliminate for long.
As the account of his travels continues, he gets more and more bogged
down in his material. The more it engulfs him, the more he runs the risk
of losing his bearings or, as the French would say, *perdre la boussole*. By the
time Pinget ends the novel, his narrator has become completely overwhelmed by the experiences, real or imaginary, that he was trying to
relate. Since he has been powerless to bring order out of chaos, all John
Tintouin Porridge can do is begin again. The reader realizes that the narrator has gone around in a circle when he repeats at the end of his
account the same phrase he had used at the beginning: "My name is
John Tintouin Porridge."

The narrator's dilemma is evident from the outset. He wrestles with
the choice of constructing an autobiography along the traditional lines of
logical development or of recording fleeting thoughts as they dart in and
out of his consciousness. He opts for the second mode of expression and
decides to use it to orchestrate the theme of birth. The subject has an
aura of poetry about it, dealing as it does with mysterious causes and a
destiny as yet unfulfilled. But having hit upon such an exciting theme,
he is paralyzed by his chronic inability to decide where to begin and how
to end. Relating even his own birth daunts him. Frustrated by his failure
to get his novel moving, John Tintouin Porridge takes refuge in whimsical musings on the nature of spiders and on two imaginary giraffes that
he had sketched on the envelope of a letter to his nephews. The next
morning he recalls by chance the Old Testament phrase "beware of the
little foxes." While pondering the craftiness of this animal, the image of
a particular fox takes shape in his mind. He quickly establishes an association between the rootless predator and the legendary figure of the
Wandering Jew. They, he decides, will become characters in a work dealing with spiritual exile.

A strange paradox soon develops. John Tintouin Porridge may have
conjured up the venerable old Jew, David, to reflect his own feelings of

not belonging, but the aged man, despite his endless wanderings, possesses a sense of destiny that the former cannot help admiring. The creature of Porridge's imagination may be physically uprooted, but spiritually he knows exactly where he is headed. This becomes obvious when the narrator-novelist has David befriend the Fox and embark with the animal on a pilgrimage to the newly created state of Israel along with a whole boatload of fellow Jews from all over Europe. While observing this motley group of passengers, the Fox, the very symbol of rootlessness, compares his aimless freedom to the sense of solidarity that propels these people forward and acts as their spiritual center of gravity:

> These people are not free, all of them keep being pushed forward by some unknown duty, all without exception, even those who are mulling over business and job plans; they are linked together to their race, even the renegades are by the shame they feel towards it. It exists, more compelling than at any other moment, just as the pores draw tighter in contact with cold; just as one has gooseflesh at the north pole they are playthings of upheavals, not necessarily persecutions but a breakdown, yes an essential breakdown basically, which reduced them to the abhorred common denominator and forces them to act. But me? I pretend to have motives, I don't have any, I float. (*LRB*, 40)

Alternating with the account of the voyage to Israel are descriptions of a huge fresco that Porridge, who is also an artist, intends to paint. This idea of a canvas that will depict the Creation arises from nowhere. The narrator appears genuinely enthusiastic about this grandiose work of art that he will fill to its farthest corners with all kinds of animals and food. Confusion arises in the reader's mind as to which project—the novel or the oversize painting of the universe—is really Porridge's priority. Far from dissipating this uncertainty, Pinget increases it by having his narrator switch suddenly and unexpectedly back to the trip to the Holy Land. What is happening now? Is Porridge oscillating between one artistic form and another in the hope of finding the one more appropriate to convey his monumental vision? Has he given up on either?

As far as the novel is concerned, the reader is justified in being perplexed. What exactly is going on? Would Pinget like us to believe that Porridge has "really" embarked on a voyage to the Holy Land and is recording his impressions with a view to incorporating them into his anticipated work of fiction? Would he prefer that we consider the events the narrator is describing as coming straight out of the latter's imagination? Or is it more likely that Pinget is perfectly happy to envelop the text in a halo of ambiguity, since every writer converts the raw material of his experience into an imaginary world. This impression of ambiguity is reinforced by the frequently scrambled time sequences. Just when the narrator seems to be settling down to relate a coherent story, there are wild swings back and forth from the present to the past. Anachronistic characters appear out of nowhere and draw their twentieth-century counterparts into a strange time warp, only to disappear and be replaced by a voluble tourist guide extolling the modern Jewish state. David and the Fox meet the Sultan Suliman the Magnificent, then Don Quixote. The weirdest encounter is probably that of the sublime sinner herself, Mary Magdalene, who, magically resurrected by the novelist and true to her original calling, continues practicing the oldest profession in the world at the time of the Crusades, and even offers her favors to a French sailor in order to ensure David and the Fox's passage back to France on one of Saint-Louis's ships.

After a while, though, questions about the meaning of these abrupt shifts in time and space become irrelevant. The novel increasingly appears to be an allegory of the search for artistic purpose. The presence of Don Quixote underscores this interpretation. As Robert M. Henkels, Jr., very perceptively observes, there is a superficial resemblance between Cervantes' insanely idealistic knight and Pinget's fervently religious old Jew, and a profound resemblance between John Tintouin Porridge's quest and Don Quixote's impossible dream (Henkels, 31). The Spanish hidalgo longs to impose his fixed, Utopian vision on an endlessly fluid reality that is refractory to it. The narrator yearns to enclose the activity of his overheated, exploding imagination within the confines of the traditional linear structure. Needless to say, the outmoded form he tries to use cannot withstand the stress of his inspiration. It simply breaks down, leaving him with no other alternative but to abandon his projected novel based on the adventures of David and the Fox.

Once Porridge gives up on this story, he finds himself back in his room, relating the humdrum events in Fantoine and Agapa, leading the reader to believe that he had never left his familiar surroundings in the first place. Once he has "landed" back on his home territory, it becomes increasingly obvious that what counts for him henceforth is not the telling of a traditional story. He concentrates now on exploring the relationship between order and chaos. He conducts experiments in the explosive potential contained in words used normally to sustain logical discourse. The outward voyage, real or imaginary, has thus been supplanted by an inner voyage, and keeping a diary to record his various discoveries becomes an end in itself.

Seen in this light, the totally unpredictable and increasingly wild swings in perspective within Porridge's narrative begin to "make sense," if that term can be deemed appropriate in such an unusual context. He is simply trying out different ways to probe his psychic resources. For a while he writes his diary as though the old shoemaker, Chinze, were commenting on the local events. He then has a harridan burst into a doctor's office and rough up a female patient who has just undergone a miraculous cure. But he reaches dizzying surrealistic heights in the episode of the medical amphitheater. Here a surgeon unflinchingly dissects the body of Joan of Arc. Suddenly spectators at this public dissection are overcome with horror as the doctor points out that the Maid of Orleans has male reproductive organs. At this point the dialogue skids like a car out of control. Words wrest themselves free from any logical connotations or connections, and in their breathless succession they constitute a remarkable display of pyrotechnics reminiscent of Eugène Ionesco's play *The Bald Soprano* (the French text is followed by my translation):

—Miséricorde, dit l'abbé. —Juste ciel, dit l'institutrice. —Mein Gott, dit le bilan. —Diantre, dit la générale. —Les vaches, disent Cécile et Michonne. —Superbe, dit Poppie. —Vice de forme, disent les jurés. —A croquer, dit le rat d'égout. —Guignolesque, dit le tailleur . . . —Sauteuse. —Fumier. —Crotte de bique. —Arbousier. —Coloquinte. —Faisan. —Faisandée. —Pebroque. —Parapluie, madame. —Instigateur. —Souricière. —Chapardeur. —Oiseleuse. —Trou du cul. —Fesses-cuites. —Bitte de singe. —Plume d'oie. —Couille d'asperge. —Verge d'arsouille. —Souille la vierge. —Perce-la-nouille . . .

Mercy, says the priest. —Good Heavens, says the school teacher. —Mein Gott, says the Balance-sheet. —What the devil, says the general's wife. —Those buggers, say Cécile and Michonne. —Superb, says Poppie. —Legal defect, say the jurors. —Looks good enough to eat, says the sewer rat. —Preposterous, says the tailor . . . —Whore. —Manure pile. —It's not worth shit. —Cane-apple. —Bitter-apple. —Crook. —Decadent woman. —Umbrella. —Umbrella, madame. — Instigator. —Mouse-trap. —Pilferer. —Fowler. —Asshole. —Cooked buttocks. —Monkey prick. —Goose feather. —Asparagus-ball. —Blackguard cock. —Sully the virgin. —Pierce the noodle. (*LRB*, 211–12)

Frustrated by his inability to get his novel moving in any direction, Porridge seeks out the guidance of Mlle Lorpailleur, the embodiment of conservatism in novel-writing and consequently the last person in the world who could understand his quest for a new aesthetic vision. She is impressed by the maxims and aphorisms he has formulated in his diary but believes they would carry much more conviction if uttered by characters in a story. She is quite astounded to learn that he has all kinds of characters running around in his mind, from biblical to literary figures, from Pharaohs to cats, dogs, the Sea of Galilee, the River Jordan and herself. What she finds impossible to understand is that her colleague does not have a specific subject in the traditional sense of the word. In fact, he does not *want* to have one. Telling a story in linear sequence does not interest him at all. It is the continuous "branching off" from a given point of departure that appears to him as the only subject worth writing about.

Mlle Lorpailleur strongly disagrees. She advises "Johnny," as she calls him, to forget about his proliferating material and ground his novel in a specific time and place. She rattles off a whole catalog of possible opening paragraphs, beginning with the words "I was born." Her colleague's reluctance to accept any of her suggestions whips her emotions up to a paroxysm. What follows is the verbal equivalent of frothing at the mouth. Simply by calling her conventional wisdom into question, Porridge seems to have pulled on a thread of Lorpailleur's so-called rational discourse and made its whole fabric unravel:

Je suis née à brûle-pourpoint (Rire d'hystérique). Autant dire que j'étais brûlée à l'avance. A qui la faute? Première-née, nouveau-née, dernière-née, mort-née, ivre-morte, aigre-doux, vert-de-grisée, trotte-menu, tire-bouchonnant, tragi-comique, sous-cutanée, pseudo-feuillue, quasi- contrate, néo-sexy, post-natatoire, avant-coureuse, semi-lunaire, intra-veineuse . . . tue-mouche, mezzo-soprano, pituite, mouline-à-vente, caf-conce, frou-frouteuse, verveine, calligraphe, cacophone, chattière, rattière, belle-manière, maniabelluaire, bagnolanière, mille-bannière, mer, mer, mer, mer . . .

I was born red hot. (Hysterical laughter). You might say that I was in heat early. Whose fault was it? (I was) first born, new born, last born, born dead, dead drunk, sweet and sour, coated with verdigris, pitter-pattering, screwing up, tragic-comic, subcutaneous, pseudo-foliaged, nearly cuntracted, neo-sexy, post-natatory, fore-runner, semi-lunary, intra-venous, . . . fly-swatter, mezzo-soprano, catarrhous, chatter-box, jukebox, show-off, verbena, calligrapher, cacophone, catlike, ratlike, ladylike, manic beast-tamer, car-crazy, banner-crazy, sii, sii, sii, sii . . . (*LRB*, 235–36)

We never find out whether John Tintouin Porridge succumbs to Mlle Lorpailleur's raving siren song or perseveres in his search for new ways of expressing the endless branching-off of life. We can be sure, though, that not only has Robert Pinget discarded the novel-writing madwoman's precepts as obsolete, but he is moving forward intrepidly in his voyage of self-exploration. In *Entre Fantoine et Agapa* he spoofed literary traditions. In *Mahu, ou le matériau* he exposed their inadequacy. In *Le Renard et la boussole* he lets us understand that in the not too distant future he will have to cast them aside for good.

Graal Flibuste

In some respects *Graal Flibuste* (1956) represents yet another parody of the traditional novel, yet another demonstration of its inadequacy. More clearly even than in *Le Renard et la boussole*, we are dealing here with a voyage that goes around in circles, leaving the travelers even more perplexed than when they set off on their adventures. While spoofing the conventional voyage narration, however, Pinget adds a dimension not present in his previous work. Through his unnamed narrator he meditates on the problem of freedom, both in the personal and aesthetic sense. Once you possess it, or think you possess it, what do you do with it? Where will it take you? Moreover, if you free yourself from traditional anchors, will you not need to find others?

As the novel progresses these questions will appear all the more urgent because what the narrator and his servant Brindon seek out is never sharply defined. Ostensibly the two are searching for the deity called Graal Flibuste, but his nature is swathed in mystery. His very name is fraught with ambiguity, suggesting two incompatible elements. The first word, "Graal" (Grail), has the connotation of a religious quest at the end of which the pilgrim will find spiritual fulfillment. The second word, "Flibuste" (Buccaneering), evokes rollicking adventures or even perils and flatly contradicts the idea of religious reverence. The closest we get to this deity is the temple erected to him in the rat-infested valley of Le Chanchèze. Decaying on the outside, sumptuously decorated but deserted on the inside, the sadness of the place is almost palpable. The description Pinget gives us seems to come straight out of a bad dream, up to and including the odors of decomposing rodent corpses, which overcome the visitor the moment he emerges from the temple. Graal Flibuste may be omnipresent, but he remains unreachable. In fact, the novel functions like a Grail quest in reverse. The more the two travelers seek out the unattainable divinity, the more it keeps receding. By the end of the novel it has become more or less irrelevant.

A similar mystery surrounds the beginning of the narrative. A foul-smelling, ugly cat and a brutal, hallucinating drunkard are locked in an attraction-repulsion relationship. Both are filled with self-loathing and feel a strange pity mixed with contempt for the other. The animal sums up the situation in a succinct statement: "We are well matched, he thinks I'm a ridiculous monster and he's a flop, which is one and the same thing."[6] When he is not throwing bread-crumb pellets at the unfortunate cat, the drunkard is obsessed by a letter he has been trying unsuccessfully to finish. Is he referring to the voyage narrative that will follow? Has he actually composed the text, or is he imagining all of these adventures? Is he a self-deluding fool or an artist anguished by the fear of failure? Could he be both at the same time?

The reader will never find out because the whole novel is a succession of dead ends. Adventures end as abruptly as they had begun, only to be followed by others whose place in the novel's architecture is just as arbitrary as the preceding ones. There is no compelling reason for the visit to the Sultan's palace by the narrator and his coachman, Brindon, to be related before the sojourn in Jasmin's domain or in the Country of the Wind. This very arbitrariness underscores the artificiality of the travel genre Pinget is intent on parodying. This outmoded literary form foists on the reader the illusion that events flow naturally, organically from one another, whereas in reality they tend to pile up without rhyme or reason in the most helter-skelter ways. The author deliberately—one might even say gleefully—gets his travelers involved in the weirdest episodes in order to dynamite this illusion. And if this were not enough, the sheer weirdness of the successive situations seems to imply that the inventiveness of fiction can exceed by far that of reality itself. Thus, while making sport of the traditional voyage novel, Pinget is demonstrating that, in regard to richness of imagination, he is capable of going it one better.

This seemingly inexhaustible power to invent comes through in the digressions as much as in the main episodes. The first one describes the stormy life of Coco, son of a nobleman, who is abducted by pirates, sodomized, becomes a male prostitute when finances warrant it, conquers the heart of his father's former mistress, marries the Sultan's daughter, and, after the Sultan's death, ascends the throne himself. Another story relates the adventures of the Duchess de Bois-Suspect. While less perilous, they are just as wild from the erotic point of view. Born and raised in a society that obliges women to kill off their husbands after the third or fourth child, the lady enjoys her first fling at 14, for which she pays dearly; is rescued from a deplorable fate by a sailor endowed with limitless virile propulsion, named "Loulou"; dumps him in favor of an ardently poetic soul who appears to pursue some transcendent idea; returns to her sailor; leaves him for good when he takes to the bottle; finds an ambiguous position as housekeeper-mistress to a self-indulgent priest; and finally marries the Duke de Bois-Suspect on the priest's recommendation.

One of the last secondary narratives in the novel relates the fall from grace of the new curate in the town of Gea. This idealistic young man sincerely believes in his spiritual mission until a rascally altar boy, nicknamed "Totoche," seduces him in the dimly lit church, before the altar itself, under the disapprovingly absent gaze of St. Chu's statue. From that moment on the unfortunate priest abandons himself to his homosexual nature, becoming the plaything of just about every similarly inclined adolescent in the parish, acquiring in the process a notorious reputation and referred to thereafter as "Bouge-croupe" (Moving Rump).

This saucy anecdote crops up unexpectedly during a conversation, which Brindon strikes up with a peasant as he proceeds on foot from the train station to the Château de Bonne-Mesure, where he plans on investigating a mysterious theft. The peasant had offered his services as a baggage-porter, and being as loquacious as he was sociable, launched into an interminable discourse on the mores of the region. After relating "Bouge-croupe's" downfall, he starts telling Brindon about the unscrupulous lawyer, Braille. This latest digression within a digression with its varied anecdotes could have easily gone on much longer had Brindon not cut off his interlocutor abruptly once they arrived at the château. It provides yet another illustration of the "branching off" of events that John Tintouin Porridge considered the essence of the novelist's task. It also provides new insights into the novelist's dilemma. Despite his longing to take in the whole fluid mass of reality, sooner or later he will have to make arbitrary choices. Sooner or later he will have to put an end to his discourse, just as Brindon suddenly had to silence his new acquaintance.

A similar dilemma faces the novelist with regard to the principal episodes. He may wish, like Mahu and John Tintouin Porridge in his previous works, to suggest the restless movement of life or display the inexhaustible inventiveness of his imagination. Nevertheless, he must interrupt the flow of his inspiration lest his text balloon out of control. The result is a succession of disconnected adventures that, however different from one another, end up by arousing in the reader a strange feeling of déjà vu. The two travelers may learn more about themselves through their new experiences, but they are no closer to reaching their goal after any of them. One cannot even apply the term "setback" to any of the crises in which they become enmeshed, since no matter what they experience, they are always marking time. Their physical space may change, but change never appears as the outward manifestation of a destiny to be fulfilled. The events they participate in simply do not add up. Spiritually, they remain immobile. Their lives seem to lack any overarching significance. In fact, as *Graal Flibuste* hurtles toward the final chapter, their initial joviality leaves them, only to be replaced by a gnawing, imprecise anxiety. Not only are they not going anywhere, despite the material distances traveled, they can *sense* that they are not going anywhere.

After their encounter with the Sultan, they eventually come upon the country of the camphor-eaters—physically repulsive but eminently hospitable humanoids who possess two virtues sorely lacking in many "normal" humans: a complete indifference toward gossip and tolerance of other people's life-styles. Brindon falls under the spell of a female creature that is broken only when his master kills her. It is a far cry from the country of the camphor-eaters to the next domain into which they wander—that of the insatiable hedonist Jasmin. This episode constitutes an "eye-opener" in the metaphorical sense for the narrator. Under the tutelage of his gracious host, he discovers an ardent sensuality lurking behind the facade of timidity. He ends up concurring in Jasmin's firmly held conviction that "the bed . . . teaches us more about someone than the longest speeches" (*GF*, 134).

One of the last major episodes, and certainly the most convoluted, deals with the Prefect Victor and the mysterious goings-on at the Château de Bonne-Mesure. The narrator arrives in a village shortly after the Prefect's wife has given birth to a son. Just before the baptism is to take place in the church, he learns to his astonishment that the Prefect has chosen him to be the baby's godfather. The whole ceremony, as Pinget describes it, is obviously a send-up of solemn religious rites that border dangerously on magic. During the course of the service the baby, a rather ungainly sausage-colored creature, is transformed into a crab, then into a lizard that nearly escapes, then into a pear, which is sprinkled with armagnac, before recovering his disgraceful human form. The infant's mother dies soon after the baptism, and the father, beside himself with grief, becomes a "necrophonique"—an emotionally disturbed person who is convinced he can speak to the dead by telephone.

Believing that he is carrying out his late wife's instructions, the Prefect orders her remains to be transported to the cemetery of her ancestors. As it turns out, however, it is the remains of someone else, the great-great-aunt of Mlle Dunu, an impoverished aristocrat who steals them along with all of the material possessions left in the funeral convoy when the so-called mourners—made up of the Prefect, the narrator, Brindon, and the local curate—stop at her château to refresh themselves with copious libations. In their attempt to shed light on this mysterious theft, the narrator and his servant decide to interrogate Mlle Dunu, as well as her supposed accomplice, Germaine Ferrant, whom they suspect of harboring sinister designs, including murder. After pursuing their investigation at some length, however, they conclude that their conspiracy theory is groundless and that their overheated imagination had tried to impose upon reality an interpretation that simply does not work.

This incredibly complicated episode in which the narrator and Brindon try their hand at being sleuths underscores one of Pinget's strongest beliefs—namely, that the way we decipher reality depends on our perception of it. Whatever we experience, we refract. We cannot reproduce it as it supposedly is. What deforms our perceptions even further is the language we use to formulate them. Words are supposed to correspond exactly to the manifestations of reality, which we endeavor to understand. At least we take comfort in this notion. In biblical texts words do not simply point to the elements of the universe. Through words, they come into being. But what if this were only an illusion? What if all words, both sacred and profane, were nothing more than desperate attempts to apprehend that which, by nature, is too fluid and complex to be encompassed? The genealogy of Graal Flibuste that Pinget retraces with devilish humor makes a mockery of our arrogance. He enumerates the names of the deities composing the endless chain of ancestors, which eventually lead to the great god himself. We never get to him, however. As though to point out the utter futility of this endeavor, the author has the enumeration proliferate and degenerate into an increasingly incomprehensible babble:

Paminoir begat Dinguetonne.
Dingeutonne begat Affaful.
Affaful begat Boute-Boute.
Boute-Boute begat Lapa.
Lapa begat Miamsk.
Miamsk begat Loin.
Loin begat Peute.
Peute begat Peute-Peute.
Peute-Peute begat Cornette.
Cornette begat Vallée-Sanzi.
Vallée-Sanzi begat Tourte.
Tourte begat Tarte.
Tarte begat Bonne-Confiture. (*GF*, 73)

As though to drive home the message even more forcefully that words cannot in themselves reproduce reality, Pinget later in the novel describes (in a special section titled "Flore") the completely imaginary flora in his completely imaginary world as though it were real. One short example will suffice: "*Les abergères*. Plantes pharmaceutiques à odeur d'ail" ("The abergères: Pharmaceutical plants with a garlic odor"). Through this miniature lexicon Pinget seems to be telling us in his inimitably facetious manner that words excel in creating fiction.

Poetic creation, then, represents the outline of a solution to the dilemma of the novelist, which was brought up in *Mahu, ou le matériau* and *Le Renard et la boussole*. If there is indeed an insurmountable contradiction between the proliferating raw material of life and the linear structures that were supposed to enclose it, why rack one's brains trying to reconcile incompatible elements? Why not simply revel in the unlimited freedom that the imagination offers, using words to express its soaring flights? At one point in the novel Brindon's horse, Clotho, symbolizes the power of inspiration, which touches off an exhilarating expansion of the narrator's mind. As he describes the animal's metamorphosis into a fabulous mythological creature, the narrator expresses a joy bordering on rapture. In this sublime moment, artistic creation becomes an absolute unto itself:

Now he is starting to grow, and grow. He goes from grey to yellow, then snow white, then diamondlike transparencies. His head touches the ceiling, it makes it burst like paper, then the roof is nothing more than a little collar around the gigantic neck, the body a cathedral, the feet pillars. A sumptuous tail unfurls and sweeps the air. "Clotho! I stammered, stay with me!" I saw his feet ready to leave the ground, they stamped, but

Clotho did not fly off. Then there was no more stable, no more village, no more friends, nothing except this triumphant horse lighting up the night, and I watching him like a weakling. The entire circulatory system appeared behind the crystal, I saw the heart beating and the arteries palpitating, the blood flowing through the veins. From red he turned to gold, he set the points of the compass ablaze. It was no longer Clotho's life, it was the life of the firmament, the movement of the world with its billions of stars, universal gravitation. Then I heard the voice of heaven thunder, but how can one transcribe a celestial word? (*GF*, 45–46)

Freedom is exhilarating. It also exacts a heavy price. However unusual the modes of thought and sensibility one may devise, they can trap their creator within their specific forms, turning him into their slaves. Practicing these indefinitely can lead to satiation and even disgust. Thus, the narrator and Brindon decide to give up the hedonistic way of life practiced by Jasmin and his friends, despite the genuine empathy they feel for these carousers. Another danger is that what was once bold and original can, in time, become outmoded or even deteriorate, since everything human is subject to change. The section titled "La Quête d'amour de la sorcière Vaoua" ("Vaoua the Sorceress's Quest for Love") can be interpreted as an allegorical illustration to this danger. Vaoua, the sea sorceress, revels in her ardent and insatiable eroticism and pays homage to her mother, Bath, the empress of the waters, for having given her "these breasts, this womb and this nice warm hole, where soft little sticks of flesh dart in and out" (*GF*, 78). But once old age sets in with the decrepitude it inevitably brings, Vaoua's sexual exploits are only a memory.

Rejecting the constraints imposed by any form does not represent a satisfactory solution either. Man may yearn for an unlimited expansion of his being, but he cannot survive for long without a center of gravity in the figurative sense, which only specific boundaries provide. Total freedom leads to an absence of intellectual and spiritual density inasmuch as the being is spread out too thinly. Floating about in a state of levitation engenders illusions. For this reason the narrator decides to leave the Country of the Wind where he was at one time tempted to put down roots:

I, who thought I'd settle in the Country of the Wind, enchanted as I had been by my first contact with it, suddenly wished to leave it at once. There was nothing genuine, consequently nothing to keep you there, neither in the countryside or the people; you didn't know in the morning if you were sleeping or had slept, unusual situations were perhaps only imaginary, you were taken in more by yourself than by others, you couldn't count on anything and these fantasies quickly disgusted me. Gloomy ideas beset me every evening instead of the joy I had expected; I even began talking about suicide. Truly, our nature is disconcerting; it aspires to freedom and as soon as it is offered to us, we feel we are caught in a vice. (*GF*, 154–55)

Thus, the novelist will always be torn between the yearning for total freedom and the awareness that structures may be a necessary evil. Necessary, because they give his being a sharpness of focus it would otherwise not have. Evil, because they force him to exclude innumerable possibilities of expression, which are equally valid. Yet despite an almost irresistible temptation to conclude—and consequently to exclude—the narrator in *Graal Flibuste* feels compelled to pursue his voyage of self-discovery. Toward the end of the novel Brindon and his master express eagerness and excitement at the thought of reaching the ocean, certainly a most natural way to bring a land adventure to its conclusion. Here land as well as sky dissolve in a common element: water. Even more than a geographical boundary, the sea is a symbolic one. Once the travelers arrive at its shore, their tribulations will be behind them. Their wanderings can finally stop.

But at the very moment the narrator seems to want to end his travels or his self-exploration, his resolve is shaken. He realizes that although the sea symbolizes a frontier, his mind is reluctant to be held back by frontiers. Any ending is artificial; therefore it is a mirage. And so, just like a mirage, the sea disappears, to be replaced by a totally different landscape. The narrator resumes his travels, moving farther and farther away from the ocean, not so much because he is afraid of not being able to describe it, as Brindon suggests, but because he wishes to remain faithful to his vision of life as an endless, inexhaustible flow.

The travelers eventually come upon a triumphal arch. It is as overpowering in its physical proportions as in its bizarre beauty. Unlike the ocean, it does not symbolize limits. With immense territories before it—the ones over which the narrator has just passed—and a city spreading out behind it, this portal represents a particular stage in a never-ending journey. On approaching it, the narrator launches into a description of its fascinating structure. And how could it be otherwise? Life flows on indefinitely, and the artist must move along with it. *Graal Flibuste* illustrates this conviction by depicting a voyage through a spatial landscape. The next novel, *Baga*, will affirm a similar point of view by relating a journey through a mental one.

Baga

The narrator in *Graal Flibuste* and King Architruc in *Baga* (1958) are strikingly similar and different. Both have very restless natures. But whereas the narrator finds an outlet for his restlessness in incessant travel, the monarch manifests his through mythomania as he fashions for himself one new identity after another. Both men feel a strong need for some inner center of gravity. While the narrator views the exercise of total freedom as being incompatible with the search for a stable identity, however, Architruc sees in it the indispensable instrument for realizing this objective. Endowed with a very fertile imagination, he uses his freedom to imagine all kinds of possible existences in the hope of eventually discovering which "version" of himself is the most authentic.

Who is this Achitruc? If Pinget were a traditional novelist, we would be invited to suspend our disbelief and imagine him as a wildly eccentric king of some run-down kingdom, a man with some pretty raunchy erotic inclinations who drifts off into mythomania to exorcise his boredom. But Pinget is a serious prankster and has conjured up a very ambiguous atmosphere around his character. As Architruc projects himself into one fantasy after another, the reader begins to question the initial hypothesis on which the novel is founded. Is Architruc really a monarch, or is he a pathetic clown pretending to be one? Are any of his avatars to be taken seriously, or are they all simply the products of an overheated imagination for which the line of demarcation between fact and fiction has been blotted out?

The accumulation of details in the novel does not guarantee the accuracy of Architruc's account of what supposedly happened because they contradict one another. At first the narration presents itself as a series of harmless anecdotes, but as the king's attempts to reconstruct his past gets bogged down in contradictions and incongruous fantasies, it ends up in generalized negation. The narrator himself does not seem to believe what he is relating, or he does not succeed in believing it, all the while desperately trying to find some landmark—the time beyond which reality somersaults into fiction. Recalling the Novocardian War, or rather the first version of it, Architruc laments, "It's painful. I wanted to go as far as possible. To play the game, as they say. You could certainly see that I didn't believe it, couldn't you? What can you believe? From what moment on is everything false? The ambassadors? No, I remember having spoken to them. Our departure during the night? My taking charge? I don't know any more, I don't know any more."[7]

In the long run it matters not one whit whether Architruc has imagined some or all of his experiences. His propensity for mythomania reveals a profound truth about his and our human condition. By projecting himself into various situations, real or imaginary, he expresses a yearning to pull himself away from the periphery of his being and move toward its core. When we consider his physical appearance, it is not at all surprising that Architruc should wish to escape so frequently into the realm of fantasy. He is an ungainly creature who views himself in the mirror with a mixture of self-loathing and mockery:

> I have a swollen, pimply head. Splotches and spots everywhere. My eyelashes fall down into my eyes. My nose looks like a potato and my ears like cabbage leaves. My hair is pale red. My teeth too. My neck is thick and white, my sagging breasts are held up under my arms by unkempt yellow hairs. I have three bristles on the sternum, which I shave every Saturday. My belly is swollen from the stomach down. In the past I used to keep it in like everybody else, not now. I can see my sex organ only when I bend forward. There is no stunning surprise. The hair is just a little less yellow there than under my arms, my penis is stout and my testicles are distended. . . . My thighs are like spindles and my rear end enormous. When I look at myself in the mirror I look like a fat white worm. (B, 66–67)

In the light of this description, it is obvious that his name or nickname, "Architruc," meaning "Huge Thingamajig," with its derisive connotations, fits him like a glove. The disgust he feels toward his body extends to his personality. Inertia and aimlessness are its dominant traits. Sleep provides an escape from boredom. At the beginning of the novel Architruc describes with self-deprecating humor the all-pervasive mess into which his mind has degenerated and his resignation to this state: "I am a King. Yes, a King. I am King of me. Of my filth. I and my filth have a King. I mean the filth of my mind. Because I have a mind. A mind that gets itself all fouled up. I've given up on having it cleaned out. You no longer feel like moving. After a certain age you no longer feel like moving. I still mean the mind, but it's the same thing. You get used to it. You find corners. You curl up. You caress your knees" (B, 7).

The company he keeps can hardly be considered edifying either. His minister, Baga, has a sinister cynicism about him. His court musicians have become besotted louts by dint of performing the same tune again and again over a period of twenty years. His royal colleague, Queen Conegrund ("Big Cunt"), who pays him a state visit, has an insatiable appetite for food and sex (as her name implies). During festivities in her honor, she takes a shine to a black dishwasher, putting on a torrid erotic exhibition with him in full public view. When Architruc grows weary of navel-gazing both in the physical and figurative sense, he imagines the comments his courtiers are making about him as he dines on his perennial menu of beef. Needless to say, they are far from flattering, with expressions like *moche* (lousy) and *vieux cochon* (old pig), being quite the norm.

To give some purpose to his rudderless existence, Architruc decides to write his memoirs for his nephews. But instead of shedding light on the mysteries of his being, his self-exploration leads him deeper and deeper into his own labyrinth. He projects a succession of incongruous fantasies on the screen of his mind, thereby raising even more questions about his "real" identity. If he possesses within him the potential for so many disparate—indeed, contradictory—possibilities of existence, how can he ever discover his authentic self?

For a while it seems to the reader that Baga will provide his master with the stability he so desperately needs. Part father figure, confidant, friend (and lover?), Baga, like the deity Graal Flibuste, remains an enigma. He is, of course, a more concrete presence than the mythological god of the previous novel, but his character and motives are enveloped in ambiguity. We never get to see this minister from the inside. He appears to us always through the deforming prism of Architruc's temperament. The king's attachment to his minister can be traced back to his coronation. Just before a solemn moment during the ceremony, the king developed an upset stomach, which Baga was able to cure. Fearing recurrences of the same malady, a grateful Architruc raised the man to the rank of prime minister, even though the Queen Mother expressed strenuous objections to this appointment. The queen's opposition is never explained, but we learn later when Architruc imagines himself being interrogated by an examining magistrate that he fell in love with Baga and appointed him to high office in order to entice him away from his mother. He even alleges that Baga had his (Architruc's) father murdered so that he could govern the country through the dead king's widow.

To thicken the mystery surrounding the prime minister, there is the issue of his shady involvement in the Novocardian War. Ambassadors from the neighboring country, Novocardie, deliver a warning to King Architruc. They will take possession of the valley of Le Chanchèze, where the temple of Graal Flibuste is situated, if the king continues to ignore their requests to exterminate the rats that have been devastating the part of the valley within their borders. Working himself up into a paroxysm of self-righteous indignation worthy of Rabelais's bilious monarch Pichrochole, Architruc denies that any such petitions ever reached him and resolves to wage a defensive war against such mendacious enemies. The ensuing battle, as Pinget describes it through his narrator, appears totally unreal and highly comical. There exists a disproportion between the inflated patriotic rhetoric spouted by the king and the pathetically inadequate forces he deploys to wage this "just" war. Architruc has no alternative but to requisition a taxi to reach the front, bringing with him provisions as though he were embarking on some picnic.

Architruc manages to achieve a brilliant victory (or imagines that he has) by bringing the maddened rodents into the enemy battalions, but a flippant remark dropped by Baga before the battle makes him eventually question his minister's honesty. While the king was haranguing his subjects to rev them up for combat, Baga had pointed out cynically that the rat population of the Chanchèze was an important source of state revenue and that much of the profits had been poured into the purchase of weapons to wage the war. This remark is enough to make Architruc suspect his minister of having withheld from him information about the neighboring country's anger. From then on, the prime minister's image becomes increasingly tarnished, his integrity called more and more into question. In fact, Architruc covers this same ground obsessively three times during the course of the novel without reaching any satisfactory conclusions about the confidant to whom he feels irresistibly attracted. It is as though the king recoils in fear at the thought that he might find irrefutable evidence to incriminate his friend, thus losing whatever stability he may have left.

Still, however powerful an influence Baga may exert on his sovereign, it is obviously not sufficient to prevent the latter from wandering off on bizarre tangents in the hope of discovering an elusive identity. After describing the victory he supposedly won over the Novacardians, Architruc relates what *really* (?) happened: a war of attrition, during which most of the population was killed off and he, as their king, contented himself with sleeping it out. Scarcely does he awaken from this long slumber when he projects himself into his first avatar, the furthest one imaginable from his royal station—that of a hermit living a life of poverty in a forest.

What are we to make of this unexpected change? Architruc seems to seek solitude in order to make some sense out of the mess of his existence.

The letters filled with anxiety, which he addresses from his retreat to the outside world—without any hope of a reply—illustrate our interpretation. Writing to a former mistress, he asks her one question after another about their love affair. His inability to remember anything suggests that our recollection of past events is short-lived at best and unreliable at worst. His correspondence with a former beloved takes on a corrosively ironic twist when he assures her that he now has irrefutable proof of their amorous relationship: he has contracted venereal disease, and so she will forever be part of his being:

> Dear pus. I had completely forgotten about our copulation of centuries ago, and lo and behold, it has come back to me through this indiscreet droplet which the doctor calls gonorrhea. So it's true after all that we loved one another! So it's true after all that we wrote verses in the meadows! My pus, my treasure. It's funny nonetheless that you should still be there, in my hut, fully alive at the tip of me, as no photo or lock of hair could ever be! I'm going to water the mushrooms with our love, I'm going to plant a bit of you everywhere and relive some marvelous hours. (*B*, 105)

Once he grows weary of this particular reincarnation, Architruc imagines another: parenthood. He disinherits his nephews for whom he was writing his memoirs and adopts an orphan, Rara. Perhaps as a father he will find himself. Unfortunately, the parental role works no better than that of the recluse. The guilt-ridden king conjures up the next imaginary experience. He projects himself into a Kafkaesque nightmare. He is a prisoner in a jail where days and nights have such an asphyxiating sameness to them that when he reaches the end of November the entries in his diary continue bearing the name of the same month while the numbers indicating the precise day go well beyond the normal 30 days allotted it. He does find Rara again in the prison's kitchen, but he cannot recall whether he is the boy's mother or father. His attempt to extend his existence through another human being has ended in failure.

A final avatar awaits Architruc, just as wild as the preceding ones, but by now the reader is not only accustomed to such transformations, he expects them. Architruc goes off with Baga to construct a splendid castle in the country when suddenly his soul soars out of his body and he is drawn into the orbit of a lesbian mystic, Sister Louise. Now the king is off on a misguided—indeed, semi-phony—mystical kick. Once he begins oozing simplistic piety, he undergoes a sex change. Architruc becomes Sister Angèle and joins forces with his Mother Superior in celebrating God in the image of woman. Inspired by his (her?) new missionary zeal,

Angèle/Architruc resolves to snatch a pure village girl, Marie, from the clutches of her fiancé in order to initiate her into the boundless spiritual love of Christ. But the language used by the recent convert reeks of ambiguity and disguised sexual lust. When Marie falls into Angèle/ Architruc's arms, their union has nothing spiritual about it except the term used by the two self-deluding zealots to describe it.

Architruc eventually recovers his male hormones, unless of course this latest adventure was just as much a manifestation of his mythomania as any of the others. He returns to his prime minister who is eager to show him the castle constructed in his absence. But Architruc is not in the least interested in inspecting it. He returns full circle to his original point of departure. He lapses once again into boredom and inertia.

From the existential point of view, then, the king's imaginary adventures cannot be considered a stunning success. They have left him as confused and unenlightened as before, since no one possibility of existence or group of possibilities can provide the ultimate definition of an individual's identity. From the aesthetic point of view, the results can appear rather disquieting. To paraphrase Olivier de Magny, Robert Pinget uses elaborate tricks to expose the novelist's trickery, thereby raising doubts in *Baga* about the feasibility of writing novels.[8] The author turns the genre of the memoirs upside down just as he had parodied the linear novel and voyage narrative. But this was to be expected. He had to demolish traditional structures that purported to depict reality before charting out a bold, new course. Henceforth, instead of demonstrating that the traditional literary forms cannot espouse the endlessly fluid contours of the imagination, he will allow this power to expand freely as he uses it to create an intensely poetic universe. By plunging into this creative process, Pinget hopes to discover more and more of his essential self.

Chapter Three

In the Labyrinth

The inner voyage of exploration through the creative process is, for Robert Pinget, the most exciting and fruitful upon which one can embark. Nonetheless, it is fraught with perils. Fathoming one's poetic universe is like entering an inextricable labyrinth. Although the possibilities for adventure are endless, so are the anguishes and frustrations. The explorer will rush impetuously along a particular path, buoyed up by the illusion that he is on the verge of making a stunning breakthrough, only to discover to his consternation and despair that he has come against a dead end. If this were not sufficiently discouraging in itself, there is also the danger of losing possession of oneself, or at least of the self that one thought one knew before plunging into uncharted depths.

To evoke this atmosphere of bewilderment in the emotional, moral, and metaphysical sense, the author has recourse—of all things—to the mystery story format. In *Le Fiston* (1959), *Clope au dossier* (1961), *L'Inquisitoire* (1962), and *Quelqu'un* (1965) he parodies the slickly written tale, which is supposed to keep the reader in suspense until the very end. But unlike what we observed in the first cycle of novels, here parody does not seem to be one of Pinget's main intentions. He simply uses the worn-out structure of the traditional whodunit to emphasize that his interest lies elsewhere. The various elements of the conventional mystery narrative are connected in an absolutely rigorous, water-tight manner to convey an impression of inevitability as the sleuth or sleuths move toward an intellectually satisfying solution. In this second cycle the supposedly finely tuned vehicle of the mystery story breaks down simply because it cannot function on the strange terrain over which Pinget is taking it. The chaos of life cannot be reduced to a mathematical formula. In each one of the four novels we will be considering, the object of the original quest soon becomes lost, or irrelevant. After a while we are not really interested in finding the culprit or uncovering a character's hidden motives. We are engrossed in a meditation on the vulnerability of the human condition.

Le Fiston (The Lad)

Obsessively, compulsively, an elderly man, half-besotted with alcohol, resumes writing the same unfinished letter to a son who ran away from home many years before. At times, his thoughts move along in clear, straightforward patterns, leading the reader to expect some unequivocal answers to the questions raised. Then, without any warning, he switches into reverse, going back over ground that appeared to have been already covered. "Facts" become distorted the second or third time around; names and people are substituted for one another. The distraught father, M. Levert, pours out an endless flow of words as much to conceal as to reveal his deepest emotions. As we penetrate further and further into the convolutions of his sick mind, the reasons for his son's disappearance, and even the question about the existence or nonexistence of the young man, lose their relevance. The novel holds our attention because it describes in gripping terms the muddled agony of a human being longing for companionship and understanding but sensing that he will have neither.

Le Fiston develops from a terse, dispassionate statement about a village girl, Marie Chinze: "The shoemaker's daughter has died." The as yet unknown narrator then gives an apparently objective account of the funeral and of the people attending it. Afterwards he relates their various activities once the service is over. Roger, Marie's older brother, and his pregnant wife drive home with another couple. During the trip Roger's wife becomes nauseated. We switch to another branch of the same family, Mme Pacot, her husband, and their rebellious daughter, Alice. The young lady meets her lover, Georges, on the street, to the consternation of her parents, who cannot stomach his coarse behavior. When the Pacots return to the privacy of their home, they reprimand their daughter for her lack of judgment. Unaffected by their indignation, she steals out of the house and seeks out the man of her choice.

The scene changes abruptly to the rectory, where the rather crabby housekeeper, Odette, is making lunch for the priest, who officiated at the Mass. After having his meal, he travels to Sirancy by bus to visit some sick parishioners. Then another scene change takes place. We are in a café where two brothers, Victor and Pierre Moule, and one of the waiters are engaged in a flippant discussion about sex. Pierre is the fiancé of Simone Brize, whom we will meet in Pinget's next novel, Clope au dossier. When they leave the café the two brothers head back for the farm, which they occupy with their mother.

The description of a villa comes next, bogged down in a welter of details. We learn that it belongs to a M. Levert. This is the first time in the novel that the old man is mentioned by name. Although we do not meet him immediately, we gain an inkling into his twisted psyche when Pinget depicts the garden surrounding the house: "The garden is situated in front, a very well-kept garden in the French manner. First there is a gravel terrace, which surrounds the house. On the street side it is enclosed by a low wall with a railing on top of it, which forms a little courtyard. On the other side it gives way to flower beds of different shapes surrounded by boxwood hedges and planted with flowers or grass. The little paths dividing them are of gravel too. Some are shaded by rare trees, which had at one time been planted at regular intervals, but since then several of these have died. Those that remain break the garden's symmetry."[1] This lack of symmetry suggests a disquieting malaise that will become more obvious as the novel unfolds.

The narrator inserts Levert in the story's context by relating his encounter with an elderly woodcutter on his property. The woman informs him that the church bells are ringing for the shoemaker's daughter who has passed away. Once he takes his leave of her, Levert begins writing in the grape arbor of his garden. The narrator notes that a bird was singing overhead. He will make this same remark many times during the course of the narrative, with the result that the past and present will be scrambled. Levert pursues his writing inside, and we are treated to an exhaustive detailing of the house's contents. Retrospectively, this unnecessary inventory will appear as an attempt on the part of the elderly man to dissimulate his anxiety. Late in the afternoon, Levert's sister and her daughter, Francine, come for a visit. For the third time, he asks them the same question to which the woodcutter and then his maid have already given the same answer: "Who has died?"

We then discover that Levert has been laboring over the same letter to his son for the past 10 years, torn between the desire to send it off and arouse the young man's pity and his inability to bring the text to a satisfactory conclusion. When the author suddenly tells us that none other than Levert himself has been narrating the novel all along, we are not unduly surprised. Like Sisyphus, he resumes, ad nauseum, the same futile task of composing a never-to-be-sent letter because this activity has become his sole justification for remaining alive. The blurred, semi-incoherent passages of the text betray not only the anguish of solitude but also the awareness that only by verbalizing his feelings can he make them more bearable:

Dear son. I'm starting again. Face discomposed, shoelaces untied, coat loose, hair unkempt, eyes weepy, head empty. This prison where I am. It's starting up again. The hand writing to you. Lost the trail. The trail of the trail of the. My head. The heading. Rush against the wall, get crushed, stairs on the wall, holes. Holes from nails. Wall studded with holes. They move away, they come back. My head studded, these holes in my head, the wall. I didn't want, I wanted. To write you. As though the night in its mercy succeeded in succeeding in gathering under the same roof in its infinite mercy succeeded in gathering under the same roof. Torment. Pierced. This letter will never be sent. (*LF*, 28–29)

At this point an imprecise yet gnawing anxiety begins to take hold of the reader. Levert has been writing an interminable letter to his wayward son in the desperate hope of softening his heart and getting him to come home. Why, then, does the old man dwell at such length on the death of Marie Chinze? Could there be some kind of cause and effect relationship between the girl's death and the son's decision to run away?

The scenes that follow seem to substantiate our suspicions. The novel focuses on Minet Chinze, the deceased girl's brother. While peeling potatoes in the kitchen of a friend's restaurant, he thinks sadly about his sister and recalls the visit of Léon, a chum who stayed with the Chinze family 10 years earlier. He remembers how Marie was attracted to the handsome, athletic young man with the northern accent. Although the two become romantically attached to one another, their relationship never quite got off the ground. Minet remembers that his sister had another opportunity to marry, but passed it up. He then returns to his potatoes.

From here, the story goes into reverse, scrambling the sequence of events. We encounter the elderly female woodcutter again after her conversation with Levert. She comes upon Sophie Narre,[2] the insatiably curious and indefatigable village gossip just as the funeral service is ending. The two women launch into a gossip session during which, through insinuating tones, glances, and silences, it is suggested that Levert may have had an affair with Mme Chinze at one time and that Marie was the result of their illegitimate union. The narrator says nothing either to corroborate or invalidate these innuendos. He does move on unexpectedly, however, to a totally different subject. He begins describing another dwelling he owns in Sirancy. Is he trying to hide his uneasiness or feelings of guilt by rattling on about this other property? In any event, once he finishes the inventory of his villa, he remembers his unhappy relationship with his wife, Mme Levert, a withdrawn, unstable woman who rejected him after the birth of their son, Gilbert. Levert confesses to having spoiled the child by lavishing too much affection on him, especially after his mother passed away. The lonely man even joined his son in drinking bouts in a futile attempt to win the young man's sympathy. Gilbert eventually ran away, leaving nothing but a terse note in which he asked his father not to make any effort to find him.

We still have not found the link between Gilbert's departure and Marie's death. But as Levert's mind continues meandering, we perceive more and more "clues" as to how the two events may be related. First, there is the intensifying feeling of guilt that plagues the distraught father. While muddling up the linear unfolding of events and mistaking one place for another, Levert continues to be tormented by an idée fixe that verges on paranoia: "What they want is for me to confess, not one spring, they plagued me with questions about that girl, that girl, she of the shoemaker, is dead, the funeral, you knew her didn't you, no letter as far as I can recall" (*LF*, 63). Then the elderly man has a nightmare in which Mme Chinze forces him to assume his guilt. It seems to substantiate all of Sophie Narre's insinuations. It is reasonable to assume that Levert did indeed have an affair with Mme Chinze and that Marie really was his illegitimate daughter. Moreover, the reader begins to wonder whether or not Marie's unhappy romance with Léon was nothing more than a camouflage imagined by the guilty narrator to repress the terrifying possibility of incest between Gilbert and the deceased girl.

Under these circumstances it is not at all improbable to conjecture that Gilbert recoiled in horror at the idea of having an incestuous relationship with his half-sister and that the unfortunate young woman was driven to suicide by this revelation:

> Aunt Pacot and Alice are sitting on the couch, old Chinze and Minet are sitting in the other two armchairs. From the bag which she is clutching like a wreckage, Madame Chinze takes a medicine bottle which she puts down on the desk next to the little lamp. She says, "They claim that your son knew her or me, you haven't seen me in nearly 10 years, now I'm willing to tell you, Marie was sitting beside him and that's how it all started. This swimming contest with Yvonne and Henriette. He took her in his arms. I knew what they were asserting, I'm passing it on to you. Your medicine. Next to the little lamp. Jealous I have never been. I liked her. I maintain that you were there. At the burial. Monsier Levert I maintain it. And Sophie Narre. Sophie Narre. So-phi-naaaaaaaare. So-phiiiiiiiii" (*LF*, 64–65)

The repetition four times in a row of the village gossip's name and the breaking down of her name into three syllables, followed by the stretching out of the vowels "narre" and "phi," create an impression of excruciating pain. It is as though Sophie Narre's very name and person symbolize Levert's moral conscience, which multiplies his torment to an infinite degree.

Since the old man seems on the verge of making a clear confession, the reader expects the story to be "wrapped up" imminently. But in Pinget's nonlinear, asymmetrical universe, events do not get tidied up neatly. Levert's discourse shifts into the conditional tense, and so-called facts evaporate into mere hypotheses. When the narrator slips away to the cemetery at night the reader again anticipates a definitive revelation. Again he is disappointed. Levert does not pour out his remorse over his illegitimate daughter's grave, if indeed Marie was the child he never acknowledged. Instead, he meditates on the enigma of the human condition and the importance of writing as a way of exorcizing death— themes that will recur with increasing frequency in Pinget's works.

In the course of his monologue Levert expresses the belief that there is no transcendent justification for any particular existence. For any one kind of life we may lead as a result of circumstances, it is easy to imagine an infinite number of other possibilities we will never have an opportunity to explore. Digging into a hypothetical past to conjure up imaginary existences one might have embodied brings with it the solace of being able temporarily to forget one's mortal condition. Levert observes, while dragging himself over the moonlit road to the cemetery, "Reduced even to imagining what one might have been. To being what one has not been. Sometimes one, sometimes the other, approximately, haunted by one's own dead, 10 years, and from this so-called lottery will come out a story mixed with what one could have been if one had not been. His father. His son. His daughter. His neighbors. His cut wood. His telephone" (*LF*, 66). Levert's gaze scans the numerous graves—Marie's, his wife's, as well as all of the other deceased now reduced to nothing more than a name upon a monument. On some stones the letters have become undecipherable. All the more reason, then, in the face of impending oblivion, to continue his rambling discourse. At least words can temporarily cover up the abyss of nonbeing into which he will inevitably fall.

After the graveyard soliloquy we find Levert in a bar laboring over yet another version of the events. For a few fleeting moments the novel seems to be lurching once more toward a "solution" to the mystery. As though to illustrate the Latin dictum *In Vino Veritas*, the semi-inebriated narrator relaxes the vigilance of his consciousness, and his blurred and unintentionally funny discourse contains confessions he would otherwise have repressed. In this present "bar" version of the letter, M. Levert repeats the initial statement he had made at the beginning of the novel about the death of the shoemaker's daughter. This time, however, his disoriented mind elicits strange resonances from the originally straight-forward words. A comparison between the two versions (both in French and English) underscores their striking differences:

> La fille du cordonnier est morte. L'enterrement a eu lieu jeudi dernier. Il y avait la famille et quelques personnes. Madame Chinze, la mère, était recouverte d'un crêpe noir, on ne voyait rien d'elle et c'était tant mieux. Le père Chinze avait son costume noir et un chapeau melon à la main.

> The shoemaker's daughter is dead. The burial took place last Thursday. There was the family and a few other people. Madame Chinze, the mother, was covered in black crêpe, one couldn't see anything of her and that was all to the good. Old Chinze was wearing his black suit and carried a derby hat. (*LF*, 1)

Here now is the chaotic yet strangely revealing version, which we find some 80 pages later:

> . . . ou disons morte la fille du nier du la fille à nier. Aveugle. A nier. La nier du mordofille est corte. L'enterdi eu a jeu linier derment. La Chinzille et pelquame ersonnes. Famère étout recrémoire un pauverte ron nelloyait mientant nieuxvelle cherpinze lostait coirume oireau echon memain lonla fetit plusemme.

> . . . or supposedly dead the daughter of the maker the maker's daughter to be denied. Blind. To be denied. The maker's girl is shead. The lurial plook tace thast lursday. The chinzily saw wether nad a pwef versons. Cher other maws vercoed ni claprep con soudn't hee er buck metter thather saw airing a sack boot dna darried aherby dat. (*LF*, 81)

It may appear far-fetched to maintain that some forms of gibberish make sense, but in this particular context, Levert's slurred, near-incoherent language betrays secrets that he would prefer to let sink into the recesses of his subconscious. The first sentence in the second French version offers a gripping example of how Levert unwittingly tells more than he intended: ". . . ou disons morte la fille du nier du la fille à nier." The verb *nier* (to deny) is really the truncated form of the noun *cordonnier* (cobbler). Thus, by dropping the first two syllables of the word Levert is subconsciously striving to deny his paternity and responsibility in Marie's death.

The question of Levert's guilt or innocence soon becomes entirely irrelevant, however. He starts up his letter-writing motor again, ostensibly to rectify errors made in the first draft, since he would not want Gilbert to return for the wrong reasons. But the corrections he adds to scenes and information, which appeared factual in the initial version of his account, alter it so radically that the reader finds them unconvincing. Far from making this original version more accurate, he is really whipping up an entirely different account. Now, he asserts, Roger and his wife did not return home right after the funeral. Moreover, Roger's wife did not succumb to nausea during the trip; it was another woman. In this new account, Alice Pacot does not run off to her lover, Georges, because he was paying a visit to his mother. The priest's housekeeper is called Martha, not Odette. He neither had lunch at the refectory, nor did he use the bus to visit with his sick parishioners. He rode over to a friend on his bicycle. The name Odette is later given to the wife of Louis, the bartender. As concerns Paul and Victor Moule, we have another total change of information. They are served at a café by a waitress, rather than a waiter. They live in a farmhouse with a third brother and his wife, not with their mother.

As Levert continues to blend the material of old episodes with their new versions, the story sinks deeper and deeper into a fog. His niece now flatly contradicts her uncle's earlier assertion that she had seen his property of "Les Roches" 10 years earlier. Marie's funeral and Gilbert's disappearance now become enshrouded in uncertainty. Levert seems more and more disconnected from reality. He jumbles up the deaths of his sister, his maid, and Marie. Even his son appears as a weird synthesis of Georges, Minet, and Léon. The old man's confusion is such that the whole edifice of his reconstruction of the past comes crashing down in derisive laughter:

> That's not all, said Levert, I still have to tell it to my son. He took his notebook but he was laughing so much that his pen dropped. The notebook too and the table too and the leftovers of the dinner and the floor too. The house was convulsed, the walls fell, the maid fell, night fell. All these fallen even so, all these graves very well kept up. With one's strength. One has strength, said Levert, with a flick of the wrist one makes everything fall and the rest. The maid was waiting for the spasm to end. With a suppository she supposed. You are going to take your suppository she said and you will sleep. I suppose, said Levert. I suppose. I suppose. (LF, 123–24)

Levert supposes so many wildly contradictory events and situations that the reader can believe nothing he says any longer. The story he had given us about Minet and Léon now becomes a visit that Rodolphe Potter paid to Georges, Alice's lover. It is now Rodolphe's turn to be the tall, blond, athletic young man, and it is the turn of Georges's sister to fall in love with him. Since anything is possible in Levert's narrative, nothing he says about the reality he depicts is necessarily accurate. Moreover, he knows that he will never send off the interminable letter to his lost son. Then why does he persist in writing it? Simply because his often confused, sometimes incoherent, endless discourse is the only weapon he possesses to ward off the anguishing thought of his mortality.

In the final analysis, it matters little whether Marie was his illegitimate daughter or not, whether Gilbert ever existed or not. What *does* matter very deeply for Levert is staying alive. Writing is proof of this determination not to perish, and, as I pointed out, throwing words into the abyss can temporarily disguise the dreaded imminence of nonbeing. Thus Levert can conclude, "Farther along the road or the roads and the mountain where one can get lost, where one gets lost, where one is lost. All that remains, a landscape, all that remains is lost. Should I continue, son, should I start again what's the use. He'll return you'll see, he's like you, this letter that I would have mailed tonight. It remains like what no longer is. Outside of what is written there is death" (*LF*, 165). A meager consolation, perhaps, but far preferable to the other alternative.

Clope au dossier (*Clope to the Dossier*)

Clope to the Dossier, published in 1961, two years after *Le Fiston*, bears some strong resemblances to its predecessor. Both novels use the mystery story as a pretext for drawing the reader into an anguishing dilemma. In both works the coherency of the narrative and the goals it ostensibly pursues eventually become irrelevant. Pinget even provides a certain continuity between the two by having several characters in *Clope au dossier* refer to M. Levert and his unhappy relationship with his son. But here the similarities end. *Clope au dossier* is far more disconcerting and, for the uninitiated reader, far more maddening in its convolutions than the previous novel. For one thing, it is extremely difficult to find the text's center of gravity. *Le Fiston* may be very confusing, but at least it has a fixed point on which one can focus: the theme of solitude and the agony associated with it. For another, the single act—the firing of a shot—that *Clope au dossier* is supposed to reconstruct, is enshrouded in so

much ambiguity that it divests itself of any "meaning" in the traditional, linear sense of the term.

   To be affected by *Clope au dossier*, one must bear in mind that the mystery story format used here is far more of a pretext than in the previous
novel. Not only does the question of the identity of both lawbreaker and
victim become totally irrelevant, but the impenetrable fog into which
the narrative sinks serves as a metaphor evoking the agony that is part
and parcel of the creative process. Indeed, the novel represents an artistic paradox. Once Pinget's narrator has dragged the reader down into a
hopelessly confused mass of disconnected and contradictory details, the
secret themes underlying the novel reveal themselves at last. They are
the anguish felt by the writer over the insurmountable barrier that separates his perception of reality from the nature of reality itself; the inability of language to truly apprehend the objects to which it refers, and
consequently the powerlessness of the writer to bring order out of chaos.

   As the episodes succeed one another, there emerges from the novel a
mounting feeling of frustration bordering on despair. As Robert
Henkle, Jr., so rightly observed, "*Clope au dossier* dramatizes a failed
experiment, a novel that doesn't get written" (Henkels, 84). Pinget has
come a long way since *Mahu, ou le matériau, Le Renard et la boussole*, and
Graal Flibuste, which parodied the traditional novel's reliance on linear
techniques to try to encompass reality. During that early period he
demolished these with gleeful irreverence and appeared to have accepted, in a rather lighthearted manner, the possibility that experience in its
proliferating complexity could not be grasped by any verbal forms. In
Le Fiston, however, and especially in *Clope au dossier*, merriment has
given way to anguished helplessness.

   Pinget devises a four-part grouping of episodes to express this failure
of human perception and its indispensable counterpart, language, to
make sense of the hopelessly tangled mess of reality. As the novel lurches from one cycle to the next, we witness an inquiry trying to get off the
ground and skidding into total confusion. The first cycle, like the other
three, revolves around a shot that was fired at one point in time. It opens
just before the noise resounds in the neighborhood. The first scene fea-
tures three townspeople—Mortin, Phillipard, and Verveine—who are
discussing Clope. From their gossip session it is obvious that he is a bach-
elor who prefers his own company. All three are convinced that Clope's
solitary existence explains his somewhat weird behavior. While they sit
in a café analyzing his personality, a flock of geese flies overhead. In the
following scene the object of this gossip shoots down one of the birds.

We are given two barely different versions of what happens after the goose is gunned down. According to the first, Kiki, Clope's dog, is finishing off his portion of the kill just as his master is storing the rest of the bird in his cold cellar. According to the second, Clope comes back up before the dog has finished his feast. Thus, there is no way to determine which of the versions is correct. The attention shifts back to the three men in the café. All three are reasonably sure that Clope fired the gun and expect his poaching habits will one day cost him dearly.

We move now to Simone Brize's apartment. She was Pierre Moule's fiancée in *Le Fiston*, and her future husband expressed misgivings at that time about marrying her, since he did not think she could satisfy his sexual needs. They are at present legally wed. Pierre works as a cook on a merchant ship, however, leaving his wife and young son, Guillaume, to their own resources. Simone let a frying pan drop when Clope or someone else pulled the trigger, so she did not hear the gun reverberate. As she looks out the window to the home of Judge Pommard, the action focuses on him temporarily. Like Simone, Pommard did not hear the gunshot because his wife covered the sound by moving furniture. He reassures the cleaning lady, who heard the noise upon entering his house, and goes back to perusing a legal document and enjoying a beer. While this has been transpiring, another man, M. Bille, has in his house been studying a legal brief while drinking coffee. Despite the noise his wife makes while housecleaning, he *does* hear the gun go off. Again, we cut back to Judge Pommard, then return to Simone, who rushes over to her child to prevent him from choking on a piece of bread. Up till now the story has been moving forward despite its jagged rhythm. Although the narrator makes abrupt transitions from one episode to the next, at least they are linked together by similar actions, situations, or verbal associations. They appear to be organically structured.

This impression of order is quickly called into question by a phrase that erupts without rhyme or reason: "Eardrum damaged."[3] It will reappear several more times during the course of the novel and may be interpreted in three different ways. It can refer to the narrator himself who was so close to the place where the gun went off that his ears are still reverberating from the bang. It can suggest Clope's insouciance about breaking the law. It can also allude symbolically to the writer whose mind gets boggled and overwhelmed when it comes into contact with an endlessly proliferating reality.

M. Toupin occupies the spotlight in the following episode. He is a half-senile, nearly blind old wreck of a panhandler stationed in the middle of a bridge, who spends his time cranking up a hurdy-gurdy without much enthusiasm. Just as two brothers-in-law pass by him, the scene shifts abruptly back to Simone Brize working in her kitchen, then returns to the bridge. The elderly beggar hears the gun going off just as the conversation of the two men trail off into silence. Like a movie camera switching nervously from sequence to sequence, vignettes follow one another at a breakneck tempo. We see Clope worrying about being apprehended by the Law, then the judge's house, then we return to the café where a carpenter says "Yes, Sir" to Pommard just as Verveine is uttering the same phrase in the presence of a customer.

At this point the narrator (is he Clope's lawyer, the author of a would-be novel, Clope himself?) bemoans the difficulty of figuring out exactly what happened before and after the shot was fired. In fact, his commentary, which is supposed to elucidate the mystery, merely confuses the situation even more. It also betrays the anger and frustration he feels over not being able to control the flow of reality (or find love?) through time, which spreads itself like some viscous blob. I will give the French text first, since Pinget exploits the double meaning of time and weather contained in the word *temps*:

> Eh oui le temps vilain temps vilain temps vilain temps de mon temps voyez-vous, et bien oui quoi le temps passe il y a beau temps je dis bien tout ce temps tout ce temps passe et quel passé ah là un temps pur tout un temps un sale temps ne trouvez-vous pas le temps d'aimer et le temps de mourir alors qu'est-ce que vous croyez bien pire bien pire on a le temps de croyez-moi mourir mais pas d'aimer il est bien temps grand temps vous m'entendez et tenez tout ce temps qu'on perd à vouloir en gagner mais oui à tant le temps qu'on a mis à ne pas le perdre vous m'entendez mais allez leur faire entendre allez donc leur faire entendre allez donc.

> Ah yes the time/weather miserable time/weather nasty weather nasty weather of my time you see, well yes what can I tell you time passes it's been a long time I mean all this time all this time is passing and what a past oh my a time for any time nasty time/weather don't you agree the time to love and the time to die so what do you think much worse much worse we have the time believe me to die but not to love it's about time high time you understand and look at all the time we waste in trying to gain time why yes when you think of how much time we spend in not wasting it you understand but fat lot of good it does you to make them see it fat lot of good it does you to make them see it what the hell. (*CD*, 27–28)

Following this explosion of powerless rage, the narrator begins a second series of episodes or vignettes. The uninitiated reader can be forgiven for feeling utterly confused, since this second cycle unfolds *before* the events described in the first. First we find out what Simone was up to before the geese flew by. We retrace her steps as she goes from one store to another, then we catch up on the activities of the three café patrons who had been gossiping about Clope: Mortin, Philipard, and Verveine. We cut back to Judge Pommard, who mispronounces a neighbor's name, then encounter Pierre Moule in the galley of his merchant ship where he is making coffee. Afterwards we again pick up Clope, who is having breakfast in the company of his dog.

The novel now moves back even earlier into Simone's morning and concentrates on what she was doing and thinking before leaving for the market. Like the narrator, this young married woman living barely above the poverty line and saddled with the responsibility of bringing up a hyperactive little son, experiences mounting rage and frustration over her inability to create and sustain a meaningful order in her life. Her attraction-repulsion relationship to her child illustrates this dilemma. She genuinely loves Guillaume. She strives to be an exemplary mother. But the boisterous child prevents her from performing efficiently the morning ritual of feeding and keeping him clean, washing herself and tidying up the apartment. Whenever she tries to move her domestic routine into high gear, her son soils himself or soils the bedcover. Compounding this problem are her sexual obsessions. Her husband being away so frequently and enjoying amorous escapades in every port his ship visits, Simone's loneliness and despair acquire a lacerating physical intensity as she soaps her body. She recalls the act of sodomy that her husband once performed on her. Although it disgusted her then, now it seems almost preferable to her present state of stagnation, because at least she was desired and excited: "She begins with her face. Next under the arms then here we are her pink breasts turning dark at their tips, let's enjoy, she rinses, then takes the soap again from its holder let's enjoy she takes the washcloth and slides it between her legs now we're at the thighs ah she's spreading them, she's bending down. Simone's ass. Meltingly plump and pink which Pete likes so much that he even tried oh yes the pig tried ouch you're hurting me you filthy lecher and he ground it in so hard all right it's fine don't yell there you see there it's better, yes" (*CD*, 51–52). After describing her scurrying about the apartment in the conditional tense, the narrator leaves her temporarily as she goes out to buy "eggs, carrots, oranges, milk, salt."

The conversation that follows between the father of Judge Pommard and M. Toupin represents another failed effort to make sense out of the mess of existence. The two wheezing, speech-slurring, half-disconnected old coots can agree on nothing except Levert's death. Just about everything else relating to their past has become as hypothetical as the events in a work of fiction:

> Ah Germaine Pisson said Pommard, she married well, Levert, remember the pasta-makers. I thought it was she who had the money, said Toupin, aren't you confusing him with his father. His father what's the matter with you, I knew him like the back of my hand, a really wild one, the Legion and all that. So then Levert's son said Toupin. If I told you said Pommard. If I told you he died last year like a dog they found him in a ditch just imagine in a ditch the handsome Levert. (*CD*, 84)

The final episode of this second series brings to the foreground another character anxious to draw some permanent, meaningful order from the chaos of his experience. He is Maurice, a young painter who spends his days redoing on canvas the same bridge on which M. Toupin plies his trade as a beggar. Much like the elderly M. Levert kept rewriting the same letter, Maurice returns obsessively to the same bridge, apparently to reproduce it to his satisfaction. As Simone crosses the bridge, an immediate and intense surge of sympathy draws the two together for a fleeting moment, expressing itself silently by an exchange of glances:

> Toupin said to Simone ah the poor fellow just look at him hard worker poor man just think he starts over again every day do you understand that? Starts what over again said Simone. Starts everything look every day a new canvas or is it a drawing you'll see go take a look, go over and take a look you'll see, do you understand that? But Simone didn't look surprised she said oh yes be quiet, but on the contrary interested, there was between her and the painter a certain way of understanding one another, he in his mess of colors she wiping her little boy's rear end and doing her cleaning jobs and waiting for Pete every day like something that one starts up again and she said what do you expect with artists of course he surely has his reasons but she didn't have the time to take a look, she pulled Guillaume who wanted to climb up on the bench and turn the handle. (*CP*, 100–101)

As this second cycle closes, the same key phrase reappears expressing the narrator's anxiousness to solve the mystery surrounding the gunshot: "Eardrum damaged. I'm listening. A kind of a kind of. No nothing" (*CD*, 101). This second path of exploration has led to nowhere. The narrator must now embark on another inquiry that will prove to be as fruit-less as the previous one. In this third cycle the narrative will move both backwards and forward, even further in time, in an attempt to discover who did what and to whom.

At the beginning of this particular investigation our attention focuses again on Maurice. Speaking in the conditional tense, the narrator imag-ines what is going on in the painter's mind. Perhaps using the young man as a pretext to express his own aspirations, he has the artist think-ing that one day he would acquire fame precisely because of all of these new beginnings, since setting off on the right path determines the even-tual success or failure of one's mission. Then he has Maurice and M. Toupin wonder (or is he speaking for himself now?) whether by working *backward* in the reconstruction of an experience they might gain the very insight into reality that has been eluding them. Why not paint a canvas backward rather than forward, with the first persons who cross the bridge coming last? Unfortunately, this hypothesis does not lead to a convincing conclusion any more than the previous ones.

To confuse matters even more, some of Simone Brize's actions, which the narrator has already recorded, will be performed by Mme Mortin several years later. First, there are Simone's sexual frustrations, which now overwhelm Mme Mortin. The milk spilling over the pot on the fire provides a very graphic illustration of this deep-seated malaise:

> She would have put the milk on the fire, dawn was starting to break, she would have remained seated or standing during the time the milk need-ed that it would have needed to boil or she would have gone to the gar-den where she would have lingered with the impression suddenly that the milk would have taken advantage of its liberty to spill over the rascal from the pot having gone back in then and seeing that in fact would say oh and would hurry over to the pot meanwhile he/the milk would not pass up for anything in the world the opportunity to seep into the cracks in the stove until he/it got to the very core. (*CD*, 105)

When Mme Mortin puts down on her shopping list the exact same items that appeared on Simone's, the reader's bewilderment is complete. We drift even further into the realm of hypotheses in the next episode, where Simone is tossing about alone in bed in the middle of the night, buf-feted by fantasies about sex, which attract and disgust her at the same time, racked with anxiety over her husband's tendency to enjoy carnal pleasures wherever he can find them. Then she has a sinister dream where divorce, suicide, and death figure prominently. The third series ends, then, with the disquieting suspicion that Simone Brize may be tempted (may have been tempted?) to take her own life, and that the gunshot may (may have?) originated in her apartment. In any event, the mystery has thickened.

The final, brief cycle opens with the narrator describing a dossier that has been compiled to defend Clope against the accusation of having committed some obscure crime or crimes. One last time the anxious narrator/investigator repeats the obsessive phrase related to the gunshot and expresses his determination to wind up the case: "Eardrum damaged. Stay calm. The brunt of it is done. They can accumulate their proofs. Dossier locked up closet. Clope's innocence. Counterproofs. Stay calm. Let's put the finishing touches to it. Come on" (CD, 124). But the narrator never succeeds in putting the finishing touches to the problematic dossier. He can neither pinpoint the place where the various people found themselves at the very instant the shot was fired, nor can he be sure that Clope himself pulled the trigger. According to some local gossip, it may very well have been Simone Brize who decided to blow her brains out in a moment of despair. As for Toupin's testimony, how can one take the words of a doddering, half-senile old man at face value?

> They are supposed to have said that he [Clope? someone else?] had gone out around a quarter to eleven and had taken a walk near the work site. When he raised his head he saw the geese and fired. They are supposed to have said that Simone Brize must have heard the shot while she boom crrrr Guillaume crrr Guillaume crrrr Brize must have heard the noise of the pot which probably fell right at that moment preparing her meal and the little one's looking toward the sea/she limp dead by this noise/act she just shot herself. Toupin was turning his crank he's supposed to have heard he would say he certainly heard Jacques Cheviot and his brother-in-law say that they could go back and see if the shot if they had heard it if they had passed by at the same time as the female student under the second plane tree if then they went then back the student would still only be let's say fifty meters away and Toupin would have thought if Jacques and his brother-in-law go back one more meter here it comes crrrrrrrrr. Buck up. (CD, 125–26)

As though the situation were not already hopelessly muddled, it becomes even more so when the narrator reexamines the evidence at his disposal and formulates a new hypothesis: Clope's mother may have been the or a victim of her son's propensity to use firearms, at least this is what Clope seems to insinuate. Behaving more and more like a Peeping Tom, the narrator penetrates into a damp shed in search of an article (could it be the firearm?) that would enable him—maybe—to prove Clope's responsibility in the death of his mother:

> The shed. First this laundry-house painted door jammed by the gravel must push, the damp smell on the sloping ground this autumn-like steam this taste for getting in out of the cold, the wash boiling in the washing machine a woman in wooden shoes leaning over the basin. The smell of wood to go down at night she will not have finished before she had never finished before, to carry the gasoline lamp. And from this steam suddenly to come out the woman saying I don't wash any more I am dead don't you see and to go lie down in the sand who slowly sinks in closing up over her slowly. [. . .] [C]ome on now, open up the dossier, there, they won't find anything against you. Suddenly she got up saying can't you see that I'm dead, she was going to lie down on the sand which slowly I had no more strength when everything would be accomplished. (*CD*, 131–32)

The narrator (detective? lawyer for the defense?) ploughs through this accumulation of evidence one more time, convinced that there is a connection between Clope, his dog, Kiki, the dead bird, and Clope's mother. This connection never materializes, however. Affirmative statements contradict one another, as do negative ones. The blurred syntax makes it extremely difficult for the reader to figure out to whom or to what the narrator is referring. The absence of punctuation compounds the difficulty. At the very end of the inquiry, the narrator, or the detective, or Clope himself deplores the lack of time to reach some convincing conclusion. But given his (or their) inability to do anything other than create an inextricable mess, the reader feels that time can only act as an enemy, drawing him (or them) further and further away from the goal they are supposedly seeking: "The truth when it/she will be dry that night was it before was it before no control over what has been said no control it is no longer the truth/she before this hand I'll cut it off she would have told me reading you see over there that's you without any power she would have said to me that's you this dossier you need this dossier plus time no more time plus time plus time plus time" (*CD*, 135).

And so these four investigations running along parallel lines all grind to a halt. We never find out exactly why the dossier is being compiled and who is doing the compiling. We never ascertain the circumstances under which the shot was fired. We cannot even be sure that only one gun blast was heard. Two people may have died from gunfire—Simone Brize (self-inflicted) and Clope's mother (felled by her own son)—in addition to the hapless goose flying overhead. But then again it may have only been the bird, the other reports being the result of gossip and mythomania. Clope himself may be the author of the dossier, addressing himself from time to time in the imperative mode, striving through his inquest to clear his name of the charges of being a poacher and a murderer. But the possibility exists that the dossier may have been put together by the lawyer hired to defend him. Unless of course, the word *dossier* is taken in one of its French connotations, meaning the back of a chair, in which case the novel's title, *Clope au dossier* could imply that the protagonist is writing a manuscript at his desk or that he is in a tight squeeze.

The mystery surrounding this dossier is all the more impenetrable because the protagonist who is its raison d'être is singularly elusive. Clope appears as little more than a name or a sound connected with actions involving the use of a firearm. If it was Pinget's intention to underscore his protagonist's ultimate insignificance by means of the name used to identify him, then he succeeded brilliantly, because "clope" in French translates into "cigarette butt."

In view of the fact that the four lines of investigation go around in spirals, closing in on themselves, formulating hypotheses rather than answers, and that the protagonist at the center of this inquest has no human presence, is the novel to be interpreted as a despairing statement about our inability to make sense out of our experience and our relations? I think not. Uncompromisingly honest it is; tragic it may be in its vision of our human condition. But at the same time it testifies to man's lucid courage in the face of death. The narrator's inquiries may be going nowhere, but in Robert Pinget's perspective, that is immaterial. What counts is the determination to keep on writing, because this creative act not only testifies to the human being's vitality, but it also weaves a magical spell that can, at least temporarily, keep death at bay. Through this spiritual process both the narrator and his creator erect a barrier to protect themselves from the anguished awareness of their own fragility, "just as one would pile up furniture in front of a door which is going to be forced a large number of memories as a defense against the intruder" (*CD*, 128). That in itself is enough to justify the writer's presence on earth.

L'Inquisitoire (The Inquisitory)

As in the two previous novels, the atmosphere of *L'Inquisitoire* (1962) is permeated by a disquieting sense of uncertainty. Ostensibly the novel describes a preliminary hearing, which will lead to a full-scale criminal investigation into the activities of the secretary at the Château de Broy.

This person is suspected of involvement in a ring of stolen and/or forged art. An unnamed investigator interrogates a former servant about the man. At the outset the reader surmises that the questions are intended to open up various avenues of approach to the problem of the missing secretary and his shady dealings. As the dialogue between interrogator and interrogated progresses, however, the original purpose of the investigation fades into insignificance. What fascinates us is the very ambiguous relationship that develops between the two. Sometimes it seems sadomasochistic; other times it strikes us as a duel between two equally cunning adversaries: the tormentor is intent on ferreting out the information he wants, while the victim is just as determined to prevent certain secrets of his private life from becoming public. By the end of the novel it is obvious that the police inquiry has been all along a pretext for probing into infinitely more crucial matters: the questioning of our ability to re-create reality through memory and words, and the recourse to art as a means of filling the void of silence.

This duel, which gives rise to such lofty metaphysical and aesthetic considerations, can be traced back to the anxieties of the author himself. I have already observed that Robert Pinget considers writing a means of self-exploration. In *L'Inquisitoire* it manifests itself in the form of a command, which he directs against the uninspired creator within him in order to get the process going again. But the relentless questioning to which the interrogator subjects the old servant also represents an illusion, which Pinget foists on himself to disguise his awareness that there is no necessity for writing, no way he can confer absolute justification upon his work as a novelist. The voice he imagines that questions and coerces him is in essence his reader or readers, without whom no author feels complete and about whom he fantasizes as he is performing the very act that gives meaning to his life. In 1972 Pinget ingenuously revealed how he forced himself to start writing his new novel: "When I decided to write *L'Inquisitoire*, I didn't have anything to say, I felt only a need to explain myself at great length. I got down to work and wrote the sentence 'Yes or no answer,' which was addressed to me alone and signified 'give birth.' And it was the answer to this abrupt question which set the tone and everything else into motion."[4]

It is hard to imagine the paradoxical implications of this situation being lost on the author. As I mentioned in the first chapter, Robert Pinget hates being hounded into a corner by interviewers, however well intentioned they may be. Yet in *L'Inquisitoire* he has his questioner pursue the old servant relentlessly to the point of violating the very sanctuary of the latter's soul. Moreover, by his own admission he created the questioning voice in this novel to provoke himself into overcoming his inertia and exorcizing his fear of silence.

Obviously Pinget responded very well to his own imperious command, since *L'Inquisitoire* is by far the longest novel he has written and, according to many specialists of the *Nouveau Roman*, including Jean-Claude Liéber, remains his most remarkable work.[5] But what imaginary universe eventually emerged once the author goaded himself into evoking it? It is one that defies analysis because nothing really "happens" during the course of the interrogation. The servant talks drivel indefinitely, so the author could have lengthened or shortened his discourse without unbalancing the novel's structure, just as the questioner orders the garrulous old man to elaborate on a particular aspect or to get to the point. The reader's interest does not focus on one particular person or group of people or on one particular event or group of events. It is spread over several hundred characters and places to the point that he or she can easily confuse principal players with secondary ones or even with the various settings. The novel does not explore to the very end any of the avenues it opens up. It whets our appetite with the promise of savory or unsavory adventures, but it never follows through on any.

Thus, the work's structure is ambiguous. It reflects the novelistic tradition to the extent that it launches a main theme along with a variety of episodes, each of which contains an excellent psychological and dramatic potential. At the same time, however, Pinget disputes the continued legitimacy of this tradition by refusing to finish what he started. *L'Inquisitoire* has no sustained plot, and the author compensates for this structural void by cramming the novel with descriptions that leave nothing to the imagination. He pulls off an aesthetic feat by turning the accessory components of the genre into the essential elements of this text. There is no way the reader can skip over the interminable accounts of the château and its contents or the region and its inhabitants because they have taken over the work. Instead of following with bated breath the unpredictable turns of a plot, we are carried along by the multi-rhythmic flow of the servant's conversation. Through it we eventually penetrate to the novel's core.

But how is one to access this fictional world in order to reach its core? Probably the surest avenue of approach is the pseudo-detective story. The reader tries to pick up "leads" from the overwhelmingly voluminous mass of information, which the questioner coaxes and coerces out of the servant. Once they all prove to be irrelevant, the terrain is cleared and the real investigation by the reader can begin.

At first the interrogator seeks details about the day-to-day pattern of living at the château as well as about the building's structure: rooms, staircases, and so forth. He also asks for information about the festivities held there. Then he focuses on different people who worked there—on their relationships with other staff members and with the townsfolk. He dwells for a while on the secretary whom the servant seems to take pleasure in presenting in the least flattering light. Without bringing forth explicit accusations, the old man insinuates that the secretary was involved in criminal practices. The questioner seems to cast doubts on the information the servant willingly provides, since he bounces back from one subject to another as though he were trying to catch his informant in a lie.

Next the interrogator probes into the lives of the château's two owners. Both are bachelors and carousers. Out of loyalty to his former masters or personal pride as their former servant, the old man is not particularly happy to reveal that they frequented younger men of dubious distinction. He mentions one Chantre as well as a hotel manager, who used to bring along with him a rather worm-eaten bunch of actors whenever he visited the place. He also remembers having chanced upon a collection of pornographic pictures when removing the contents of their car, and the rather distasteful impression these images made on him. For the time being, the interrogator does not pursue the matter of the owners' sexual inclinations, including possible homosexual tendencies. He turns his attention to the more distinguished company that the playboys invited to their domain. He observes that none of the dinners held there were for mixed company. Again, out of loyalty, the servant is unwilling to give details about his former masters' predilection for all-male parties.

Questioned about the townspeople, the informant names several doctors among the other inhabitants with whom his masters used to hobnob. This enables the interrogator to switch back to Chantre. Why did the medical student decide to do his internship at Douves rather than Agapa, which is so much closer? Although hounded by the detective's relentless questioning, the servant persists in giving evasive answers. For a while it appears that the questioning voice will succeed in demonstrating the existence of a criminal operation using the château as its base. This will remain only a hypothesis to the very end, however.

It is not without significance that the interrogator lets his informant out of one corner after another. Is he waiting for the very instant when his victim will relax sufficiently to divulge some terrible secret? In any event, as soon as the old man lets down his guard, the questioning voice goes after him again about medical matters. He wants to know why the château owners avoided the town doctor, what injections they used, whether syringes could be found around the property. The kinds of key questions he then asks about visitors from abroad suggest that the playboys might have been involved in drug trafficking. When the investigator again demands details about the doors and corridors of the château, it becomes apparent that the servant had omitted the secretary's office. Did he do it on purpose? And what about the man himself? Was he in collusion with Minette, the homosexual, to run an illegal antique business? Or was he in league with Ballaison, the realty agent, to pull off a shady land-speculation scheme?

The investigator's questions keep circling around the old servant, as though they were being asked for the sole purpose of catching him off guard and revealing his mendacity. Eventually the secretary's dubious conduct recedes into the distance to be replaced by a probing into the servant's past. The ruthless questioning voice compels him to reenter certain rooms of his memory whose doors he would have preferred to keep tightly bolted forever. Succumbing to this unabaiting mental torture, the old caretaker finally discloses that he lost his wife 10 years ago. He also informs his inquisitor that M. and Mme d'Eterville, the masters for whom he and his wife used to work, considered themselves mediums in contact with spirits beyond the grave. Mme d'Eterville even offered to summon up the ghost of the servant's little son who had died at the age of eight. Revolted by these practices, which he considered infernal, the distraught servant sought to put an end to them, but to no avail. When his wife died, he held the d'Etervilles and their black magic responsible for her death. Later, as the inquisitor applies more pressure on him, the servant confesses that he finds frequent solace in the bottle. Totally rattled by now, he hallucinates, imagining that the devil is going to take him away.

After this brush with insanity, the servant calms down somewhat. But not for long. The inquisitor goes after him with questions about some necrophilic murders that took place in the area. For a while it seems as though his tormentor is trying to extort a confession from him of complicity in these particularly gruesome crimes. The interrogator goes as far as to insinuate that there may be some connection between the servant and one of the known murderers, but backs down when it becomes obvious that the servant and the convicted necrophiliac, Johann, had merely worked for the same people.

The inquisition drags on interminably—the cross-examiner striving to back his adversary into a corner, and the victim using the most artful verbal dodging to outwit his aggressor. When pressed to give detailed information about a wing in the château that he had maintained was unoccupied, he vents his pent-up rage at what he considers a completely futile exercise, since it consists in going around in circles without ever capturing anything essential:

> Twenty more rooms and then there'll be still more and you'll tell me to describe them, and more and more kitchen servants gossipy stories bedroom escapades families miles and miles of streets and stairs and lumberrooms and junk-shops antique dealers grocers butchers of wretched poverty everywhere in our heads how depressing it all is, it's always starting all over again why, all these dead people around us all these dead people we grill to make them talk when will you have finished I haven't asked anything, will I always have to start again the evenings in the bistro in the street what why.[6]

The only other confession the inquisitor can wrest out of the old servant is his veneration for a saintly recluse, M. Pierre, for whom the château owners had provided a refuge in one of the towers. An astronomer by profession, M. Pierre spends his life charting the movements of the heavenly bodies. He represents for the old man an otherworldly serenity, stability, and dignity in stark contrast to the futile agitation of daily life. In fact, M. Pierre is probably the only person in whom the servant has ever completely believed. This sympathy he feels toward the astronomer is all the more poignant because he knows that his own existence is singularly lacking in significance.

In the final stages of the novel the inquisitor demands of the servant that he describe the spectacular party that his masters throw once a year on the grounds of their castle for townspeople and employees alike. Once again the old man dredges up all of the scandals that the investigation has been associating with the owners and their motley band of friends. For a moment there is even the hint that all of the elements may coalesce into a credible synthesis: the two playboys' interest in members of their own sex, the secretary's involvement in a dope operation with the castle used as its headquarters, and the suspicion that one of the employees had taken part in a series of particularly gruesome murders.

But this synthesis never takes place. None of the theories or hunches can either be corroborated or invalidated. All that remains is a bullying interrogator and his increasingly recalcitrant victim, caught in a labyrinth of irrelevant questions and equally irrelevant answers without any hope of ever finding the way out.

The dialogue ends just as arbitrarily as it began: the questioning voice badgers the servant mercilessly, while the latter, alleging his extreme fatigue, refuses to go on. The inquisitor tries to worm more information out of his prey about his relationship with M. Pierre, and the inquisition continues along its futile course until Pinget decides to terminate it:

> Answer, have you envisaged a way of seeing Monsieur Pierre again
>> Never I wouldn't dare disturb him unless
> Unless
>> As I dreamt one day one morning I was walking along my little paths.
> Go on
>> I took one I didn't know and I see Marie in a garden with our child and she says to me come in come in and I go into the kitchen where I find Monsieur Pierre
> Go on
>> He invited us to dinner we had the whole night to talk about the stars and another night and then another and
> And
>> We were going to talk for a long time
> Go on
>> I could hear everything I could hear everything I was telling him all the names Cyrille came to shake me
> You were dreaming in the café
>> I don't remember
> You had fallen asleep in the café
>> I don't remember
> Did it ever happen that you fell asleep in the café. Answer, had you fallen asleep that day in the café
>> I don't remember
> Answer
>
> Yes or no answer
>> I'm tired. (*I*, 488–89)

Having depicted in some detail the perverse relationship linking interrogator and interrogated, we are in a better position to zero in on the core of the novel. Obviously it is not to be found in the pseudo-detective story dealing with the disquieting events that unfold around the castle, since none of the so-called "leads" lead anywhere. Nor is it to be located in the innumerable neo-Balzacian inventories of objects. In Balzac's fiction, descriptions of places are vital in creating the psychological atmosphere in which the action develops, whereas in Pinget's work, the old servant rattles off information about the castle and the surrounding area in response to questions with which he is continuously badgered. It is rather the dialogue/relationship itself between tormentor and victim, and all that it implies, which gives this apparently shapeless novel its unity and purpose.

Like M. Levert and the investigator in *Clope au dossier* before him, the old servant is doggedly determined to stay alive and confer meaning on an existence that he suspects may very well be devoid of it. The best way he can ward off his fear of death and emptiness is to start talking and keep talking, especially since he suffers from almost total deafness and its inevitable corollary, solitude. Hence the role of victim, which he willingly accepts despite the occasional flare-up of indignation. On the surface, the elderly servant is subjected to nonstop bullying, even when it takes the form of cajoling or commiseration. Confessions are wrested from him without his ever being allowed either to pour out his heart or to conceal his humble secrets. But as Michel Foucault pointed out, truth acquires authenticity from the very obstacle and opposition that it has had to overcome in order to express itself.[7] In *L'Inquisitoire* the artificial struggle between a ruthless confessor and a talkative patient is indispensable in the search for truth. The experience of baring one's soul becomes all the more thrilling when an aggressor threatens to break into its very sanctuary. In fact, the accused clamors for an attentive listener and an omnipotent judge. Although he is an object of scrutiny, he acquires through the sheer ruthlessness of the interrogation inflicted on him, the status of a subject resplendent in his very guilt.

For this reason the elderly servant would have designated himself as a victim had the questioning voice not chosen him first as the target of his bullying. Moreover, despite the appearances, the deaf old man is actually running the show. He exploits his naïveté and hardness of hearing to avoid the traps and ambushes his tormentor sets up for him. Through denials, digressions, and phony denunciations, he prolongs the inquisition. His unsatisfactory answers compel the interrogator to ask more questions that in turn enable him to continue talking indefinitely and thus anaesthetize his awareness of his unhappiness. He runs the show even when he complains of weariness and balks at giving any more answers to futile questions. At one point during the interrogation, he is forced under threat to provide information on Mme Lemove, née Golard. It would appear that here at least, he is caving in under pressure, but his conduct reveals the opposite. Bristling with anger and indignation, he turns this command to his advantage. His verbal torrent allows him not only to occupy center stage again but to bury his tormentor under a mass of unrequested information. "I'll answer you'll get your fill," he screams, then hurtles himself into a dizzying genealogical account of the Golard family where procreation and the delicatessen trade compete with each other in volume production: "They used to sell pork sausages sauerkraut potted meats blood pudding bacon prepared foods. . . . They made five children two boys and three girls Daniel Alexandre Lucie Dorothée and Patricia Golard" (*I,* 304–305).

Even when he complains of exhaustion, the last thing the deaf old man wants to do is stop the inquisition. Were the merciless questioning ever to come to an end, he would no longer exist. Nevertheless, while he clings tenaciously to life by throwing words into the void, he realizes that these evanescent sounds are powerless to re-create the events on which he is being interrogated. It matters not at all that his words are being recorded exactly as he speaks them. This so-called objectivity is an imposture.

Acting as Pinget's spokesman, the servant, in one of his moments of exasperation, expresses a profoundly pessimistic view of man's ability to re-create reality through memory. Far from resurrecting the intensity of past experience, our faculty of recollection produces inauthentic results. In attempting to reconstruct our past it invents something that never existed. It does not recapture our acts but cuts us off from them. Our past may continue living on in our minds, but this past has very little to do with what actually happened, since the events we participated in have been interpreted, and consequently, transformed, by our imagination. Worse still, it is words that create reality and not vice versa. Reminiscences are all false. Once words are used to recall the past, roles can be switched around, and parts taken by one person can just as easily be assigned to another:

> All the while you're questioning me it seems to me that I'm back in the café on my chair as if I were talking about something else something else somewhere else I'm not here any more we could invent other people no matter who they are yes make them say anything we wanted it would be just like what happened between the real ones all of them in our heads

they're dead, I feel your questions are forcing them to talk but mistakes
are of no importance they'd talk exactly the same way whether it's true or
false and we'll still be in the same boat when other people ask questions
about us [. . .] and perhaps that's what our life is all about, like a sort of
closet where we pile up things we don't need any more we say they're our
memories it's helped me get where I wanted to be and 20 years later we
find them again and we no longer know what they mean, papers photos
notes all these notes. (*I*, 299–300)

As though to underscore the fragility of the very words on which we
count to re-create reality, Pinget has his elderly servant distort through
ignorance many references to bourgeois culture. Because the results of
these distortions are hilarious, we do not dwell on the frightening
prospects of a language that could lose its referents and no longer mean
what, by common agreement, it is supposed to mean. The sexual innuendos that he produces unconsciously by misusing literary and mythological terms illustrate this tendency. Although the old man's
consciousness represses the eroticism in him ("there are all these barriers
in my head," he declares), it gains the upper hand surreptitiously by substituting its own symbolic manifestations in his discourse for expressions
he has completely misunderstood. Describing the dramatic entertainment provided by the two playboys at their huge outdoor party, he
relates that a group of actors performed before a lewd audience "Les
Foutreries d'Escarpin." Those familiar with the comedies of Molière cannot repress a chuckle on reading this. The correct title of the farce to
which the servant alludes is *Les Fourberies de Scapin*, meaning "Scapin's
acts of deception." In the old man's misinterpretation, it becomes
"Escarpin's acts of fornication." The word *foutrerie* is especially comical
because it is one of the most vulgar expressions available in the French
language for sexual intercourse. As for *escarpin*, it is nothing more than a
low-fronted shoe.

Then the servant talks about the large pond surrounded by bronze
sirens and tritons, in the center of which the goddess "Amphibite" displays her nudity to the fountains spraying water over her. The prudish
caretaker never expected he would invent an obscenity by referring to
the Greek deity Aphrodite as an amphibian phallus, but this is exactly
what he does by using inadvertently the French slang expression "bite"
for the male sex organ. Further on the disgust he feels for homosexual
relations manifests itself when he calls "L'Apollon du Belvédère" (The
Belvedere Apollo) "L'Apollon du Réverbère." Since the word *réverbère*

means "streetlamp," he has sullied the greek god by insinuating that he is a male prostitute who pounds the sidewalk in the hope of soliciting customers.

If the servant's many spoonerisms show how easily language can be threatened through misuse, Pinget himself conjures up, through the servant's bumbling character, a far more frightening prospect for the creative artist: the possibility of failure. This is evident in the episode relating the marriage of Marthe's niece. The elderly servant is invited to this celebration and even helps organize it, since he and Marthe, the château's cook, have been friends for many years. The narrative is completely unnecessary for the architecture of the novel. It can be isolated without the overall context suffering at all. Yet it contains such a pile-up of bizarre happenings and unintentionally comic utterances that it becomes an allegory of aesthetic creation that disaster plagues at every turn.

Since Marthe and the elderly servant have worked for many years in elegant surroundings, they are placed in charge of protocol for the whole proceedings. They put together grandiose plans for the wedding's success. Nevertheless, they completely misinterpret the code, applying it in ways that transform it into a parody of itself. During the course of the "memorable" day, both of them sense that by pooling their resources they have concocted a first-class fiasco. Yet once the process is set into motion, it functions under its own weird propulsion and can neither be stopped nor reversed.

From the outset things start falling apart. The wedding procession has problems getting under way. The bride misplaces her pins, her father breaks the stem of his carnation, and Mme Dumans loses her purse. A drunkard starts some shoving during the ceremony that nearly turns into a brawl. The children cannot wait until the Mass is over before grabbing the bag of candies. While trying to assemble the group for pictures, the photographer fails to maintain decorous behavior. To make matters worse, unwanted guests invade the premises. First there are the minor characters or stooges: Cyrille, Cruze, and the waitresses. Then some spoilsports appear: Blimbraz and "Little Drippings." They are followed by unwanted suppliers: Tripeau, Lantoy, Monachou, and Gorin. Finally, creatures from the past materialize at the worst possible moment to haunt the wedding party: Pipi and Tourniquet. Before long, the whole village is participating in the event. Even the author invites himself under the guise of his first name ("le petit Robert").

If a wedding celebration offers any family the opportunity to show off its *savoir-vivre*, then this one covers Marthe and her relatives with shame.

A hole in the stained glass window of the church depicting the life of St. Chu marks the "beginning of the end." In a bizarre misapplication of the rules governing the organization of the nuptial procession, she and the elderly servant have the groom walk down the aisle first—unaccompanied—and require that the bride make her way toward the altar at the very end—alone. Then the servant comes up with another unworkable idea. Inspired by his masters' seating arrangements at their castle parties, he, too, would like to have a male not only sit next to every female, but opposite one at the banquet table. Unfortunately, there are 16 guests in all, which leaves him no choice but to place two women and two men together at either end. An even more embarrassing result of this plan is that the bride and bridegroom sit opposite each other rather than next to each other, and worse still, opposite their parents. Needless to say, the latter take advantage of this unexpected opportunity to continue their meddling.

Had the meal been outstanding, it might have blotted out all of the preceding faux-pas. Being rather mediocre, it simply aggravates the malaise. In fact, it betrays the organizers' stinginess. Instead of the three meat dishes with vegetables, preceded by the three hors-d'oeuvres and followed by the three traditional desserts promised, the guests must make do with only two main courses, a scrawny-looking roast, one lonely vegetable, one salad and cheese plate and two desserts. To foist upon their guests the illusion of plenty, the organizers add pastry shells and cheese-topped foods, which even the servant considers stodgy stuff. Instead of the traditional wedding cake, the participants can look forward to nothing more than a four-level ice cream concoction in which the servant sees a symbol of the disaster yet to come.

And the disaster is not long in coming. The guests devour their food like ravenous beasts. Even the priest and the mayor's wife lose control. The ice cream dessert begins to trickle under the heat, the father bursts into tears when his jacket gets stained in the sauce, and the shawl of another guest gets soaked in the wine. As though fate were determined to make an exemplary mess of the proceedings, the children at the wedding meal trample on Marthe's hat.

The customary speeches that follow the meal are so incoherent or ludicrous (or both) that they foreshadow the collapse of the whole bourgeois order. Inspired by the garlands that decorate the reception hall like some country fair, the father of the bride hails "the great wedding day with everyone gathered around a new Chinese lantern" (*lampion* in French). The priest's turn is next. Not to be outdone, he mixes metaphors from the realms of alchemy and religion to such a degree that his speech verges on the obscene: "A woman is a treasure or rather a vase that contains a treasure if the husband does not make the effort like Jesus-Christ the treasure disappears little by little and the church enters a state of collapse he put them on their guard" (*I*, 242). Finally the mayor, representing the state, appropriates the marriage for secular ends. Marriage means procreation and procreation means supplying the future managers, which a country needs to continue flourishing. This is the substance of his speech expressed through the outlandish metaphor of the egg: "The family is the cell of the egg of the country and without it nothing holds, each marriage is another cell and another egg that gives the country its leaders" (*I*, 242). He brazenly distorts a quatrain by the local poet, Louise d'Isimance, in praise of love to exalt the Republic, the supreme secular and democratic institution. The verses are certainly trite: "Love is great and promises the after-life / To pilgrims who stay on beaten paths" (*I*, 243). But the connection he establishes between their content and republican virtues is phony.

Notwithstanding the ludicrousness of the wedding, it affects the old servant as well as Marthe. But the author does not share their sentimentality. He gives vent to derisive laughter as an order based on worn-out conventions decomposes. The same reaction is forthcoming at the end of the novel, when Pinget describes the nighttime celebrations at the castle. It simply echoes on a more grandiose scale the same agitated preparations, the same headaches involving etiquette, and the same orders placed with suppliers that we noticed in the world of the "little people." Moreover, the phenomenon of decomposition appears far worse. It matters little that the playboys and their cynical friends present an elegant facade. Their actions are far more reprehensible. The celebrations serve as a pretext for an orgy of drinking and sex. Thus, at the top as well as at the bottom of the social hierarchy, one observes the same failure.

It is significant that Pinget chose the so-called realistic novel as the most appropriate vehicle to depict the wedding debacle, just as he pressed the worn-out literary form into service to draw up his interminable inventories. In the first case he demonstrates that a tightly organized plan, unfolding in a linear sequence, does not necessarily ensure a mastery over reality where the unpredictable regularly takes over. In the second case, he forces us to acknowledge that describing every conceivable object we can perceive does not bring us any closer to understanding our relationship with our surroundings. These descriptions are based on words, groupings of weightless concepts, and beneath these concepts lies the void. This consciousness of the emptiness lurking behind human discourse can engender despair. Rather than tears, Pinget prefers laughter, because it represents a victory of sorts over our imperfect condition.

Quelqu'un (*Someone*)

Heretofore in this discussion Pinget and his various characters have been conscious, while wandering through the verbal labyrinth, of treading on shaky ground. Beneath the words used to evoke their experiences they have discovered silence, and beneath silence they have sensed the far more terrifying presence of death. But what if words could, through their sheer weightlessness, produce the magical formula, the dazzling spiritual illumination that would exorcise the horror of the void? What if they could make us whole again? This is the question for which Mortin, the principal character of Pinget's next novel, *Quelqu'un* (1965), seeks a solution in vain. Here the author's restlessly searching voice acquires a new tone.

In his anxiety to make some sense out of a wasted life, Mortin gropes about like a blind man for the kind of redemption Pinget would express magnificently 17 years later in "Propos de New York." As I mentioned at the beginning of Chapter 2, in order to enter the realm of legends where time never flows away, the author insists that it is necessary to travel light. In fact, the baggage must be virtually weightless, humming with words, which distill the treasures of our collective unconscious. Mortin senses obscurely that he must get his suitcase packed as neatly as possible for the voyage to the other shore, but he is not sure what should go in it and what should be thrown out. This uncertainty is compounded by the realization that as old age is inexorably approaching, so is death. His is the time for recapitulations. As he continuously pours over his past, however, he keeps reaching different conclusions. Foraging into the recesses of his memory means bringing up more and more things. How does one reduce these to the size of a bag that can be easily carried? At the beginning of the novel, the narrator deplores his inability to pack his suitcase once and for all:

> as though it were always necessary for your existence to form a compact little parcel that you could pick up right away and take along with you everywhere. And that's not even an image, I shouldn't say as though, that's the way it is. That's the way it happens. One's existence in a valise, nicely arranged, well cataloged so that one has what one needs just in case. So one packs one's valise continuously, one is always in the process

of making something into a package. Even when talking about good weather. There is something in my valise that is not in the right place. You repack, sort out, remake the package, you're again prepared but then look what happens, the weather is no longer nice, you get wet, you get soaked to the bones. So you open up the valise again. You'd think you were doing it on purpose, that you were waiting to open it up again every second.[8]

Mortin's metaphysical anxiety is triggered by an apparently banal incident: the loss of a sheet of paper on which he had scribbled some notes. He is barely seated at his desk when he notices, panic-stricken, that he cannot find this paper without which it is impossible for him to pursue vital research. Actually, what the reader eventually figures out is that *Quelqu'un* has started off with a quid pro quo. The missing document the narrator is so desperate to recover has nothing whatsoever to do with the novel, which is unfolding. Mortin refers to the latter as the "exposé" or presentation. The paper forms part of a botany project, which he works on as a hobby and which he calls his manuscript. Yet this lost object becomes the novel's reason for being, and the search it touches off constitutes the purpose of Mortin's/Pinget's writing.

As obsessive and compulsive as M. Levert, the narrator goes over and over the events of the day, trying to figure out how the scrap of paper got lost. Chronological and typographical details pile up on one another. As he gathers up his recollections, he puts forward various hypotheses as to its disappearance: the maid might have misplaced it; Fonfon the retarded adolescent might have thrown it out; a neighbor might have picked it up. Mortin really seems intent on retrieving the insignificant object. His mind sweeps through every corner of the boardinghouse, every interval in his schedule. He continues hoping against hope that somehow during the course of his exhaustive investigation his mind will slide momentarily out of control, and through a gap in the rational structure of his language the longed-for discovery will emerge.

Why all this fuss over an ordinary scrap of paper? Obviously we must look to the symbolic level for its significance. It is a mere pretext for a search of spiritual proportions. Mortin doggedly tries to track it down because he cannot put his finger on exactly what he is yearning to find. During the course of the day other lost objects will take the place of this first one, the most noteworthy being a book entitled *Thérèse Neumann*, which may be a detective story, a work of religious mysticism, or, according to the maid, a piece of pornography.

After a while Mortin is no longer completely convinced that he lost the scrap of paper. Once he returns to his manuscript, he realizes that the missing article is really not indispensable. But, if such is the case, then who lost a piece of paper? And which one was it? Could it have been the one where the name and telephone number of another servant were jotted down? Was Marie the maid the one who misplaced it? If so, she is certainly not the only one in the boardinghouse who loses things. Throughout the novel everybody seems to be losing and forgetting everything. Gaston forgets to call the plumber, Marie forgets to buy the cheese, Monsieur Cointet cannot find his suspenders. Life in the narrator's dwelling seems to be one big, continuous memory lapse. Mortin feels that his brain is a real sieve. To counteract his chronic forgetfulness, he concocts all kinds of memory-joggers—telegraphlike sentences that he subsequently forgets to use: "Ask Gaston: wine and Apostolos Canary Wine, canary, light bulb, what else? Tell Reber Marie" (*Q*, 83). Mortin even dreams of being a reincarnation of St. Anthony, who supposedly used his supernatural powers to help people recover lost articles.

Actually, the theme of the misplaced paper is a metaphor for a deep-rooted obsession in Pinget as well as his narrator: the ebbing away of one's memory, and along with it one's existence. Confessions are dangerous to make because they drain you of your vital substance. Drawing up exhaustive inventories of one's surroundings in the hope of reaching the rock bottom of the subconscious gets one nowhere either. Referring obliquely to his previous novel, *L'Inquisitoire*, the author has his narrator denounce the futility of lengthy descriptions. All they do is prevent the mind from focusing on the secrets of memory. For this reason, he refuses to describe the shed where he happens to be foraging at the beginning of the novel:

> I enter the shed. Now to be honest I should name everything there is in the shed and that I inspected and walked around. But I don't want to give myself over to inventories any more. I did it before with such conscientiousness and patience! In my other exposés, to help me concentrate, hoping that it would clear out my subconscious, that it would open up avenues toward the essential. Nothing doing. Completely useless. Objects are of no use when you're aiming for the soul. You might think at the outset that they help us orient ourselves, concentrate, I repeat. Bullshit. You get caught up in the game, you fuss around with the description, you revel in it but in the end you're back to square one like before. (*Q*, 22–23)

Limiting one's subject, as Pinget and his narrator try to do in *Quelqu'un*, is a precautionary measure taken to prevent the flushing out of their psychic and emotional systems. Neither is yet quite ready to pack his suitcase in the metaphysical sense. Neither can as yet figure out the answer to the anguishing question concerning our presence on earth. Consequently, through his character Mortin, Pinget sets a far more modest and attainable goal for himself. By scrutinizing one of his days, Mortin endeavors to solve one specific problem: When and where did he misplace the piece of paper? If he can answer this second question, not only will he have unlocked the door leading to the treasures buried in his subconscious, but he will be in a better position to resolve the first one.

Strapping himself up tight into the structure of a narrative does not work for very long, however. His descriptions simply cannot exhaust the time or space he initially circumscribed. He even ends up succumbing to the temptation he swore he would resist: baring his soul. As he dredges up the events of the day, they trigger associations of ideas, which lead him deeper and deeper into his past. Almost despite himself he is compelled to name names, to explain how the boardinghouse project got started, to uncover the causes of the deterioration of his relationship with his business partner and friend, Gaston. In short, he finds himself trying to give meaning to his life. With some alcoholic stimulation, he opens wide the floodgates of confession, offering up to the reader his own often less than attractive secrets, along with those of his boarders. Obviously, then, this middle-aged man who seems to treasure solitude and silence yearns deep down for an audience before which he can reveal all. Indeed, he launches into a veritable orgy of self-depiction that leaves him as weary as the elderly servant at the end of *L'Inquisitoire*.

Hence Mortin's contempt for the *Art poétique*, a treatise on the art of writing by the seventeenth-century author Boileau. The latter extols the virtue of clarity. He even goes as far as to say that it is the inevitable corollary of rigorous thought. For Mortin, it is not clarity that makes writing possible but the opposite: "It's because you don't understand anything about it that you talk. If people understood, they would be only too happy to remain silent." As Mortin abandons himself to his verbal inebriation, he discovers that what counts in any narrative is not so much truth as plausibility. Each new interpretation he brings to bear on his past becomes the new reality. It matters not at all that these successive hypotheses may be at odds with one another, or that they may be in conflict with what actually happened. The narrative he is producing at any given moment is the only event really taking place. No one statement ever remains invariably true because it can be replaced by another, which appears equally plausible. Mortin and Pinget give us the key to understanding their imaginary world in the following paradox: "What is said is never said since you can say it in another way" (*Q*, 45).

The deep sadness bordering on despair, which leads the narrator to bare his soul and reinvent his past at the same time, can be explained by the company he has been keeping for too long. As half-owner of a run-down boardinghouse, Mortin is in daily contact with a bunch of decaying old failures. Terrified by death but unwilling to admit it, they seek refuge in memories of happy experiences so embellished by their imagination as to be unreal. Although physically still alive, they are already spiritually embalmed in a past that never existed. The building they inhabit is thus a halfway house between being and nonbeing.

Unlike his boarders, the narrator has an almost biological integrity, which makes it impossible for him to lie to himself. Because of this ruthless lucidity, he cannot stomach his fellow man's propensity for self-delusion. In his dealings with the pathetic human wrecks who inhabit his building, he is constantly torn between pity and disgust. His present isolation and misanthropy do not result from hatred of all those people who spend their time running away from themselves, but from a disillusioned awareness that trying to empathize with them is fruitless. Rather than play the role of the compassionate saint, he prefers to withdraw within himself. As he observes sorrowfully,

> In the past, when I wasn't doing my little research, I was like everybody else, I talked, I made experiments, I lived as they say. I bored the shit out of myself. That's the right word. Or rather not quite. I bored the shit out of myself but kept telling myself that I was going about it the wrong way, that my views were slanted, that I didn't see things as they are, that I could get much more out of them and that the situation would change. I mean things and people. Especially people. So I made the pleasure last as they say. I floundered around in other people's crap all the while telling myself that I couldn't see clearly, that I had to pay more attention, be kinder too, forget myself a little, love them a little, help them a little, so that they would open up a little. What bullshit. The more they opened up, the more of it there was. At one point I couldn't stand it any more, I was suffocating. And I withdrew into my own. (*Q*, 10)

This insurmountable revulsion the narrator feels explains the scatological imagery appearing frequently in the text, which has scandalized more than a few critics since its publication.

If the reader is at first inclined to think that Mortin is guilty of over-reacting, the description of a typical lunch, which brings the boarders together, amply justifies his misanthropic attitude. This is indeed the longest, funniest, and most significant episode in the novel. It is dupli-cated at the end of the book by the much shorter dinner scene into which it blends. It functions as a link between the description of a morn-ing and afternoon so weirdly similar that we end up confusing them. The novel seems to go round in circles, swinging from lunch to dinner to breakfast and back during the very same day. It is as though Mortin's reminiscences were foul-tasting food, which he simply is unable to digest properly. In any event, chewing the same fragments over and over again allows him to finally swallow them. Since there is nothing he can do to change the course of his nauseating existence, at least he has the satisfac-tion of mocking it.

Mortin begins his description of lunch by going around the table clockwise, identifying each of the participants in this pathetic yet side-splitting psychodrama: "On my left there is Perrin, we share the end of the table which is oval. . . . On Perrin's left there is monsieur Cointet. . . . Next to Cointet his wife. . . . To the left of madame Cointet, madame Apostolos. . . . To the left of Apostolos there is monsieur Vérassou. . . . To the left of Vérassou, at the other round end as well, is Gaston. . . . To the left of Gaston there is monsieur Erard. . . . He is next to her at the table and his wife is next to Fonfon who is on my right" (Q, 125–30). During the summer holidays the scaled-down lunch has only five partic-ipants: "Me [the narrator] in my place, that is to say, with my back turned to the kitchen, Apostolos opposite me, Reber at the other end, Gaston opposite her and Fonfon next to me" (Q, 254). Even when the majority of the boarders are away, they still manage to make their pres-ences felt like ghosts returning to their old haunts.

The menu remains invariable: eggplant, steak, salad, cheeses, peach-es. At dinnertime fried eggs replace the meat. During certain seasons certain courses may be modified. The conversation is as invariable as the menu. Its subjects come in series: holidays and fashion; the best butcher and the Borromean Islands; travel and accidents. The series mingle and even feed upon one another. On Sundays and in the evening Vérassou, who works at the hospital, describes for the boarders' edification and enlightenment the accident cases that have come to his attention. His lurid descriptions obviously enhance their dining pleasure: "He talks about what he has seen at the hospital or what he has heard, the incur-able cases, the amputations, the car accidents with details which take my appetite away or what's left of it, but them, not at all, especially the women. Like mustard or pickles, it makes them salivate, they ask for more, they want more details. They masticate their carrion while licking their chops. Does their subconscious imagine that it is in the process of eating up a sawed-off leg or a ripped-off ball?" (*Q*, 138).

The combination of meat and the Borromean Islands provide for even more tantalizing conversation. An aging couple, M. and Mme Cointet, invariably bring up the subject of the Italian islands and the succulent roast beef they enjoyed while honeymooning there. As soon as the foul meat course is brought in a Pavlovian reflex is set into motion, and they begin to wax rapturously not only about the unforgettable roast but about the flowers whose scents they inhaled 30 years before. Even when the Cointets are not present at lunch Mortin can hear them talk about Isola Bella as though he were hallucinating: "This devious life they had, the Cointets, in any case, which takes the place of the present one with such precision that they can almost smell the flowers and the aroma of the menu of June twenty-fifth, isn't it enough to get one aroused?" (*Q*, 137).

Reminiscing about an idealized past is how Mortin's boarders manage to anaesthetize the horror of their condition. By fixating themselves on experiences they once enjoyed, they obliterate the present and become oblivious to death. In fact, they treat themselves during their earthly existence to a foretaste of eternal bliss. Of course, all they are doing is foisting a monumental fraud on themselves that the narrator is quick to expose. Their lyrical recollections are nothing but empty talk: "Just hearing them talk about these things proved that they had understood nothing about them, that they were elsewhere when they saw them, in their country-fair paradise, which was slipping through their fingers . . . that's why they would close their eyes when looking at the azaleas" (*Q*, 139–40). Taking pity on them despite his disgust, Mortin offers them a new dream to keep them going, one much more within their grasp than Isola Bella or a succulent roast beef: the purchase of a washing machine for the boardinghouse.

Within this immutable mealtime ritual occur other incidents, which prevent life from becoming totally monotonous. The adolescent simpleton Fonfon, whom Mortin has unofficially adopted, can always be counted on to unleash chaos. He blows his nose in his napkin, pours water inadvertently over his shirt, drops eggplant over his trousers or gets them soaked, or spills red wine over the tablecloth. Clumsy in deportment and afflicted with vulgar manners, he brings the maid, Marie, to the verge of tears and makes the cantankerous old Mme Reber so indignant that she fakes a choking spell. Fonfon's transgressions can be pitied and explained by his slow-wittedness. Mme Reber, however, who takes an almost sadistic pleasure in persecuting him, is unforgivable. Casting away her last shred of dignity, she greedily sucks up the remnants of dessert: a mixture of peach juice, sugar, and third-rate wine. Mortin observes her, heartbroken and sick to his stomach.

It is understandable, then, that the narrator should yearn for some form of spiritual deliverance. For a while he hopes for an illumination through the act of writing. Who knows—a miracle might take place. Through associations and plays on words something "unexpected" or "dazzling" might well up from the abyss of his subconscious, suddenly conferring a transcendent meaning on an otherwise purposeless existence. Perhaps the written word would eventually loosen up the taciturn introvert he appears to be and reveal a soul overflowing with generosity as well as an eloquent interlocutor. Like the new being heralded by the Gospels, a new Mortin might emerge—a splendid creature, "a being all pure, all grace, all smile."

Mortin does not entertain this illusion for long. He gives up on the longed-for upheaval that would free his bottled-up soul. Since no spiritual transformation is possible, there is at least the saving grace of honesty and the freedom to create a work of art. Depicting reality as he sees it is a way of rising out of the quagmire of mediocrity. Resurrecting his experience of life and expressing it in a lasting form will dispel the feeling of dejection and failure. When the author describes what exists around him, however ugly it may be, he triumphs over it. The vulgarity we find throughout the novel is not gratuitous. It reflects the writer's determination to face unflinchingly the truth about our human condition. That is why he compels himself to continue foraging in the garbage heap of life, to pursue the act of writing, just as the infant remains seated on the chamber pot until he produces the appropriate results: "I'll stay on like a child on his chamber pot, he keeps wanting to get off it, his mother checks to see if he's done his job, he hasn't done anything yet, she plunks him back on until he makes his deposit. I want to be the child, the chamber pot and the mother all at the same time" (Q, 170).

Another passage in the novel illustrates Mortin's unshakable resolve to confront his existence, however repugnant it may be. Still searching for the useless yet elusive piece of paper, the narrator plunges unflinchingly into the garbage accumulated over several days, made up of all the foul-looking, foul-smelling leftovers and kitchen remnants:

I emptied the garbage can, a filthy job, I got another look at everything we had eaten over the past three days, how did I manage to do it in this heat, the smell was overwhelming me. All the zucchini and eggplant peelings, the rotten tomato parts, the spit out nerves of the beef steak, the nauseating leftovers from the kitchen pots, the lettuce cores, the egg shells, the mouldy ratatouille remnants . . . the tattered pieces of the rag-bag mixed with fat balls of dust already greasy from sauce left in the plates, sheets of paper stuck to the bottom for God knows how long, everything, I looked at everything. Reber yelled at me put on gloves to do that. Gloves, gloves, I had to have gloves, do I handle life with gloves? (*Q*, 214)

This uncompromising honesty tinged with self-deprecating humor fully justified Dominque Rollin's description of the novel as "a fictive operation that makes sordidness spill over into courage, meanness into lucidity, and rottenness into love, without apparent transition."[9]

For the narrator, however, courage and integrity are not sufficient in themselves to help him cope with his existence. His moral qualities may make him a "someone" in his own right, but he still yearns for another human being, "someone" who might understand and sympathize with his aspirations. He expresses this poignant yearning twice during the course of his day of soul-searching: "Let them understand me, let them put themselves in my place. I wonder whether someone would want to. Someone. . . . If only I had someone! Someone to read over my shoulder, but that would be too good to be real" (*Q*, 52, 195).

Jean-Claude Liéber has correctly pointed out that this "Someone" is obviously the interpreter, which every book needs in order to come alive. It may be ennobling to face the truth that there is no escape from the drudgery of our condition, but this unpalatable truth becomes easier to bear when shared with a sympathetic reader. Creating endless illusions based on reality may be a highly gratifying activity in itself, but it becomes infinitely more so when someone else can in turn re-create them in the light of his/her own imagination, thereby extending their fragile life.

For a few fleeting weeks, Mortin and Fonfon revel in this very role of the sympathetic interpreter. Indulging in what for him is an extravagant luxury, the narrator rents a television set to entertain the simpleminded adolescent. The two viewers immediately get hooked on a series called "Capitaine Corcoran" whose every adventure they await with bated breath, in whose destiny they actively participate:

I thanked heaven for having given me this idea. I was perhaps going to save Fonfon like that, with the television. But I was saving myself, too, perhaps I might have been able to save myself. We talked of nothing but Capitaine Corcoran, we imagined all day what he was going to do at night after dinner. [. . .] And then the show came on, a bedazzlement, paradise. [. . .] And for one month it was like that, we were the television, we saw coconut trees wherever we walked, sunsets on the minarets, perfumed nights, ships decorated with cushions and we set sail for the tropics. Fonfon remembered from one time to the next, not I, he was the one who ended up telling me the story. We were coming back to life. (*Q*, 219–20)

It is a noteworthy paradox that Robert Pinget has recourse to the traditional story with its linear unfolding of plot, cause-and-effect sequences, and clearly delineated characters to revitalize temporarily these two lonely souls. All of Capitaine Corcoran's adventures have a beginning, a middle, and an end. He is a flamboyant, self-assured romantic hero who knows exactly where he is heading, rushes forward to meet the most perilous of challenges, and triumphs inevitably over all adversity. In fact, both he and his adventures are the exact opposite of Pinget's characters and aesthetic intentions. Was the author contradicting himself without being aware of it? Hardly likely. Although the television series that thrills Mortin and Fonfon nightly conforms to the conventional principles of storytelling and appears to be plausible, it is a pure product of the imagination. It delights the two precisely because it frees them from humdrum reality, allowing their minds and hearts to soar through time and space. It gives them access to the realm of dreams. It provides them with the sensation of weightlessness and the possibility of infinite expansion. One wonders, then, why Pinget did not avail himself of this artistic vehicle, however traditional, to draw his readers along with him in soaring flight. As one of his earlier novels, *Graal Flibuste*, attests, he can be a superb storyteller when he chooses. Who knows? If he had chosen to explore this more traditional approach, he might have drawn a far different category of "someones" to his fictional world.

Chapter Four

Exorcizing Anguish

In many respects the title of this chapter could apply equally well to the previous one. M. Levert, Clope, and the deaf servant in *L'Inquisitoire* wander about in a labyrinth of words to forget the pain of solitude or the terror of the void. In *Quelqu'un* Mortin shuttles back and forth between a half-imagined past and lackluster present in pursuit of the magical formula that will make him whole again, thereby bringing him lasting solace. But as a title, "Exorcizing Anguish" is even more appropriate to describe the atmosphere that prevails in Robert Pinget's next two novels, *Le Libera* (1968) and *Passacaille* (1969). In these works the anguish is no longer latent or intermittent. It is an integral part of a theme that the author orchestrates continuously on various registers: the omnipresence of loneliness and death. Moreover, in these subtle and, indeed, "musical" orchestrations, the reader discerns a new tone emanating from the same recognizable voice. Once he captures it, he finds himself moving even further along with Pinget on the voyage of self-discovery.

Le Libera (*The Libera Me*)

At the beginning of this study I spoke of "the swirling configurations" of Pinget's imaginary universe. Of all his novels, *Le Libera* is probably the one that best illustrates the description. Its restless, circular movement backs up against itself, yet at the same time it opens up continuously onto endless new possibilities. Up until the last 10 or so pages it is very difficult if not impossible to determine where the author wishes to take us. Successive versions of the same event contradict one another as they multiply like living cells. Episodes get tangled up. Different characters get involved when a particular incident or drama recurs. Then, retrospectively, in the final stages of the novel, the scattered fragments all come into focus as the prayer "Libera me Domine" is uttered with overtones of derisive laughter. We realize that the whole text is an exorcism devised by Pinget to make the inevitable disasters of failure and death more bearable.

While grappling with his metaphysical obsessions, the author is simultaneously pondering over the age-old dilemma he must confront as a novelist: How does one balance the two opposing requirements of expansion and closure? On the one hand, he is fascinated by the ideal of a narrative with an indefinitely extendible structure, propelled by its own momentum. On the other, he knows that this forward thrust carries within it the yearning to conclude and to confer some kind of unity on a production, which he could otherwise no longer control. A first reading of *Le Libera* can be a very disconcerting experience. The sheer proliferation of its material, the innumerable criss-crossings of its themes and motives, seem to frustrate any attempt at analysis. After careful perusal, however, it is possible to uncover the novel's complex structure and inner tempo. We are much indebted to Jean-Claude Liéber, whose insightful interpretation of this work has helped guide us through its intricacies.[1]

The first 20 or so pages deal with the Mlle Lorpailleur obsession. The reader will recall having met this madcap schoolteacher back in *Mahu, ou le matériau* and in *Le Renard et la boussole*. In *Le Libera* an anonymous person is out to "get" her. He seeks out the pharmacist, Cruze, known as "Verveine," and tries to persuade him to have the spiteful, gossipy woman committed, since she has been spreading rumors to the effect that he (the anonymous narrator) was involved in the murder of a child. As Tony Duvert pointed out in his masterful analysis of the beginning of *Le Libera*, its whole expository sequence is contained in the phrase "the Lorpailleur woman is mad."[2] After being repeated several times, it gives birth to a complete episode.

This accusation leveled against Mlle Lorpailleur is the pivot on which the novel swings. Eager to denounce the madwoman in order to vindicate himself, the anonymous person sets in motion a process of paranoia, which seizes the whole town in its grip and gives rise to various forms of collective madness: "The word cataclysm or catastrophe, it's said that this kind of thing works on them, delusions of grandeur, delusions of misfortune, they see traps everywhere, they're all in a whirl trying to get out, to extricate themselves, to escape, something is going to swoop down on them, they feel bound hand and foot, this is what madness is about."[3] This initial statement about Lorpailleur's madness confers on the narrative the dimension of the irrational. Since the imaginary world of Robert Pinget thrives on contradiction, the child whose murder has caused such a commotion could have been disposed of in a variety of ways: he could have been strangled, kidnapped, he could have had his throat slashed, or he might have been run over by a truck. As it unfolds, the text proposes any number of destructive possibilities. All the child has to do is slip away from his parents to be doomed. His very disappearance endangers the whole child population. Conversely, any tragedy that can befall a child—be it abduction, sickness, or accidental death—is inflicted on this particular one. As his family name, Ducreux, indicates, the child serves as a mold for the whole series of victims to come.[4]

Being the perpetrator of the first attempt at blackmail, it is only natural that Mlle Lorpailleur be victimized in turn by the murderous imagination of the narrator. As she rides her bicycle to work, he constructs various scenarios to satisfy his craving for revenge: he has her fall to the pavement, frothing at the mouth and wriggling in a fit of epilepsy; then he imagines her struck dead by an oncoming truck, or seriously injured. He even has an eternal bystander, Mme Moineau, corroborate his assertion that the harridan has gone off the deep end. The teacher's fall, combining an epileptic seizure and an accident with a motor vehicle, illustrates the technique of literal associations by which the text moves forward. Other examples abound. Mlle Lorpailleur passes by on her bike, stiff as a ramrod, watched by a neighbor who is perched on a stool washing her windows. Without warning time skids; spring is left behind, and summer falls upon the town. Although there exists no cause-effect relationship between Lorpailleur's presence and the Ducreux murder, the switching back and forth between episodes links them by a strange kind of interdependency. All the madwoman has to do is appear in order for disasters to be unleashed. At the mere mention of her name, her mother passes away, and her father falls victim to an accident. Her name carries with it as much of a curse for the village as the month of July when dreadful events are wont to occur.

Another child who loses his life is mentioned at the beginning of *Le Libera*. The little Bianle boy gets crushed under a car and is confused with the Ducreux offspring through a memory lapse of the narrator. The latter blithely mixes up dates and victims, giving the following pathetic excuse: "We couldn't even remember that misfortune strikes us always in July, a car accident, a drowning, a fire, it must have been a Saturday, I can still see Mme Ducreux washing the bakery store windows [. . .] what am I saying, crushed, it happened to the little Bianle boy" (*L*, 20–21). The narrator does make an effort to differentiate between the Ducreux child, lost forever during a picnic, and the Bianle boy, who dies under the wheels of an automobile. Shortly afterward, however, the "picnic" version of the Ducreux child's disappearance is challenged and replaced by another unhappy event, which does nothing to clarify the situation: the Bianle family picnic during which their innocent little off-spring vanished and was never seen again alive. The Ducreux family's affliction sets them up as a target for village gossip. Malicious tongues half-accuse the parents of complicity in their child's death. The gossipers insinuate that connections exist between the tragedy, on the one hand, and the parents' unsavory business dealings, their less than blissful marriage, and their constant dissension, on the other. The murder, then, is just a ploy, a pretext to float out any number of hypotheses to sustain the reader's curiosity. Just like the window washer, the reader savors the morbid pleasure of being a voyeur.

This first sequence comes to an end as the narrator fulfills his most deeply rooted fantasy: he has the satisfaction of witnessing the confinement of his arch enemy, Mlle Lorpailleur, in an insane asylum. But he is not the only one who revels in revenge. Pinget, who created the madwoman in the first place, takes an almost sadistic delight in using her as a scapegoat to denounce the sheer folly inherent in the act of writing itself, the inextricable mess that ensues when an author is overcome by the compulsion to express himself over and over again in words:

> No one went to see her at the asylum, besides it was discouraged, she was subjected to cold showers and was put in a straitjacket on certain days and was given the electroshock treatment and medications [. . .] she didn't take the trouble to go to the bathroom, I mean the crazy one, doing it right on the floor, at the foot of the bed, and there were manuscripts everywhere, loose sheets covered with illegible handwriting, it boggles the mind just thinking that we endured that creature for 15 years as the person responsible for our children. (*L*, 27)

Let us bear this judgment in mind. It will recur toward the end of the novel when the whole creative process disintegrates in a self-mocking play on words.

A collective voice comes to the foreground in the second sequence, which extends for roughly 14 pages. It represents the consciousness of the town, the synthesis of the townspeople's conversations. It relates just about all of the anecdotes which make up the novel. As can be expected by now in a Pinget novel, *Le Libera* is not based on one major story, unfolding in successive stages till it reaches its conclusion. Instead it contains a profusion of narratives moving along parallel lines, overlapping from time to time as though the reader were bouncing back and forth from one newspaper column to another. The new narrators, referring to themselves as "we," allude to events rather than flesh them out. Episodes get started but never seem to get finished. They color and condition one another to the point that the mind, utterly confused, finds in their sources nothing but uncertainty and contradiction. Coming on top of the murder of the Ducreux child and the tragic death of the Bianles' little son is the murder of Serinet by his brother-in-law. In addition, we follow a series of disputes over issues such as land property, construction sites, or rival candidacies for municipal office. These generate antagonisms between local clans.

The murder was announced at the beginning of the first episode and served as a model for that of the Ducreux child: "We hadn't seen a drama like this one since eighteen hundred and seventy-three" (*L*, 9). Actually, the date does nothing more than confirm the predilection fatality has for the month of July when it comes to inflicting misfortune on the town. The crime acquires its immediacy through its contextual proximity to the murder of the little boy. The mention of the "little blond boy with chestnut-colored eyes strangled outright" leads to the announcement of "Serinet killed by gunshot." In both cases a wooded area provides the backdrop for the ugly deeds. Still, these murders are given a comic treatment. Pinget very accommodatingly has a hearse wandering about the town from noon till 6 P.M., at the disposal of the police officers, who are rather slow in bestirring themselves. In fact, the author's irrepressible sense of humor is ever-present in the narrative, softening its often gruesome aspects. Not only is there the always-available coffin for the suddenly deceased, but the local curate remains on duty day and night, always ready with a quick prayer, and the narrator, commenting on the dilemma of Serinet's widow, coins a proverblike statement to conclude the anecdote: "She returned home with a husband to mourn rather than a reveller to beat up."

This dispute theme precipitates a chain reaction of rivalries between various narrators. Mlle Ronzière pulls the carpet from under the feet of the madwoman Lorpailleur, who is forced to make do with a sermon on Providence. Then Mlle Ronzière upstages Latirail, who must content himself with a political analysis. This double upstaging in turn gets both the curate and the secretary of City Hall into the act. Obviously, then, the quarrelling between various townspeople provides the narrative's momentum. The rhythm is sustained when the notion of homicide leads, through an association of ideas, to that of bloody spectacle: the horrifying motor accident where the Bianle boy loses his life. At first, the accident is barely averted through the driver's quick thinking. Then it is more and more strongly foreshadowed by details of the setting in which it will occur: rue de Broy (from the verb *broyer*, meaning "crush"), bazaar Tripeau (from *tripes*, meaning "guts"), rue des Tanneurs (the verb *tanner* means "to thrash"), and the butcher's wife (*la bouchère*) substituted for the baker's wife (*la boulangère*). This whole lexical field draws the young lad to his death like a magnet. Here again the author's sense of humor attenuates the tragedy of the situation, arranging skillful transitions between the flower pots at the burial and Ariane de Bonne-Mesure's window boxes, or between the child's splattered brain referred to as "*détritus*" (rubbish) and the cat's droppings.

The episodes that follow are organized around the theme of man's relationship to nature. Each one of them ends and leads into the next with the appearance of a cyclist. First we have a ludicrous theological discussion between the chatelaine, Ariane de Bonne-Mesure, and the curate, inspired by the former's cat, and adumbrated by Lorpailleur's discourse on Providence in the previous section. Their conversation already points to the rather raunchy anecdote of a homosexual priest, referred to as "the RP" ("Révérend Père," or the monogram of the author himself), bent on seducing the village youths. Ariane, or her niece Francine, scolds the cat, depending on whether the recalcitrant feline leaves her droppings in the hortensias, the vegetable garden, or the flower box in the salon. These variations will appear each time the lunch sequence at the Château de Bonne-Mesure recurs. And it does indeed recur, with the result that the guests get back on their bicycles once the meal is over in order to take part in the next chapter.

There follow two more episodes in which nature's influence is celebrated. The first involves the Bianle family, for whom the enjoyment of natural surroundings and fresh air are vital necessities. This leads to the picnic version of the lost child, which will engender the sequence describing a school excursion later on in the novel. As in the Ducreux affair, the father is suspected of wanting to do away with his son. It is to no avail that he calls upon Mlle Ronzière as a witness, even though he mistook her for Francine on her bicycle. The second story is centered on Dr. Mottard, a perfectly stoical gentleman who otherwise would have every reason to reproach nature for its injustice, since his daughter is both lame and slow-witted. But she loves plants and birds, and so the doctor comes down against the confinement of Mlle Lorpailleur (of all people) in a mental hospital, rather than of his daughter. This decision, needlessly to say, gives rise to all kinds of malicious gossip. Then, in two symmetrical paragraphs, the influence of nature is extolled and ridiculed.

Finally, the curate drives past the schooleacher's window on his motor-bike, indicating that these two episodes are concluded.

Immediately thereafter the Ducreux affair reappears in its initial version, according to which the little boy wanders away from the yard where he is playing. The poetic and slightly syrupy depiction of the child's roundabout is very similar in tone to the Simone Brize episode in *Clope au dossier*. In a dazzling display of virtuosity, Pinget has the baby undergo a speeded-up transformation until he reaches adulthood. Thus, aside from his unusually introspective temperament, the trauma he undergoes as an infant will not leave an indelible imprint on him. The affair does not end there, however. In the final pages dealing with the theme of nature, Verveine and Lorpailleur present rival versions of the same events that make all townspeople connected with them appear guilty. Paranoia and madness sweep through the collectivity. Since there is no character to provide a focus for the plot, it is impossible to put it into perspective. Everyone becomes a target of suspicion.

The next section dwells on disloyal relationships and misfortunes. This theme undergoes a double orchestration. The first concerns itself with a case of inheritance fraud. It centers on the Doudin family and is monitored by Judge Maillard and the notary. Etiennette Piédevant, wearing a flamboyant dress, disturbs the legal consultation by her inopportune arrival. Her presence spells danger, since she has jeopardized her reputation through her involvement in the affair and has had to go into exile. Now she further complicates the situation by bumping into Mlle Doudin, who is on her way to a secret meeting with the judge. Then Etiennette compromises him by figuring out what is really behind all this secrecy. Meanwhile, people rally to the defense of the City Hall secretary, Monnard, who is implicated not in this particular affair but in the Ducreux boy's murder as a result of Verveine's accusations. Finally, the townspeople draw a parallel between Mlle Lorpailleur, whose cynical maneuvers in the inheritance scandal have been thwarted, and Mlle Moine, whose devotion has not been rewarded by the executor of the will.

In the second development on the same theme, Pinget emphasizes his belief, through the use of fiction, that individual lives, far from being unique, are interchangeable. The names may change, but the succession of events making up a person's destiny are more or less alike. The author describes the shabby treatment that the Moignon children have meted out to Mlle Dondard (or Mottard), then taking the opposite tack, he relates how nasty the Mottard children (Eliette and her brother) behaved toward Mme Moignon. The author has the different people assimilate each other's characteristics to such an extent that the distinction between victim and persecutor gets erased: "Madame Moignon was a Mottard," states the narrator, blithely indifferent to the discrepancies that are slipping into his discourse. In this inextricable maze of alterations and contradictions, we never reach the end of the listing of the Mottard family's 12 children; we are never quite sure how they are to be ranked. For example, Jean-Claude goes forward from sixth to tenth place before going backward from sixth to fourth in the next-to-last sequence of the novel.

Names, too, undergo surprising deformations. Mlle Mottard, a relative of Dr. Mottard and his half-witted daughter, has a female cousin afflicted with a hunchback. The unfortunate woman used to gather horse dung along the roads for her garden. So Pinget has her stricken with dysentery and gives her the very graphic name, Crottard (*crotte* means "droppings"), evoking the biological operation to which the woman is henceforth condemned. In an unabashedly scatological yet uproariously funny passage, he has the village's collective "voice" describe Mlle Crottard's Calvary as it prattles on about the exchange of words that took place on the very subject between Mlle Moine and the doctor:

> What might one do to rid her of her cross, it got hold of her in the middle of communion, such a worthy person and all that, the doctor is supposed to have said for her to come and see him about it, we'll look into it, there may be a chronic appendicitis, let her come and see me, which he shouldn't have said but with such an old acquaintance he wasn't suspicious, because Mlle Moine had the time between nine and ten o'clock to tell everybody about this incurable disease that at 11:30 bordered on a shameful illness, so that in the evening when the poor Crottard woman went out again to buy some jams for her mother's "biscottes" people barely acknowledged her greeting and on returning home she was so overcome she barely had enough time to rush into the lavatory, one more second and it would have been too late. (*L*, 75–76)

This scatological episode is not gratuitous. The excrement motif will recur toward the end of the novel to devastating yet hilarious effect. It will symbolize the disintegration of artistic ambition within the sewer of existence.

After this episode Pinget repeats in several very complex pages all of the anecdotes on which the novel is based: the drunken driver, the rivalry between the various contractors, the destruction of a building with the street number 12, as well as the disappearance of the Ducreux child in its picnic-drowning version and the tragic accident involving the Bianle boy. The village voice sorrowfully concludes, "death was among us" (*L*, 77). The double development comes to an end as the various elements fall into place. Judge Maillard condemns Mlle Doudin in the inheritance case. Mme Moignon accuses Eliette Mottard of having jinxed her daughter. Now that the two developments have fused, they can unfold again. But this time it is Verveine who calls out to Eliette as she walks down the street with a cardboard box containing her dress under her arm.

Having unraveled the skein of twisted relationships and interchangeable destinies in the town, the author now launches into the largest section of *Le Libera*, taking us up to the concluding pages. It has as its framework a meal at the Château de Bonne-Mesure, which is interrupted at various times by other sequences and then resumed without ever really coming to an unequivocal end. The sequences are as follows:

Lunch at Bonne-Mesure
The picnic
Continuation of the lunch at Bonne-Mesure
Lunch at the Mortin boardinghouse
Lunch at the Château de Broy
Account of the audition
Continuation of lunch at Bonne-Mesure
Dinner at Bonne-Mesure

Here for the first time in the novel the narrative acquires a linear structure. As it unfolds in a sequential pattern, however, it becomes very complicated. The repetition of episodes allows for all kinds of substitutions and superpositions: events are modified, and characters assimilate each other's tics and traits or get so altered as to appear in contradiction with themselves. Even places and textual fragments get switched around. The results of all these changes can be very startling. The presence of Mlle Lorpailleur next to the curate during the second account of lunch at the Château de Bonne-Mesure gives the sequence an entirely different orientation. This time round Arianne and her niece Francine try to worm a confession out of the schoolteacher, whom they suspect of being linked to all of the town's dubious activities: the Doudin inheritance, the feuds between the various building contractors, the relationship between Ducreux and a Vernes or Vernet.

Through textual osmosis Francine herself begins to act more and more like the Lorpailleur woman she despises. They are rivals for the attentions of Monnard, the elegant City Hall secretary. They both indulge in the disgraceful mannerism of smelling themselves under their armpits. Tourniquet, the adolescent initiated into homosexuality by the RP, yields his apprenticeship to another youth, Pinson, whose latent erotic tendencies the same priest will be only too happy to bring to the surface. Ariane glides flippantly from one personality to another, by turns disputatious, serenely indifferent, and salacious, whereas the curate holds forth on the subject of fornication despite his assurances that he is incapable of following up his words with action.

As we have observed, there exists no transcendent justification for human actions in Pinget's imaginary universe. The chain of events constituting a so-called destiny is nothing more than an illusion, since for every act an individual performs there are any number of others he could have performed at a given moment. The author once more illustrates his aleatory conception of the unfolding of human existence in the lengthy prelude leading up to the meal. Here he gives Francine the choice between two itineraries and four stages in which to reach her destination. She can either take the path bordered by rhododendrons, which cuts across the commons, or she can proceed through the main alley, which will bring her straight to the terrace and the guests. The four stages are as follows:

Francine interrogates the cook about Lorpailleur's presence at the meal.
Francine changes her blouse in Ariane's bedroom.
Francine reads the letter on Ariane's dressing table.
Francine greets the guests on the terrace.

Gleefully deploying his mental dexterity, Pinget juggles with these hypotheses, arranging them in different combinations. Thus, the so-called chain of events gets short-circuited and conjectures skid into one another as the narrative moves forward or in reverse to suit the author's whims.

The meal itself undergoes the same aleatory combinations. It cannot seem either to get under way or come to an end, since the narrator himself is unable to decide if the scene on the terrace will serve as a setting for the aperitif (before the meal) or coffee (once the meal is over). The problem is not resolved until the end of the episode when Francine removes the porto instead of the maid and brings the coffee on the terrace. Once the guests are seated, the meal unfolds "normally," moving from main course to dessert. The menu itself varies with the narrator's fancy, however. The soufflé is replaced by artichokes or by cold consommé. The *matelote* vies with the small sausages and the fricassee of game in wine for the attention of the guests' palate. And the narrative nearly gets bogged down hopelessly in decisions about what kinds of coffee are to be served with or without caffeine.

Not only does fantasy preside over the meal, social blunders, vulgarity, and even scatological references do as well. These echo the disaster that befalls the wedding celebration in *L'Inquisitoire* and portend the disaster that will overwhelm Pinget's imaginary world at the conclusion of the novel. Ariane de Bonne-Mesure's cat sets the tone by persistently defecating in the wrong places. Not to be outdone, the bumbling and voracious curate spills the wine, gets gravy all over his napkin, pulls a bone out with his fingers, lets out a burp, and has a choking spell. He indulges in a Rabelaisian play on words, confusing *"le service divin"* (divine service) and *"le service du vin"* (wine service) and comparing *"la scène"* (the scene) with *"la Cène"* (The Last Supper). The successive courses of the meal are punctuated by references to the cat's biological emanations: "They were on the second course after the droppings." The guests are treated to the very artichokes that the cat had repeatedly dirtied: "They were being used as dung heap that year." The curate deplores "having to do everything through the same canal"—the words that set the reasoning process in motion are blocked by the bolus. The organs that take in and evacuate food get inverted: "The Lorpailleur woman opened up her chicken ass to swallow a mouthful."

In the final analysis the lunch with the local aristocrats turns out to be a figment of the schoolteacher's imagination, a fantasy she keeps replaying, all the while embellishing it, erasing some of its elements or replacing them. The first version of this social climber's deep-rooted yet unfulfilled wish has as its setting Mortin's boardinghouse. Lorpailleur fails in her attempt to see the master of the house or to be introduced to the nobleman, M. de Broy: "Arrival of the Lorpailleur woman, Mlle Lozière asks her how it is that she did not see Mortin" (*L*, 146). Her dream materializes when M. de Broy receives Lorpailleur, who first refuses his invitation, then either accepts it or wrests one out of him. But in the last variation on this fantasy she pays dearly for her social ambitions: she is dismissed from the elevated company whose favor she tried so hard to curry. Moreover, the lunches at the two châteaux, Broy and Bonne-Mesure, are fused through a series of repetitions. When Mlle Lorpailleur approaches both dwellings, they appear with their windows open to let the morning sun stream in. At both meals the servants are stationed in the corner of the terrace, and the same conversations about cattle raising and farming are heard. Each time either the cat emerges from the hedge or the gardener's wife comes out from behind a shrub. This creates an ambiguity that the novelist is in no hurry to clear up: "She was disturbed while doing you know what [. . .] in fact, she was weeding."

Referred to in a conversation during the meal at Bonne-Mesure, the Révérend Père actually appears during the second. The second lunch naturally reproduces the first, up to and including the same indecision as to the courses to be offered: "cold consommé or artichokes, matelote or fricassee of game." The narrator tries to put an end to this indecision by proposing all of the dishes together, mixing the heat of the summer day with the cool summer foods: "raw vegetables from the garden and cold fish in this heat." The curate's act of clumsiness in the Bonne-Mesure version is repeated by guests in the Broy scene. They, too, let their spoons drop into the sauce. Even the gardeners' names take on similar yet distinctive resonances according to whether they work at the Château de Bonne-Mesure (Amédée), Mortin's boardinghouse (Irénée), or the Château de Broy (Araignée). One version of lunch without Lorpailleur's presence is symmetrical to the first. The conversation in both cases is lighthearted "since in reality the Lorpailleur woman wasn't there."

We are then treated to a third description of lunch at Bonne-Mesure, this one unfolding after the meal at Broy, which has just ended. Here textual proximity counts for much more than precision in time. Now that Mlle Lorpailleur has been the object of the nobleman's mock gallantry, Francine can legitimately torment her. She no longer attempts to make her confess her involvement in the local scandals. She refers to the schoolteacher's recent humiliation in order to witness her reaction. In the context of this particular meal, we are also informed, through the ensuing conversation, about the audition organized by Mlle Lozière at Mortin's boardinghouse, and we learn more about the debauched adolescent, Tourniquet.

Since the sequence of events in Le Libera remains fluid, lunch at the Château de Bonne-Mesure flows naturally into dinner. Just as the meal at the Château de Broy borrowed elements from a previous one hosted by Ariane, so that last dinner arranged by the chatelaine of Bonne-Mesure reproduces, to the point of parody, the informal lunch arranged by her cousin, M. de Broy. Mlle Ariane receives the schoolteacher with the same flippant familiarity bordering on contempt: "No formality

between us," she insists with an overtone of diabolical irony. After breaking the ice, the chatelaine asks, in the very same order, the very same
questions that the Révérend Père addressed to Mlle Lorpailleur about
the latter's mother and sister. It is obvious by now that the text is going
around in circles. In its compulsion to retell what has already been told,
to nail down once more events in time, to repeat them in order to snatch
them from the void, is the novel not implicitly foreshadowing its failure
in particular, if not the death of the narrative in general—a death that
will become apparent in the conclusion?

Having buttered up Mlle Lorpailleur to put her completely at ease,
her hostesses, Ariane and Francine, bring up the subject of picnics, thereby interrupting the account of the meal. This is a trap cunningly set to
catch the unsuspecting schoolteacher and incriminate her just as the first
narrator had tried to do: "That she's crazy, there's no doubt about it. But
criminal, who can prove it" (*L*, 107). What follows is the relating of not
one but two different school expeditions, which from time to time merge
into each other to the point of being indistinguishable. Here again
Pinget emphasizes in how random a fashion events align themselves in
human lives and how interchangeable they can be.

The picnic per se takes place on the last Sunday in July, under the
supervision of Mlle Lorpailleur and her assistant, Odette. It takes place
before or after the schoolteacher's illness—an ominous sign of things to
come. The Bianle twins participate in the venture, one of whom, Henriette, turns out to be a tyrannical little hellion. The group of schoolchildren pass by Mme Tripeau's notions store, where the lady allows
them to filch some candy, then they turn left into the rue Ancienne. The
first school outing is set for Easter. For this particular expedition the
assistant is Monette Dondard—chosen, it seems, by fate itself to be the
urchins' scapegoat. Odile and Frédéric Mortin are substituted for the
Bianle twins and nearly get themselves run over at the start. The group
passes by the Tripeau general store and makes a right turn onto the rue
Ancienne. Despite certain noticeable differences in seasons, people, and
incidents, one perceives an illusory continuity linking the two episodes.
There are in both the same shoving and pushing, the same selfish whims
and infantile simpering. Monette retrieves the purse, which Odette had
gone off to find. Henriette torments both teaching assistants, but that is
understandable, since the bratty child not only carries the same first
name as Mlle Lorpailleur but embodies the same kind of nastiness. The
schoolteacher demonstrates her ugly, irrational character when she takes
the whip to the children while promising them some lemonade.

Mlle Lorpailleur's irrational nature—imposed on her by a mischievous author bent on having a good time at her expense—manifests itself in the contradictory pedagogical theories she tries to implement during the course of the two school outings. Comparing her pupils to animals, she describes them as "reserved, on the defensive," or "kind" and "spontaneous." She calls herself an advocate of competition and altruism, she waxes lyrical about ecology or shows indifference toward it, she gets on her high horse of principle or climbs off it in favor of empiricism. She is indeed torn and disgraced. She cannot choose between the panorama or the countryside. She favors both the snack bar and the miraculous statue. Consequently, she botches her lesson and, instead of having it both ways, loses both ways.

To complicate matters, a third picnic is described—one organized by the Bianles—causing an overlapping with the first two. Criss-crossing and blending occur. The same threat of the lost child now hangs over the schoolchildren. After the parents, it is the teacher who is accused of heedlessness and irresponsibility, just like the little Bianle boy's father. The reader perceives echoes, textual parallelism or imitations: the Bianle child on his father's shoulders mirrors Henriette riding piggyback on the teaching assistant. Madame Bianle passes on her leadership qualities to Odette and goes back to her homebody existence, just like M. Ducreux, who detests outdoor activities. The narrative eventually sinks into confusion. We never determine exactly what happened to the lost child. Who was he? The little Bianle boy or his cousin who was of school age?

The anecdote centered on the Révérend Père, begun in the first version of the lunch and postponed until now, seems to imply as much. The choirboy's broken cruit is a metaphor of lost innocence, which suggests far more than it conceals. This time Mlle Ariane does not talk about her cat performing behind the bushes but makes a transparent allusion to an unusual sexual initiation occurring there: *"La Scène du parfaitement derrière la haie"* ("The Scene of the exactly behind the bushes"). To defend his colleague, the curé falls back on the concept of nature—an incongruously atheistic term in the vocabulary of a so-called man of God. But by now obscene references seem to multiply. The collective voice prattles on about the policeman and the railway worker caught in the urinal, the mystical soul Monette carrying on a lesbian relationship with the Doudin girl. Purity and softness inevitably beget cynicism and perversity.

Neither the curate nor the schoolteacher is of any help in solving the mystery of the child's disappearance. The class outing and the meal that reconstructs it do not produce any conclusive evidence. There is no dead body to be found in the bushes or the pond. The only mishap is a case of indigestion suffered by a female pupil overexposed to heat and cold. Latirail's attempt to break through the conspiracy of silence leads nowhere. Ariane yawns as Francine holds forth; Mme Dumans barely pays attention to what the Lorpailleur woman is saying. Having reached a dead end, the narration seeks out a new direction. The narrator latches on to the Duchemin succession, no doubt triggered by association with the Doudin girl. The story manages to bounce back to life with the anecdote of Lorette's madness, this young woman being the third rein-carnation of the teaching assistant. It is possible, however, that the anonymous narrator may be referring to Lorpailleur herself or her equal-ly bizarre sister. Lorette's internment or burial (neither the reader nor the text is sure which report is accurate) brings us back to the point of departure. Now that one madwoman has been permanently silenced, we can move on to her rival, the fatuous poet, Mlle Lozière, who will be the heroine of the audition sequence.

This abysmally bad performance put on by the self-styled great artist and her pupils is given at Mortin's boardinghouse and is preceded by a buffet luncheon for the guests. It is only natural, then, that the account of the recital be inserted between the description of the two lunches at the Château de Bonne-Mesure. Mlle Lozière's "gala" performs the same function in *Le Libera* as the wedding celebration in *L'Inquisitoire*. Here again art serves as a pretext to exalt the dominant ideology founded on simplistic patriotism, family solidarity, and nationalistic revenge. Needless to say, Pinget has a field day making fun of it.

The audition unfolds like a religious rite and adheres strictly to the program. The various presentations have, however, such a monotonous sameness to them that they become interchangeable and confuse the spectators. Mlle Lorpailleur's wicked assessment of the afternoon for Ariane de Bonne-Mesure confuses matters even more: "A pilgrimage, that's what it was, a poetic pilgrimage, followed by a sentimental one, or the opposite" (*L*, 202). Having started off in a ridiculous fashion, the afternoon gala rattles on in its ludicrous way. Several of the guests get into a fight over preferred seating; others try to gate-crash; still another pretends to be the guest lecturer and sports a phony Legion of Honor medal. At least Mme Apostolos, a fugitive boarder from *Quelqu'un* now transformed into a Argentinean exile, is honest in her devastating com-ments about the performance, unlike the pupils' parents, whose remarks take the form of treacherous insinuations.

Although Mlle Lozière's audition is supposed to proclaim the triumph of the spirit and of artistic endeavor, the afternoon gets dangerously mired in the material and the prosaic. Idoménée, the gardener-turned-singer for this manifestation of high art, cannot resist patting Miquette's rear end. The performance takes forever to get going. The individual numbers are interminably long. The scenery is incredibly shabby. The pupils who are supposed to represent the Muses of Poetry are far too rotund, made up, and ungainly in their costumes to project a convincing image. As the narrator malevolently remarks, they look like "communicants who turned out badly." But the prime mover of the event, Mlle Lozière, comes across as even more laughable than her pupils, because she is far more pretentious than they could ever be. She carries on like an artist of international repute, but some members of her audience at least are not taken in by the illusion:

> They applauded again and Mlle Lozière came out from behind the curtain to bow, the hats she wears off stage, as well as on, are created by Brivance, it was written in the program, now according to Mme Moineau they could only be hats of several seasons past, they got fobbed off on her for nothing, besides people at the boardinghouse have never seen more than two on her, the white one she had on that day and the black one she wears in the winter. (L, 166)

The anonymous narrator's comments on the performance are all the more devastating because they seem to register the spontaneous reaction of an inexperienced spectator witnessing an artistic event for the first time and bringing to it the naively positive attitude of the neophyte. By simply calling the shots as he sees them, he inadvertently exposes the recital for what it is: a pretentious flop. Miquette performs some graceful arm and leg movements; what a pity, then, "that she already has such fat thighs and that one could see her yellowish feet." Irénée makes his entrance, interpreting a song written by Mlle Lozière on the solitude of autumn: "Everybody applauded and he sang—how shall I say it—not all that well but it was touching that he made the effort, he's attracted to spiritual things, he kept moving about while singing because Mlle Lozière believes in the movement theory" (L, 164). The narrator invariably expresses his approval ("Mlle Lozière knew her trade") whenever a technical error is committed or a theatrical cliché is presented as a stunningly original touch, such as the scene with the poet gazing at the clouds.

The show bristles with so much symbolism that it degenerates into a veritable riddle. For example, it takes a while for the audience to figure out that one of the gaudily dressed pupils represents the Muse. The performance scales new heights of ludicrousness when Mlle Lozière flaunts her royalist convictions. Yet here, too, the allegorical allusions remain rather muddy: "We wondered afterwards who was the Sleeping Person, if it was Youth or History or even France who had been aroused by the racket" (*L*, 172). Whatever the interpretation, it is obvious that the purpose of the recital is to celebrate the official ideology. Poetry, music, and dance are requisitioned for consciousness-raising of the most blatant kind. This patriotic mass reaches its climax when the postperformance speaker, Professor Duchemin, conjures up grotesquely distorted episodes of World War I to work the audience up into an orgy of chauvinism.

Once the celebration is over, the various guests taken an almost sadistic pleasure in running down Mlle Lozière to the point of indulging in scandalmongering. According to them, she has neither talent nor moral elevation, and they will make sure that all the châteaux dwellers know it. Mortin's reaction is radically different but equally intense. He sinks into despair, because the poet's pitiful aspirations mirror his own failure as a writer. Ruthless in his self-judgment, Mortin refuses to entertain the thought that the artist's powerlessness in the face of the transcendent deserves compassion and respect.

Thus, the afternoon performance, followed by the patriotic lecture, have inadvertently exposed the emptiness of a society's moral and aesthetic values. It has also underscored the inability of the artist—and this includes the writer—to impose a meaningful order on the sewerlike chaos of existence. What else is left, then, but to celebrate this universal collapse and end the novel with funeral rites? It matters not at all who is going to be buried. Everyone, from narrator to reader, will plunge into the valley of tears or the abyss of nightmares against a farcically apocalyptic backdrop. Just as the recital was marred by all kinds of hitches, so is this Last Judgment ceremony sullied by the triumph of the inappropriate, and a seemingly vengeful one at that. The bier is late in arriving; snot keeps coming out of little Jean-Claude's nostrils; and the organ, which has been whining away, stops dead when the heavy church doors are slammed shut.

As a final touch to the spirit of sardonic vengefulness that presides over this funeral litany, the excrement motive reappears once more. As though to tame death, the narrator parodies the solemn prayer *"libera me domine,"* asking not for release from the terror of eternal damnation but from the permanent asphyxiation of our existential dung heap: *"de merda aeterna."* He knows full well, however, that there is no escape possible from the enormous blob of crap that will be thrown in our faces on our day of reckoning. The only solution is to indulge in the overkill of black humor and to withdraw into silence. As the novel lurches to its conclusion, fragments of previous paragraphs reappear, implying that the narrator's train of thought has become disconnected, and that, having given up the struggle, he has accepted failure.

Passacaille (Recurring Melody)

Le Libera confronted failure and death by means of snickering self-mockery. Passacaille (1969) attempts to neutralize the ever-present anguish of mortality through incantation. These divergent approaches to the same obsession go a long way in explaining the radically different structures of the two novels. Le Libera expands indefinitely through contradictory accounts of the same event, thus giving the reader the illusion that something is happening. Passacaille questions every hypothesis it puts forward, returning again and again to its point of departure. In the final paragraph of the novel recurs the same statement that had appeared for the first time on the second page: a man of undetermined identity throws the clock mechanism out of order. But this last recurrence leaves us as unenlightened about the personage as at the beginning. When the reader finishes the novel, he has the impression of being back at square one. Being devoid of anecdotes and characters, the action never gets going. What we have instead is a poetic meditation on the omnipresence of death, which resembles a musical composition.

Much has been written about the similarity that supposedly exists between the novel's structure and J. S. Bach's Passacaglia. Robert Pinget may have inadvertently encouraged many commentators to seek out profound resemblances between the two works by a statement made during an interview with Jean Roudaut: "While writing it I listened continuously to the great Passacaglia for organ [by Bach]" (Roudaut, 91). Taking her cue from the author himself, Jane Davidson argues that one of the leitmotivs of the novel, "The calm. The gray," echoes the rhythm of the repeated two-bar phrase of the ground bass in the German composer's piece.[5] I would agree up to a certain point. The Passacaglia is a composition of pure movement, a formal combination of evanescent elements, and in that respect and that respect alone, Pinget's novel bears a certain resemblance to the work of the baroque master he so admires. It would be dangerous, however, to carry the comparison any further for the simple reason that many other equally important leitmotivs keep coming back as the text unfolds. I would concur with Jean-Claude Liéber's view that the musical composition that comes to mind when analyzing *Passacaille* is Maurice Ravel's *La Valse* (Liéber, 250). There, as in Pinget's poetic meditation, fragments of different themes swirl around under the mottled orchestral surface, but the reader, just as Ravel's listener, would be hard pressed to reconstitute them in their entirety.

The novel's principal themes are stated in a condensed form at the very outset. The disquieting atmosphere first suggested by the two elliptic phrases, "The calm. The gray," is prolonged by the symbolism of the clock on the mantlepiece. With its "black marble, gold-encircled dial and roman numerals," it evokes the very tomb into which time is swallowed up.[6] The diffuse feeling of terror is confirmed by the immutable order that reigns over the countryside. Neither human beings nor objects can be seen anywhere. Has life suddenly come to an end? Has some unnamed disaster plunged the domaine into solitude and shadows? The idea that "something must be broken in the mechanism" even though nothing is visible, suggests the irreparable. The chiasma at the beginning of the third paragraph—"The gray. The calm"—underscores the sense of a rending within this strange world.

To add to this generalized disquiet, an anonymous character bursts upon the scene. His existence may still be only hypothetical, because the French text indicates his presence by the conditional tense: "Someone may have just entered the cold room, the house was closed, it was winter" (*P*, 7). Now ambiguity, both semantic and grammatical, will suffuse the narrative. The sentence describing him lends itself to two diametrically opposite interpretations: "The man seated at this table a few hours before found dead on the dung heap" (*P*, 8). If one pauses in the reading of this sentence after the adverb "before," it implies that the owner of the dwelling succumbed to an attack soon after he returned there. If one leaves out the punctuation, the intruder or visitor can appear as a ghostly presence. The ambiguity is heightened even further when the guardian ("the sentinel") designated to watch over the man, slumped in his chair and chilled, maintains having seen the so-called deceased person wreck the clock.

But who is this person slumped forward in a chair, with his elbows on the table and his head in his hands? Could he represent the author/narrator, overwhelmed by despair in advance at the thought of his impossible mission of deciphering the ever-proliferating complexity of reality? Or has he, like his predecessor in *Le Libera*, already tried, failed, and let himself be engulfed by depression? Or is he allowing himself to be pulled into his imaginary universe where he just might decode some of the universal symbols linking him to the collective unconscious? In any event, the spiritual signals are difficult to capture and even more difficult to decode. The narrator acknowledges as much when he asks himself, "How can one trust this murmur, the ear is at fault" (P, 8). Elucidating this murmur becomes an all-consuming obsession, especially since death is always lurking in the shadows, ever ready to pounce on its prey.

At frequent intervals the narrator refers to this almost inaudible sound "broken by silences and hiccoughs" (P, 9, 30, 99). Like some dogged astrophysicist tracking down a radio signal from some distant star, the narrator attempts to pull in clearly, through the depths of his inner universe, impulses from the realm of his subconscious, knowing full well that "the source of information [may be] weakening at every instant." Moreover, the reality of his soul from which spring forth all of the fantasies of fiction interest him infinitely more than the so-called outside world. The fountain on his property with its spout in the form of a chimera symbolizes the grip his imagination exerts on him.

After immobilizing itself in the evocation of an inanimate, glacial country, the narrative gets moving again by switching abruptly to another season. It is suddenly and inexplicably springtime, exploding with its many colors. The anonymous owner arranges as best he can some irises in a bouquet. But the reader begins to be wary when this rather clumsy attempt to justify the change of season is called into question by the narrator's remark that perhaps the bouquet was made up of orchis and picked in the heart of the summer. At once the tone of the text becomes sinister, inasmuch as the Greek etymology of *orchis* is testicles, and the term *harvest* is used to describe the gathering of these particular flowers. Rather than being elucidated, however, the mystery thickens. The female goatherd who is supposed to relieve the male guard fails to notice what is happening.

With the third repetition of the initial theme ("The calm. The gray") we return to the winter setting and the corpse on the dung pile. Although the testimony brought forward by the neighbor's child seems conclusive, the victim's identity once more proves to be elusive: "That was surely it, the other was already stiff." Meanwhile, the unidentified man who was seated on a chair, slumped over the table, gets up after a temporary malaise, or "absence," as the text describes it. When he goes out into the garden, it is he who sees the child coming back from school in a kind of hallucination, since the latter appears as a ghostly presence (the French word *revenant* can be construed as either the present participle of the verb *revenir*, meaning "to come back," or as a term for phantom). A final version of the corpse on the dung pile, this one in a nocturnal setting, seems to corroborate the death and clarify this bizarre episode, but the neighbor, refusing to take any risks, questions its reality: "nothing betrayed the accident, there had been no witness or person who supposedly knew that the owner had returned on this grayish winter day for inspection, he put the key back in the keyhole and opened the door again, you never know, let's be cautious, then went off toward the village" (*P*, 11–12).

This questioning of events purported to have taken place is typical of the way in which the novel functions. It is condemned to endless repetition, as illustrated by a phrase that recurs again and again: "Turn, return, go back." Erasing itself word by word as it advances, the novel reaches the very frontier of abstraction. It is well-nigh impossible to latch onto any concrete references here. All we have are suppositions and pretences. We can explore the workings of the mechanism itself, however, and show how it combines the various elements whose existence it subsequently calls into question.

The nucleus of the novel consists of an initial hypothesis: An unnamed person sees a corpse lying in a given place. So far the situation seems straightforward. All kinds of substitutions take place within the text, however. First, the witness is a child, then the sentinel or the female goatherd, then the mechanic or his apprentice, then the owner himself. There is even an anonymous observer present referred to as "the other," "the person." The cadaver changes identities as well. In some places within the narrative it is a human male—either the owner, the postman, or the young idiot. In others, it is a cow or a scarecrow. The dead body does not remain stationary either. It moves from outdoors—the dung pile, the swamp, the terrace—to indoors. We find it either in the stable or the dwelling, and, once there, the author has it slumped over the table or in a chair, or lying inert on the bed or in an armchair. In fact, the wanderings of the corpse give the novel a grotesquely comical dimension. Pinget even thought of calling his book *Le Simulacre* (*The Sham*), to underscore the unreality of the situation. In the end, however, it is the nightmarish aspect of the text that prevails.

Death is conjured up here in various ways. Sometimes its presence is understated: "Someone is dying" (*P*, 127); other times it appears as an apocalyptic exaggeration: "The whole countryside is decomposing" (*P*, 93). Whatever the statement put forward, it is sooner or later invalidated. At one point the testimony is rejected: "he doesn't see," "he didn't see anything," "he could have confused one with another." At another, the circumstances in which death occurred seem fabricated: "He disappeared in the morning, but on the dung pile, no he did not put it." Then there is pure and simple denial of the event: "It isn't that," "It couldn't be that." Or the inquest stops dead in its tracks for lack of evidence: "Besides why the corpse, it could be a body that would pick itself up several minutes or several hours later, a fainting spell" (P, 86). In the final analysis, there is not one statement made that does not give rise to its opposite. The mutilated cow has not the slightest trace of a wound, and the legatee has no survivor. The dead man himself had spent a lifetime perfecting a system of affirmations and corresponding negations founded on impeccable logic, just like the narrative that protects itself against potentially explosive situations by negating them afterwards.

Death appears in three different guises during the course of the novel. As though to attenuate the horror of the event, Pinget presents it as a social ritual entailing funeral preparations, burial, and the reading of the testament. Grief inscribes itself in an everyday setting, allowing the survivors to dominate their emotions and preserve a cherishable image of the deceased: "the doctor in his flowery picture frame" (P, 132). The next form in which death appears, however, is absolutely terrifying, because the author emphasizes the physical decomposition and rotting away the ritual strives to eradicate. The human being is overcome with disgust at the idea of this "fermentation until the grave." In a riveting hallucination the narrator visualizes his remains superimposed on his still-alive body: "A child's cranium covers a senile face, the mouth still says I love you while the death knell sounds in the ear." Given the decay and disintegration to which this tragic event leads, it is inevitable that the author designates the dung pile as a monstrous synonym of death and the most appropriate place where it can assert its presence.

Somewhat less frightening, but no less powerful, is the symbolic representation of the event. Pinget draws upon the many traditional images of death embedded in the Western psyche, such as skeleton bones, crows, crucifixes, and scarecrows. In themselves, they may not be highly original, but the author uses them in such a way as to reawaken the primeval terrors lying dormant within the recesses of our subconscious. The owner scrutinizes an engraving in an old book of a pine forest where a completely white skeleton is swinging amidst bird carcasses. The first childlike evocation is later reinforced by the spectacle of a scarecrow hanging from a tree and resembling, from a distance, a man subjected to the horrible punishment of crucifixion:

Because actually the body or was it a corpse glimpsed by the owner had disappeared a few minutes after, the maid when questioned affirms having heard the noise of a motor and the same for the goatherd except that she didn't see anything on the dung pile even though she passed by it, did the gentleman take a close look, he doesn't distinguish things clearly from far, or rather, he confused it, this is the opinion of the doctor who didn't say it right away, with a vision of a scarecrow with its arms stretched out like a cross which had nearly shaken him up the day before, they were still laughing at it now. (*P*, 76)

Is Pinget trying to help the reader exorcise his fear of pain and death by conjuring up these dreadful simulations? Is he trying to outwit the inexorable agent itself by evoking it under these different illusory guises? At any rate, his character, the master, certainly is. The elderly man revels in relating over and over to his friend the doctor, and in minute detail, the episode of his burial. He also loves to play games in regard to his testament. Instead of bequeathing his worldly possessions to his nephews, the master designates deceased people as his heirs. In this way he can delight in the illusion of not only outliving his relatives, but himself as well.

The gullible souls in the village label him a sorcerer, convinced that he possesses magical powers. The skeptics brand him an imposter and manipulator. We are never sure whom to believe. Like any creator, the master tries to transcend the haphazard unfolding of life by uncovering the secret order within the universe. He then translates his findings into a number of symbols, either mathematical, typographical or calligraphic. By practicing this intellectual alchemy, he can seek refuge in a realm that is luminous, untouched by impurities, and devoid of peril. Here he can glide about in total freedom, like some "old-fashioned, stubborn skater in the sempiternal morning of his mania" (*P*, 48). He can even delude himself into believing that he has forever eluded death by identifying himself exclusively with his activity as a writer: "He would have no history other than a written one, no breathing other than literal" (*P*, 97). As long as he keeps reappearing in his works of fiction, he will remain alive.

There exists in *Passacaille* another obsession that, like death, betrays an irreparable loss: castration. Although not quite as tragic in its implications as the dissolution into nonbeing, it constitutes, nevertheless, a nightmarish fantasy that preys upon both writer and narrator. It is not surprising that the master and his lifelong friend, the doctor, talk endlessly about their fantasies, including this very terrifying one, and do so with a kind of puerile compulsiveness. By evoking freely their nocturnal terrors, they can come to grips with them more easily, regardless of how ridiculous their childlike chatter may appear: "You might have wondered { . . . } if you weren't dealing with children so babyish was their conversation, they told each other everything including their dreams, a most insipid thing to say the least, or how many times they had urinated at night or a certain thing their mother used to say or memories of love" (*P*, 67). Uninhibited, they indulge in verbal outpourings in order to conjure away their subconscious night and expel phantoms that have haunted the abyss of the mind from time immemorial.

The castration fantasy harkens back to the oedipal trauma and implies fear of punishment from the father for having violated the taboo of incest. In the novel a sleeping person is hunted down, even in his dreams, by transbiological memories of massacres or epidemics. The myth of the primitive hoard crosses through the book, carrying with it a reverberating sense of guilt for a "crime without end" (*P*, 96). Even though castration may represent punishment of the first outrage committed against the father, it does not dispel the child's anguish. The "bloodied codpiece" symbolizes not just the loss of the sex organ but a perpetual emotional wound. As the novel unfolds, this primeval terror expands to nightmarish proportions. It is symbolized by a knife, a pair of pruning shears, an ax, and the blade of an ice skate before solidifying itself in the form of a motor-driven chainsaw that mutilates the idiot youth.

An earlier scene adumbrates the idiot's horrible accident. Abandoning himself to his wild imagination, the narrator dismembers the unfortunate idiot then glues back the latter's various bodily parts: "I could see him fracturing an arm or a leg or an ear falling off, I would call him quickly so that he would smile at me, a recourse which I didn't have with broken dishes" (*P*, 106). When the mutilation takes place, the master collapses on the bed, a victim of the scene he has just witnessed. As though to reassure his horrified reader that the image presented was simply a means of exorcizing a deeply rooted terror, Pinget, however, has the bloodstain dry up, then transforms it into nothing more frightening than a red rag that had fallen off the scarecrow: "I can still see the red rag that served as a belt, the blue jean that is unraveling, the jacket torn apart on the stake" (*P*, 125).

Perhaps even more frightening than the castration fantasy is the obsession with cannibalism that recurs just as frequently in the novel. It is all the more disturbing because of the difficulty we still encounter in defining its boundaries, despite the fact that it is a universal theme in stories and mythology. Cannibalism can betray not only the fear of being devoured but the desire to incorporate someone else's being into our own. It appears for the first time in the novel as just one bizarre phenomenon taking place in the locality among many others (a female cat devours its kittens), and it reaches its terrifying climax in the final pages where the doctor is metamorphosized into a rapacious beast. In between, the eccentric master is used by the mothers of the village as a threat to keep their children in line. In their young, impressionable eyes, he becomes the old ogre who swallows naughty children. Then there is a meal during which a female nipple is devoured while milk and blood run down the chins of the feasters. Finally, death seems to bring out the beast in people. After Momolphe dies, his friend, the master, samples a jar of jam which the former had prepared. Although the jar may be a eucharistic symbol, the act of eating its contents produces a parody of the Christian belief. In the morbid atmosphere of the novel, the eaters do not gain spiritual sustenance from this ritual. On digesting the jam, they are overcome with disgust to the point of wanting to vomit, inasmuch as they have the distinct impression of reliving Momolphe's burial.

This act of ingestion takes on a metaphorical connotation in the scene to which we have already referred, where the doctor abandons himself to a paroxysm of gluttony. What appears at first as a frenzy of necrophilia turns out to be the dogged search for the secret contained in the literary text: "Then the doctor leaning over the cadaver pulled out of the wound with one bite a bloody thing that he called the connoisseur's morsel, with his jaws moving and his tongue clicking, he plunged once more into the hole and removed the manuscript intact, a true miracle, put on his spectacles and reread the sentence in which the other found a bitter taste, our predators are at work" (*P*, 124).

Despite Robert Pinget's avowed distaste for romanticism, this cannibalistic image obviously recalls Alfred de Musset's often-quoted evocation of the writer as a pelican who tears open his entrails in order to uncover sublime truths he will share with his reader. Unlike the romantic poet, however, Pinget can extract nothing more than morbid fantasies from the depths of his being. Does this signify that the voyage of self-discovery implied in the act of writing is doomed to failure? Not necessarily. By awakening our most terrifying, repressed obsessions, the narrator, in his own words, dredges up, "midnight in broad daylight" (*P*, 130). He compels himself and us, his readers, to face our unconfessable nightmares. We all come out stronger and more lucid for it.

Chapter Five

Toward Redemption?

The horror of failure, decay, death, and mutilation, orchestrated so eloquently and on so many different registers, leads inevitably to its opposite theme, the yearning to remain in some permanent form, thus justifying one's presence on earth and ensuring one's spiritual redemption. Lucid awareness of his condition, however noble in itself, does not suffice for Robert Pinget. Through the various narrators of his last four novels, he searches for ways of preventing his being from decomposing into disconnected fragments swallowed up by time. He seeks out an atemporal unity—one that will not simply justify his existence but redeem it from the incoherent morass into which it can so easily degenerate. At certain intervals in these texts the author suggests that artistic creation may very well be the avenue to redemption. While expressing such a hope, however, Pinget sometimes implies that it may be nothing more than an illusion. Hence the question mark that accompanies the title of this chapter, and the disquieting ambiguity the reader perceives in *Fable* (1971), *Cette voix* (1975), *L'Apocryphe* (1980), and *L'Ennemi* (1987).

Fable

This deceptively simple title conceals a work of redoubtable complexity. Like the traditional literary genre, Pinget's *Fable* is a narrative rooted in the imagination and drawing on myth to propose an explanation of our human condition. The author imposes, however, his own arrestingly original interpretation on the legends of Narcissus and Osiris. Moreover, the text represents a break with the neorealistic aesthetic so evident in works such as *L'Inquisitoire, Quelqu'un*, and *Le Libera*. Here there is not even the slightest attempt to foist upon the reader the illusion of reality. The universe of *Fable* functions as a closed circuit, leading Jan Baetens to view the text as an example of the *Nouveau Nouveau Roman*—that is a work that resolutely excludes all references to anything outside of itself.[1] Obviously *Fable* derives its spiritual "energy" from Greek mythology; but, aside from this dependence on sources from without, the text creates its own reality and remains self-sufficient.

Using, then, the ancient story of Narcissus as a catalyst, Pinget has produced a meditation on broken love and lost happiness unfolding in counterpoint to the theme of a yearning for wholeness. The forsaken lover rehashes his past, bemoans the fatal rending of the relationship, striving in vain to repair the damage. The poignant sadness that pervades the narration is sustained by the contrast between the nostalgia for a lost innocence and the nightmarish vision of a world in ruins. On the one hand, we have touching, childlike images symbolizing purity: oat and poppy fields, clumps of delphiniums, flaming meadows, luminous landscapes. On the other, the author conjures up scenes of desolation: cities covered with ashes, crushed and smoking, lava spreading its destruction as it advances, fields strewn with rubble where refugees in exile live in makeshift camps, stench emanating from vacant lots and cemeteries. Pinget suggests in turn a vanished paradise and the fall from grace.

This contrast between innocence and sin, sweetness and bitterness is heightened by the antagonism between religious spirituality and eroticism. There exists a very ambiguous relationship between the moral teachings of the church and the individual's sexual urges. In *Fable* the Christian faith does not succeed in sublimating the libido. It simply imposes its taboos on the latter, and by so doing it intensifies the desire to violate them. As could be expected, Eros overwhelms religion, the floodgates break down, and sacrilegious allusions mingle with expressions of religious fervor, underscoring Christianity's failure to truly exalt and edify. It is as though the principles of catechism learned as an adolescent haunt the consciousness of the adult where they are permanently tainted by sexual obsessions: "There will be no grounds to separate that which since childhood has been united, Sacred Heart and sacred ass."[2] Naturally, this association of the sacred and the obscene leads to a degradation of everything connected with the Christian faith. The image of the child-god in the *Salve regina*—"the blessed fruit of thy womb"—is transformed into an object of revulsion: "The blessed fruit was nailed there."

Far from retaining its transcendence, the Word, on becoming flesh, is reduced to a phallic symbol. Indeed, it becomes singularly pagan. Not only is Christ's virility glorified—"The most beautiful among the children of men. The most beautiful organ which has ever been"—but it is exhibited as a sexual symbol of the Indian god Shiva: "The tabernacle. He didn't even bother buttoning up anymore, the whole works were displayed in the sun and the people started singing O salutaris" (*F,* 57). Since Christ's sexual organ has become the focal point of worship, it is inevitable that he should offer it to the faithful in lieu of the eucharistic bread: "He is there in front of the kneeling person, points to his circumcision and the latter lunges toward it, he partakes of the Sacrament" (F, 42).

Once religious fervor expresses itself in the form of erotic lust, the narrator draws out all its gruesome conclusions. The Communion table is the place where a witches' sabbath unfolds. A hideous sorceress raises to her lips "a stiff member that was moving close to her" (F, 33). A huge penis is used to fish for souls: "And the worshiper clung to the Lord's organ, imploring his mercy" (F, 42). The imagination of supposedly devout women runs wild as they peer, transfixed, at the evocative form of "you know what" hidden behind the loincloth. Prayer degenerates into masturbation. Nevertheless, the wicked laughter elicited by these perversions betrays a deep-seated terror. Circumcision, which is openly exhibited or concealed, represents a threat of castration. In a strange transfer of meaning, the loincloth of the crucified Christ becomes the white cloth Veronica places on his face. Thus, the text equates Christ's countenance, twisted in pain as a result of the torture he is enduring, with his circumcised organ. Then, the two motives, head and penis, come together in a particularly horrifying scene: the leader of a barbaric horde suspends the head of the corpse from his saddle or his belt where it bounces about like a sex organ. Further along in the text the image is retransmitted in another grippingly ugly form—that of an octopus whose head nestles between its thighs (F, 77).

The Virgin also undergoes a number of sacrilegious metamorphoses. Prayers addressed to her are a "whining litany whose words are strung one after the other like a rosary of dung droppings in the infinity of nightmare" (F, 42). One of her favorite pastimes consists in distributing prurient pictures to sex-starved, pious old maids—the same kind who reach a high by focusing on Christ's sex organ. When she "incarnates herself" as a plaster statue, it is to indulge in questionable conduct with sexually deprived sailors, toward whom she extends her "thousand deceiving arms." Deceiving, indeed, because in the final episode, this "Maris stella" (star of the sea), transforms herself into a starfish that emasculates male corpses.

In this desecrated, irreversibly degraded world, man blames his powerlessness on the divine. Far from lifting the human creature up to sublime heights, the Word has brought about a crumbling of values. As Miaille declares, "nothing equals zero" (F, 75). Christ's self-sacrifice has not produced man's redemption. Prayer offers no solace. The only possible escape from the anguish of loneliness is through the violation of religious taboos and the triumph of Eros. Obviously this can and does lead to a flirtation with the powers of evil. The disillusioned believer in need of a new faith abandons himself to Satan. He is happy "to exchange the soul of the old man for these bodies of ivory and ultramarine" (*F*, 75). The devil offers his services under the guise of a mysterious gypsy traveler, who appears to be a divine guest. He deceives his gullible prey by reciting a verse taken from the Psalms: "I have chosen your dwelling, I will work as the maid and the gardener and the guardian." With the stranger's arrival, all restrictions and moral laws vanish—or, rather, the only law he proclaims is that of pleasure: "We will break down these enclosing walls so that each one may find enjoyment" (*F*, 37). Proclaiming the glory of erotic love, the gypsy:

> Proposes his merchandise
> Opens his habit.
> The good Lord will repay you.
> Brings out the Holy Sacrament. (*F*, 35)

Transplanted into this new sinfully fertile soil, Eros flourishes again. Frolicking, frenzied embraces, unbridled fornication continue unabated in the forest. Censorship, represented by the gendarme, is powerless to stop this unleashing of elemental energy. In a sense, this orgy of universal proportions satisfied man's nostalgia for the state of innocence that preceded the existence of sin. The sexually aroused archangels amid the luxuriant vegetation mark the return to a primitive paradise. As though to symbolize man's new (ancient?) harmony with nature, "poppies grew on their foreheads and cornflowers on their groins."

In this orgiastic explosion Pinget has created the perfect setting for the orchestration of the myths of Narcissus and Osiris. As Stephen Bann has pointed out, myth for Pinget is a way of transposing his narrative and preventing the reader from discovering biographical references in it. To appreciate the book's depth, it is necessary to examine it in its mythical context.[3] While illuminating the depths of a writer's consciousness, the two legendary figures confer unity on the individual elements of the text. This is not to say that the author reproduces the legends with scrupulous accuracy. He avails himself of the creator's right to reinterpret them in order to present his own vision of our human condition in a more striking manner.

According to the ancient myth, Narcissus was an incomparably handsome youth infatuated with his own physical appearance. In fact, so
obsessed was he by his own beauty that he remained indifferent to the
appeals of the nymph, Echo, in Ovid's version of the legend, or of his
lover, Aminias, in the Conon interpretation.[4] As a result, he incurs the
wrath of Nemesis, or the god of Love. They punish him by condemning
him to become enamored of his own reflection in a pond without ever
being able to satisfy this passion. He withers away and dies in Ovid's
text, and commits suicide in Conon's version. On disappearing, he gives
birth to the flower that bears his name. While being afflicted like his
earlier counterparts by the same erotic fever, Pinget's Narcissus, unlike
the former, responds to the call of universal love and participates in all of
its frenzied frolics. He resembles Echo in that he is abandoned, "transfixed, at the edge of the pond." His worn-out body leans over the water,
"his face gnawed by vermin, the sockets of his eyes empty holes" (F, 96).
It's as though Pinget had forgotten to transform him as the legend
required.

At this point in the narrative the myth of Osiris enters into play, profoundly modifying the Narcissus legend. The corpse of the sublimely
beautiful young man is torn apart and sliced up by the barbarians. He
becomes the hero of a cult celebrated by numerous processions, because,
having incorporated traits of this other mythical figure, he is worshipped
as the god of resurrection, the inventor of wheat and barley, who abolished cannibalism. Indeed, after having been dismembered by the bestial
hordes, he endeavors to put the scattered parts of his body back together: "He will go groping about in search of his arms and legs trying to
reunite them with his beloved body then to breathe life back into his
corpse" (F, 82). But Pinget's reworking of the Narcissus story does not
end there. The cannibalistic episode preceding this rebirth and rebirth
itself harken back to another chapter from Greek mythology, that dealing with the god Dionysus. The divine embodiment of energy was cut
up and eaten by the Titans, whom the lightning bolt of the father of the
gods, Zeus, reduced to ashes, and from these remains arose the human
race. The only portion of Dionysus that escaped the Titans' devouring
fury was his heart. Being *the* vital organ, it made the god's rebirth
possible.

In addition to enriching the Narcissus legend by superposing elements from two others, the author substitutes another flower for the traditional one named after the self-adulating youth: the delphinium. Why,
one might ask? Simply to inscribe within the new emblem the sorrow of

loss: "Let the delphiniums turn blue, unless it be his tears, the sky being reflected in them" (*F*, 14).

Far wiser than Narcissus, the protagonist of *Fable*, Miaille, has the courage to wrest himself free from the illusion of self-love. Rather than fall under the spell of his reflection in the water, which is a sham, he prefers facing reality. Hence his heroic decision to destroy the very instrument that has led him to cultivate self-delusion—his eyes—as well as the part of his body which generated erotic self-obsession. His self-inflicted blindness and castration constitute the turning point of the story, which functions henceforth on another register, and leads to his assuming another identity, that of Miette: "I am the Narcissus of a new kind he said, deprived of his eyes and his favorite organ." Through this self-mutilation, Miaille wants to free himself from the tyranny of appearances and to spare himself the agony of witnessing his being decomposed as it moves through the successive stages of its existence. Most important of all, however, he yearns to recover his unity, which the very fluidity of life prevents him from grasping. The razor blade he has turned against himself will allow him—at least he hopes it will—to open up the eyes of his spirit, "those which the sun does not dazzle" (*F*, 82).

In the long run, though, Miaille's self-mutilation is in vain. Like Narcissus, Miaille cannot be reconciled with himself indefinitely. No sooner has he reached his spiritual haven when he is cast out into the exterior shadows or, worse still, is thrown back onto the wheel of reincarnation: "The whole creation was spewed out again" (*F*, 69). This reversal, however unexpected in the context of the narrative, can be easily explained by the author's deep-seated distrust of edifying moral decisions. Miaille's conversion is a spectacular theatrical act and nothing more. Both he and Pinget refuse this advent of a completely regenerated personality.

Yet the temptation remains to seek out some transcendent unity that will confer upon the being this longed-for wholeness. Not unlike Mortin in *Quelqu'un*, Narcissus/Osiris/Miaille would dearly love to discover the magic word or phrase that would illuminate his being by defining it once and for all. To accomplish this feat, he is willing to take the biblical route in reverse. According to the New Testament, the Word became flesh. Miaille longs to transform his flesh into a transcendent verbal expression. Although he never expresses this exorbitant wish explicitly, Pinget's technique of verbal recurrences in *Fable* justifies this interpretation. As the author asserted in "Propos de New York," one of his principal endeavors as an artist consists in rediscovering atemporal time—that of myths and legends—that remains embedded in the collective subconscious. Chronological time represents the very opposite, since it is an irreversible flow, swallowing up in its wake the successive stages of human existence, thus reducing the individual to a mass of scattered fragments. To stem this tide, Pinget has devised a very complex network of verbal echoes. Through their semantic and affective reverberations, words link the various themes and images of *Fable* from beginning to end. Whenever the text seems to repeat itself, it launches itself on a new beginning, thereby negating time in the chronological sense and illustrating the very watchword of the narrative, "to retell everything in order to renew everything." With the help of a computer, Robert Henkels set up a dictionary of concordances for *Fable*, which emphasizes the polyvalency of its images and the subliminal relationships between its narrative cells.[5] For Jan Baetens, *Fable* is based on an anagrammatic program—one that wrests the text from its linear development and composes chains of intratextual linkages. These, in turn, reverberate within the narrative.

The anagram seems indeed to be the source of a number of plays on words that enable the reader to apprehend the reverse, and often disquieting, side of familiar surroundings: *Zéro* (zero) under *rosée* (dew), *ruse* (trickery) under *azur* (azur blue), *magie* (magic) under *image* (image), and *toile* (canvas) under *étoile* (star). The word "EVA" changes to "VAE" and then to "AVE" to show how the curse connected with the first woman on earth, Eve, is transformed into a blessing by the presence of the Virgin Mary. In the interplay of word series, we see the same letters used to summon up radically different concepts—*exil/élixir/lieux* (exile/elixir/ places)—or we observe that Pinget uses different words containing the same general concept to suggest different nuances of meaning: *l'huis* (door)/*seuil* (threshold)/*Prolégomènes* (prolegomenae).

But is this complex network of verbal interplay created for the purpose of abolishing chronological time anything more than an illusion? At various places in this text Pinget does seem to doubt the effectiveness of his artistic venture. "The pure and simple game of a lunatic," he exclaims mockingly at one point; at another he has the Sibyl and Miaille look at each other laughingly, once their magic tricks are exposed. Each is the ludicrous mirror image of the other: "Old bearded, crapping nanny goat / Old bearded, twitching fathead."

As he ages, Narcissus slobbers, groans, and has trouble breathing. The yearning for some kind of immortality seems, then, to crumble into dust. And yet it cannot be said that the narrative is totally pessimistic. The word structure Pinget has created does succeed in revitalizing the age-old myths lying dormant in our unconscious—myths that express our secret yearning for physical resurrection, wholeness, and eternal youth. That the author could orchestrate them so eloquently in a poetic narrative "as hard as a rock" suggests that, at least within the spiritual space occupied by a work of art, time can indeed be made to stand still.

Cette voix *(That Voice)*

Although the magic of art can suspend the onslaught of time, death, toward which time moves inexorably, is always lurking around the corner. We have seen how frequently it preys upon Robert Pinget's mind. In *Cette voix* it is the overriding obsession. Not just content with meditating on its omnipresence or conjuring up its various horrors, the narrator actually takes up residence in a tomb in a cemetery. The author's purpose appears twofold: (1) he seeks to conquer his anxiety about death by viewing it unflinchingly as both an agent of decomposition and an agent of liberation; (2) he uses the cemetery as a metaphor to evoke the writer's production and to reflect upon the theme of immortality through art.

Given the omnipresence of death in *Cette voix*, it is not at all surprising that the setting of the novel should be a gigantic necropolis (the narrator's tomblike dwelling is situated at the bisection of path no. 333 and service road no. 777). Here the author exploits to the hilt the idea of disappearance. We find abandoned vaults, outdated burial plots, faded names on tombstones. In fact, one of the novel's major themes is that of the disappearing trace, to be understood metaphorically as the fate in store for every book perused by a reader—doomed to burial within the reader's memory. From the outset the term *funeral monument* refers far more to a work composed of words rather than of concrete materials. While pretending to attack the style of funeral epigraphs by his remarks on "the vanity of elegantly worded inscriptions and the whole lot,"[6] Pinget is really taking a shot at literature. He scoffs at the writer's claim to escape the lot of ordinary mortals. Every self-respecting writer, including Pinget, bets on immortality, but this may be nothing more than a pious illusion, an artificial garment of which he will be stripped on the fateful day.

Even with such a ruthlessly lucid attitude toward death, it staggers the imagination that the narrator should choose a cemetery vault as his place of residence. The reader is shocked to discover this singular creature sliding out of his tomb, with his skin in bad shape, half-crawling, half-stumbling as he moves over the flagstones. It seems even more incredible that he should feel completely at home there to the point of inviting a companion to share the space with him. But for archaic societies, this familiarity with death was perfectly natural. Like them, the author forges a link between the worlds of the living and the dead. In *Cette voix* the squatter-narrator effects the osmosis between the two, but his function in the text does not end there. In view of Pinget's constant concern over the fate of the writer vis-à-vis posterity, it would not be far-fetched to see in his narrator a metaphor of himself, entombed in his own words, which hover precariously over abysses of silence. Authors themselves enjoy just temporary reprieves from death. It is their written works, remaining behind them, that represent their cemetery plots. Only these can be leased in perpetuity as a protection against nonbeing.

The fascination with death is such that it leads to all kinds of acts of desecration that, in their bizarre way, actually pay homage to its omnipotence. The family vault is the scene of a syrupy courtship leading to a formal engagement and marriage. As the maid babbles on to her niece,

> You mother was putting flowers on her parents' grave just as she did every first of November she tried to meditate but a man nearby was watching her, subjugated, he approached her and asked her something or other where was the plot of such and such a family she replied pointing out the direction but the pot of chrysanthemums which she had just put down was overturned by the wind and he put it back in place the conversation started up about death you see what I mean was it really the place to strike up a courtship it didn't matter he went on they returned home together and got engaged two months afterwards had I been your mother I would have been afraid of the evil eye the cemetery lovers just imagine but they were very happy as you know. (*CV*, 50–51)

It is also the spot where a rather ambiguous relationship between uncle and nephew develops: "The old idiot thought I was gullible but I had him figured out right away first his hand patted me on the shoulder your cares will pass and then caressed my thigh and then you see what I mean the crowd disappeared liberties taken" (*CV*, 156).

In some instances the acts of desecration are far more direct, more aggressive, as though their perpetrators were determined to dominate death by heaping insults on the dead. People coming to the cemetery begin by placing flowers on the graves and end up by "crapping on the deceased," even though the maid wonders anxiously whether it is the appropriate place for relieving oneself (*CV*, 140). Just like All Souls' Day, the corpse seems to draw excrements to itself: "A perfectly shitty All Saints' Day."

By association, the idea of death brings forth the spectacle of decomposition, which fairly permeates the novel. There are "rotten" children, the old woman is "spoiled." The miserly uncle already has one foot in the grave: "a distant relative he would see him only once a year, smelling in his hole." From decomposition, we move on to the agony of death itself. Pinget spares the reader not a single aspect of what can be, and often is, a ghastly experience: "white phlegm farts convulsive movements," and the ugly mess of the final moments of life. But even before death stakes its claim on the aged, their deterioration is continuously stigmatized, as though expressions of horror and disgust could, in themselves, push back the dreadful hour. The novel fairly swarms with derogatory terms designating old people: "impotent old man," "old idiot," "old bastard," "old sap," "old fogey," "old fool," "old fathead." For pages on end, we are treated to descriptions of senile old bodies that can no longer contain their secretions or bad odors, which spread themselves indecently on the sidewalk, "disgusting swollen masses that should be hidden from sight." Through the sheer vehemence of his language, Pinget seems to want not so much to punish old people for falling victims to the inevitable ravages of time as desperately to exorcise the dreadful specter of old age, whose coming, he knows, is unavoidable.

Practicing disgust overkill is not, however, the only way to exorcise this obsession. The victim can in turn become the aggressor. A striking example of this reversibility can be found in the cannibalistic depiction of death. At one point, the narrator imagines himself being thrown defenseless into the jaws of the "triumphant ogress humanity nightmarish mother Ubu." At another, hyenalike slugs launch an attack against the body trapped in the tomb dwelling. But then the theme turns itself around, the female devourer gets devoured, and the slugs are transformed into edible substances similar to ordinary snails. Housewives get into the act as well. "Tireless carcasses," they have no fear of death. In fact, the prospect makes them drool. For lack of corpses to chew up, they clamor for crunchy little shrimps. "Is it edible at least?" they ask. When the primitive hordes tear through the narrative, just as they did in *Fable*, these women fight it out with the flesh-eaters to get hold of their share of the prey: "You can see them with their mouths full clamouring for more leg of venison."

In another scene a phantom carrying its bones at the end of a string begins sucking one of them to cheat death, just as a person would take a drink to quench his thirst. It is as though the best way to confront the legendary flesh-craving bogeyman is to transform oneself into such a creature and attack in turn. If I howl as loud or louder than the monster, I will ward him off. Herein lies the meaning of the strange refrain that occurs again and again during the course of the novel: *"Reprendre du poil de la nuit,"* which means literally, "to snatch fur from the night." It is a paraphrase of the idiomatic expression *"reprendre du poil de la bête"* (literally, to take back fur from the beast), meaning to regain one's strength. In *Cette voix* night is synonymous with the beast, and the beast is none other than death.

In sharp contrast to this nightmarish image is a whole development hailing death as the great initiator into another world and the instrument of transformation. Hence the reverent and almost religious tones in which Pinget refers to "the great night, its unpronounceable name . . . profound indiscernible night of being and love," or the fervent invocation to "the Lilies of the Great Slumber" into which the world yearns to merge. Underpinning the book's structure is the theme of initiation. The narrator must conquer the powers of darkness and triumphantly overcome spiritual agony: "a trial such as no one has ever endured not me at least" (*CV*, 11). Like young people of ancient societies, the narrator must confront the successive phases of a ritual that tests his physical and mental stamina: abandonment in the wilderness, pursuit by a flesh-eating monster, symbolic dismembering, and mock-burial. Since he is being hurtled backwards to a timeless past, the cemetery where he resides is no longer just a place to bury the dead. It is the meeting ground for him and his ancestors. Situated at a point where the world's great avenues intersect, his vault is not just an unusual dwelling. It is an initiatory chamber: "Here is where I come to find my ghosts again." This chamber may be closed in the physical sense, it is wide open in the spiritual one: "This chamber closed to the eye / window open onto the night."

The initiated person goes through the experience of regression right back to the embryonic state, while awaiting "this new time which I do not yet know and which I will have to handle gropingly work over organize according to my needs." Initiation is thus a second birth. The narrator's descent into hell implies simultaneously a return to the uterus.

Naturally, this initiatory rite is to be interpreted in the metaphorical sense. The narrator/author hurtles himself backwards to his prenatal condition in order to plug into the collective unconscious which he carries within him and apprehend his mythical self. *Cette voix* is in fact founded on the process of anamnesis, which, in psychiatric terms, signifies the voluntary evocation of the past. The novice's initiation implies his encounter with this original Self and his identification with the ancestors he embodies in his temporal existence. In order to accede to this heightened self-awareness, he must experience depersonalization. Only then will he be able to make contact with the Other within him, to capture the resonances of this immemorial voice, and to acquire in the process the strength and knowledge that lies beyond time. Pinget's characters have this timeless consciousness of life: "We will all have been in the same boat and that's really comforting" (*CV*, 212).

As though to illustrate this timeless dimension, the narrative jumps from one generation to another. Theodore, the nephew, succeeds his uncle, Alexandre Mortin, just as Francine is in a significant sense the reincarnation of her aunt, Ariane de Bonne-Mesure: "[Mlle Francine] is no longer in the prime of her youth she resembles her Aunt Ariane more and more the same kind face same corpulence same gait and also the intonation of the voice you'd think the deceased woman were speaking" (*CV*, 175). One would venture the opinion that for Pinget, humanity is constantly reembarking on the same journey, regardless of which individuals are alive at any given moment: "On such and such a page the season to love on another to give up one's place" (*CV*, 83). The recurrence of the same activities over any number of lifetimes gives the world a coherence that is reassuring and comforting.

Time in the chronological sense represents the very negation of the timeless dimension to which Pinget's narrator so yearns to accede. In fact, it is a hellish experience:

What is the moment
It is the crap where you find yourself while hoping to get out of it only to fall again into another moment. (*CV*, 205)

This unbearable feeling of discontinuity destroys our perception of reality. Since all of our acts are disconnected from one another, they disappear once they are performed. Torn as we are between contemplating an act and experiencing regret over its passing, we can never quite bring it into being. Squeezed between a hypothetical future and an irretrievable past, the present hardly exists. How, then, can one perpetuate the fleeting instant and restore its flavor? Reproducing the routine of a person's existence is no way to go about it. Mortin's nephew is determined to bring his late uncle back to life by accounting for every hour of his day. But whatever vital energy the latter possessed was squandered away

in mindlessly repetitive actions. His nephew can hardly hope to regener-
ate the old man by relating one insignificant detail after another: "I see
him in the morning opening his shutter at eight o'clock then toward
nine he takes a walk around his garden. . . . Then I see him reenter and
he goes out again around eleven and he does the walk again and reenters
and goes out again around two o'clock and then around five and finally
around seven until the moment when his maid calls him for dinner in
her rasping voice" (*CV*, 186).

Not only does chronological time sink the present into insignificance,
but it leads inevitably to decay. Pinget transposes onto the comical register the allegory of the ages of life. The brain, he suggests, is like a soufflé.
You shove it into the oven when its owner reaches the age of reason. It
rises slowly, puffs up, and expands until he reaches maturity, which
varies according to the individual. Then it caves in progressively until it
ends up completely flat or burned. Later on the author compares time to
an old doughnut that gets burned up on the frying pan (*CV*, 224). Even
when the calendar year moves toward spring and renewal, then summer
and full-blown maturity, it is nonetheless coming closer and closer to the
unavoidable: death. Hence the metonymical link between the month of
June and this final tragedy. The floral avalanche is the furthest thing
from a symbol of euphoria. It is, in the words of the narrator, a "horrid
avalanche." The floral motive here seems inseparable from funeral rites
and the heartbreaking buzzing of insects ("maybugs of despair"). The
month of July, with its harvests, symbolizes the end of life (*CV*, 227). In
fact, the narrator as well as his narrative will not last until the beginning
of August. When the final catastrophe arrives it is conjured up by the
traditional images: darkness, cataclysms, dizzying drops into the abyss.
Gradually the slate upon which the narrator was writing falls to pieces,
a portion of his memory crumbles, the ceiling of the burial vault collapses, and the cemetery is thrust into the void as the world returns to
primeval chaos.

Perhaps more than anyone else, the writer is agonizingly aware of the
curse chronological time leaves hanging over human existence. The
chaotic disorder of his manuscripts reflects the unresolvable mess of his
life and of life in general. As he sadly acknowledges, everything is hopelessly mixed up in "the drawers of the flood" (*CV*, 182). With this statement he is telling us that all the elements of the universe, which once
emerged from chaos, seem condemned to return to it. The book the narrator is preparing resembles this universe: "it is going down the drain. It
is futile to even try to find some semblance of order within these bloody

files." The scattered segments of the book would love to come together as a tightly knit unit, but to no avail. The completed book is nothing more than the fantasy of the writer "lost in the hurricane of his pages." He will never see the beautifully bound, finished product. His successors will have to try to make headway with the mess, to be followed by others at some future point in this same accursed temporal span. As though to evoke the profound dissatisfaction the writer experiences when confronting the disorder of his manuscript, chaos engulfs the text of *Cette voix* almost halfway through its course. The twists and turns of Pinget's style and his narrator's contradictions and regrets invade the novel to such an extent that it becomes muddied. As he admits himself, "you can't make heads or tails of it" (*CV*, 98). The reader has the weird impression of witnessing the death of a text. Words get crossed out then erased, sentences peter out ("In what whose tomb"), terms get mixed up ("vestiboule" instead of "vestibule"). At one point the narrative comes almost literally to a dead end: "Then suddenly nothing more on the slate nothing more in the dossiers the registers not a line blank sheets" (*CV*, 97).

To escape chaos, literature must turn its back on chronological time. But then another problem bedevils the writer: the structure of language itself. Contrary to what one may think, when one tries to create a literary work one is not necessarily in control. Someone else pulls the strings, either Fate or the "Manitou," as Pinget calls him. The Manitou refers to the mysterious intricacies of language, acting in association with the vital forces of the subconscious, which exert a preponderant influence on the writer's activity. The proper noun used in *Cette voix*, or any other novel written by Pinget for that matter, does not designate any specific individual but an indefinitely modifiable person. When Théodore describes his uncle Alexandre, he is in essence evoking a mythological figure that at one moment borrows that individual's name. Alexandre can insist on the reality of his existence from today till tomorrow, it still remains problematic.

Indeed, no name or character can encompass the existential space that language creates. As the narrator protests impatiently, "Who is this Albert again didn't we have enough with Alphonse Alfred and Alexandre?" (*CV*, 114). The individual's singularity gets swallowed up in the universality of the language used to describe him. Someone can be anyone, and ends up being anyone. Théodore cannot escape his fate any more than his uncle can. His character decomposes into childish utterances that convey the primary urges he shares with everybody else: "Theo Dodo Toto Zozo Popo" (*CV*, 223).

This apparent liability of language is an asset, however. Its very universality makes it the ideal vehicle for expressing the timelessness of myths, consequently, for connecting us to our collective unconscious. Very frequently during the course of the novel the characters find themselves oscillating between their purely human existence—prone to fragmentation and disintegration through chronological time—and their cosmic being—"wired in" permanently to their human condition and therefore unalterable. This explains the shifts in tone one perceives as they swing from hope to denigration. At the end of a particular period in his life, Mortin exclaims, "Ah yes the end of an epoch quickly to the next and shit to our nephews." This oscillation between human and cosmic time creates an ambivalent, boundaryless space where the two coexist. Some disquieting encounters can take place here between the living and the dead. Witness, for instance, the episode of the maskers at the very center of the text: "The procession of maskers filed through the corridor then went out through the garden and got back into the cars that moved off noiselessly leaving the master alone under the arch" (*CV*, 114). With a stunning sense of the supernatural, Pinget evokes in his novel a venerable tradition in archaic societies: the visit of the dead.

Once the frontiers between the living and the dead are broken down, death ceases to be a frightening entity. Far from representing the end of life, it marks a fresh, new beginning. Rot and decomposition signify a break with the past and an orientation toward the future (*CV*, 220). Continuity is everywhere, all one has to do is be on the lookout for it and decipher it. At one point in the text Pinget conveys an almost material vision of survival as he exalts life's power of self-renewal through the planting of seeds: "a package of seeds in the spring I mean for vegetables and we'll be saved." But the horror of death can also be exorcised by making destiny go backward rather than forward. Buoyed up by the exalting myth of regeneration through an "ineffable dive into the water of dreams, " Pinget's characters can recover their childhood and thus conquer chronological time. The old man "recovers the voice of the well-behaved little boy he once was," and the old aunt regains "her little girl's voice with the perfect diction." Obviously the logic of folklore rather than reason is prevailing here. Nevertheless, it reflects a deep-seated yearning on the part of the human creature to become fully integrated into the cosmic cycle, and, as such, it is extremely moving.

In *Cette voix* Pinget seems to be telling us that it is perfectly legitimate to entertain the notion of rebirth as long as one bears in mind that it is a fable—a fable no different from that of the phoenix on its pyre or the

transformation of the pumpkin into Cinderella's carriage. To believe anything beyond would be sheer madness. An aging, half-senile Mortin cul-
tivates alternatively hope as though it were an orchid or its opposite, "his
really daffy little despair" (*CV*, 168). Dreams get bludgeoned by reality.
The sister-in-law "is not a princess," and the dying man will end up as a
corpse. Lest one turn in desperation to the solution proposed by Marcel
Proust, the narrator warns the reader that rebirth through the resurrection of chronological time is a mirage. Pinget's spokesman remains poles
apart from the hero of *A la Recherche du temps perdu*. He refuses to con-
template from the vantage point of the present the whole fragile edifice
of his past: "To rediscover time in the innermost depths of the self what a
sinister joke. One might just as easily believe in the fragrance of horse
manure just try discovering the flowers that make it up; for how much
longer will they make of memory a substitute for eternity" (*CV*, 160).

Then what kind of rebirth, or immortality, is left for the writer, especially when he is haunted by the specter of death as is Robert Pinget? His
books—a kind of symbolic tomb from which "no one will have the gall to
throw him out"—represent his hope of remaining as a living presence
beyond death. Not that his books contain any earth-shattering messages
to enlighten and edify future generations. In a significant sense *Cette voix*
constitutes a parody of the writer who deludes himself into believing he is
a prophet with a splendid secret to divulge to a breathless humanity. The
so-called revelation takes place in a cardboard decor, amidst all kinds of
theatrical tricks, and the message itself is gibberish: "And this revelation
they are waiting for pchllpchlll you can hear the clap of thunder upheaval
cataclysm and the whole works" (*CV*, 158). Pinget's ambitions are far
more modest yet, nonetheless, very lofty. He seeks to mirror his fellow
men's secret fears and yearnings and to remain in their memory through
a stunningly original and inimitable expression of the human condition,
which, for lack of a better word, we will call style.

L'Apocryphe (*The Apocryphal Book*)

Pinget's unending meditation on death, the creative process, and the
possible immortality it can bring with it takes on an unusual twist—
even for him—in his next novel, *L'Apocryphe* (1980). The title of this
work presents a paradox. An author cannot normally bring forth an
apocryphal book inasmuch as the term designates a text whose authenticity is questionable. The most he can do is edit one. It is up to posterity, and posterity alone, to determine whether or not a work bears the

mark of a given writer. Scrutiny of the novel's structure, however, confirms the appropriateness of the title. The book does not have the appearance of a definitively composed text whose various components were put together by one author. It seems a compilation of one or several collaborators entrusted with the task of ordering, deciphering, retranscribing, reworking, and commenting on a virtually undecipherable first draft referred to as a "Grimoire" in French, meaning either a piece of mumbo jumbo or a book of magical spells.

Obviously this impression of incoherence is only an illusion. Pinget has put his text together exactly the way he wanted to and had no intention of relinquishing his prerogatives to his reader. But the novel does function in a bizarre fashion. It is constantly torn between the demands of two protagonists, the uncle and his nephew. The former delights in making alterations in his text, in recording the ravings of his mind, and the fantasies of his imagination. The latter strives to bring harmony out of this apparent chaos and to weed out the incongruities. *L'Apocryphe*, then, relates the elaboration and subsequent revisions of a supposedly posthumous manuscript during which both author and editor express their conflicting reactions. While committing his work of "fiction" to paper, the uncle jots down in telegraphic style all kinds of reminders and instructions to himself as well as to the reader:

> Verify meaning apocryphal
> Distrust literary tone
> Abandon term château
> Urgent fill void February-April

As for the nephew or editor, his comments swing so wildly in favor of or against the text he is revising, that one wonders at times whether or not he has delegated a part of his responsibilities to a subordinate. When the editor's judgments are derogatory, he seems to invite the reader to play the editor as well, suggesting that the successive paragraphs and episodes of the book are little more than the hopelessly jumbled pieces of some jigsaw puzzle that is hardly worth putting back together:

> Imagine what the master wanted to make of his manuscript.
> That old jerk and his unbecoming jokes.
> Following pages, same clichés about the flight of time and the damaging effects of the conscience. Eliminate.

Thirty or so pages before the end of the work comes the most damning commentary of them all: "there's not enough material here to make up a novel."[7] At other moments, however, the nephew affirms the opposite. Through its different versions, the book is perfectly well constructed and focused: "Not the slightest trace of chance in all this," he exclaims. To which he adds, later, another highly favorable opinion: "The old man had more than just air in his cranium."

This old man remains an enigmatic figure. Depending on the narrator who happens to be portraying him at a given moment, he comes across as a self-deluding fool with no talent whatsoever for creation or an artist haunted and tormented by an unattainable perfection, conscious of his failure yet tenaciously pursuing his dream. In this respect, he bears a fraternal resemblance to the protagonist of *Quelqu'un*. Both these reincarnations of the omnipresent character, Mortin, yearn to fashion through the alchemy of words the magic formula that will illuminate the night of their soul, uncovering its secret unity, making them whole again, and perhaps guaranteeing them immortality:

> Poring over his book of magical spells, the old man studied with a magnifying glass the cabalistic figures that illustrated it and dreamed of mysterious transfers, or signal relationships between things making up his memory, a small number of them and those that one discovers during privileged moments of consciousness, quickly vanished fireflies whose trace however remains somewhere or other and leads us. . . . (*A*, 151)

His failure to unlock the treasures of his inner realm explains his obsession with death. Since the old uncle realizes that he cannot achieve immortality through art, he is determined to leave an indelible imprint in the minds of his inheritors through the shocking surprises he has in store for them in his last will and testament. He imagines with malevolent relish his funeral procession at which he is an omniscient mourner. He depicts the visceral hatred seething within his relatives and seeping through their facade of hypocritical grief. Then he savors in advance the vengeance he will wreak upon them as he gets to the part of his imaginary script where they discover in the notary's office that they have all been disinherited:

> Ah there he comes out of his house feet first in great pomp, I'm not exaggerating, pinch me so I'll keep a straight face, pinch me I'm asking you, d'you realize this whole big show is being put on for that piece of shit,

half of our inheritance I'll bet you, we've lost absolutely everything but
I'm having a good laugh, we're not in the will, the others don't know it
yet, they've put on their phony expression of bereavement, we're going to
die laughing at the notary's office, darn it, did you see the flowers and
wreaths? to our beloved uncle, to our adored great-uncle, to our faithful
friend, to our brother, to our . . .
    In favor of the insane asylum.
    They won't get a bloody thing as we put it bluntly. (*A*, 67)

As for the old man's death, the reader has his choice of possibilities.
In one version he is ambushed by a band of thieves who rob and wound
him before doing away with him. In another he is murdered in his bed
by an unknown assailant who makes off with a precious statuette. In
yet a third, the author (or is it the nephew-editor speaking?) assures us
that no such murder ever took place. The potty old gentleman was simply trying his hand unsuccessfully at writing detective stories. Which
version is the most plausible? Any or none at all. We have emphasized
at various points in this study that for Robert Pinget, the unfolding of
events in a person's life is purely aleatory. Since no individual existence
has a transcendent justification, the circumstances making up its successive stages in a work of fiction can be altered indefinitely. It is no
more far-fetched to believe that the uncle ended his days in an insane
asylum (which the novel seems to imply on more than one occasion)
than it is to maintain that he was a victim of premeditated murder.
Indeed, given the pitiful form of immortality for which he settles, the
idea of the asylum is perhaps not the least implausible of the different
hypotheses.

    Given the diverging accounts of the uncle-master's life and character,
the chaotic state of his manuscripts, and the radically different reactions
they elicit from his editor(s), it is a tribute to Pinget's consummate skill
as a novelist that the text actually does have an underlying unity and
does reach a number of conclusions. The metaphorical glue holding all
the scattered fragments together is the figure of the shepherd. He
embodies the author's/narrator's yearning for order and serenity, his
search for a spiritual sanctuary where at long last the tormented wander-
er will find peace. In *L'Apocryphe* a man reflects on his past, making
clumsy efforts to bring into focus the fragments of his personality. Just as
the shepherd draws his herd back into the fold, so does the protagonist
strive to gather together his ideas into a coherent whole. In other words,
he is embarked on a voyage of self-discovery, which has as its final destination the center of his being.

The expression "five paces ten paces," recurring like a leitmotiv at various stages of the novel's development, refers not only to the uncle's medicinal walks around his miniature garden but above all to the ritual of self-exploration, which he performs regularly in the hope of uncovering the unity lying beyond the chaos of contradictions his life represents. Even the very detailed descriptions the uncle gives of his two homes— one in town and the other, a château, in the country—can be interpreted in the symbolic sense as an attempt to explore the dwelling of his soul. That he arranges the various rooms on paper in the highly complex form of a cathedral rose-window or according to the equally intricate pattern of the houses of the zodiac attests this symbolism.

The overarching importance Pinget attributes to this shepherd figure is obvious from the frequency with which it recurs during the novel, as well as the many transformations that it undergoes along the way. At the very beginning of *L'Apocryphe* the reader has the illusion of scrutinizing a frontispiece like the ones placed at the front of volumes printed centuries ago, which adumbrated the crisis to be evoked: "Very simple the image at the center. A man seated on a pile of stones. Perhaps a shepherd, with a cape and a stick next to him. He appears to be young, the lines of his body are supple, his elbows are resting on his knees, his head leaning forward, his chin in his hands" (*A*, 9). Of course, it is not a frontispiece per se, but the description of the kind of engraving found in ancient texts, which the uncle/master takes pleasure in leafing through. From this point on, the author indulges in a collectorlike mania. Copies of the shepherd spring up in one form after another: in paintings, tapestries, flower boxes, photos, and statuettes. Two manifestations of the figure are especially noteworthy during the unfolding of the novel: the image of a shepherd on an ancient goblet—"skiff of the imaginary realm"—and the silhouette of a goatherd viewed through a pair of field glasses by the master or his servant. The image on the drinking cup precedes the living person and seems to engender the latter, but it is out of reach, inscribed in the lens of the viewer.

It is significant that this emblematic person always appears enclosed in some way or other, as though placing him within a given framework could immobilize him for good. He is seen only through an optical device, which limits the field of vision—be it a "perfect circle" in the first part of the novel or a "banal rectangle" in the second. His body and the décor against which he stands out blend into each other. Either the landscape follows the curve of the man's back and the edge of his cape or his body is shaped by the curving lines of his surroundings. Even more striking is the parallelism between the modifications to which the shepherd figure is subjected and the innumerable corrections imposed on the manuscript. Just as traits are modified, added, or restored in the figure, so are details changed, deleted, or corrected in the uncle's text. In order to emphasize once again the process of permutations and combinations that life implies, the shepherd and his surroundings get radically altered as the novel unfolds. He is, by turns, young and aged; his flock is made up of nanny goats or sheep; he sits under either an olive or a beech tree; the countryside where he watches over his animals is either scrubland or cultivated fields. His elusiveness is explicitly willed by the author, who insists that "an ideal figure must remain inaccessible." At the end of the novel he reaches the height of moral grandeur. Dressed in white amidst his flock, he symbolizes redemption through Christ. It matters not whether this redemption will or ever did take place for the uncle or the narrator. What *does* matter very much is conquering serenity through a series of ordeals: "The chimeras fade away with the setting sun, the wounds of the imagination heal."

This yearning for redemption explains the tension the reader perceives in the novel between two systems for measuring time—the calendar and the liturgical. Stephen Bann was the first to point out the competition between these diametrically opposite temporal orders.[8] On the one hand, the protagonists are buffeted about in time that passes. On the other, they refer to an absolute time that, being invested by the sacred, bestows a supreme significance on human existence. In contrast to the eternal cycle of "nature before its salvation," as it is depicted on the portal of the collegial church, stands triumphantly the message of Christianity. Although the latter was expressed in a historical context, it transcends history. The myth of the eternal recurrence is therefore supplanted by a singular event—the Incarnation, which gives a revolutionary meaning to the concept of human destiny. Christ's birth heralds the reign of the new law. The attentive reader can pick out many signs in the text suggesting a break with the past and the progress of divine grace. Images of destruction and decay (thunderstorms, gales, the withering away of July), as well as images of cleansing, rebuilding, and renewal, suggest the triumph of redemption manifesting itself, in the words of the narrator, by an "overabundance of signs" (*A*, 157).

The shepherd-turned-Christ-figure also accounts for the double system of quotations borrowed alternatively from Scripture and Virgil's *Eclogues*. As Pinget emphasizes, the old master spends sleepless nights rehashing the famous verses interspersed with liturgical references, longing, no doubt, to uncover in these timeless texts the key to his own enigma. Not only does the novelist quote the first three words of the poem—*"Tityre, tu patulae recubans sub tegmine fagi"* ("You, Tityrus, lying under the shade of a large beech tree")—but he also reproduces in a very mysterious fashion the first two words of the last verse: *"Ite domum"* (Return home").[9] These two quotations frame yet a third, the very famous line of verse from the fourth bucolic, in which Christianity has traditionally seen the pagan world's prophesizing of the birth of Christ: *"Ille deum vitam accipiet"* ("This child will participate in life of the gods"). This is no doubt the poem by Virgil on which some unknown scholar makes comments in a book found by the uncle at a second-hand dealer's shop.

Passages drawn from the Bible are equally prominent. According to Bann, the recitation of the Psalms punctuates the religious calendar and offers the Christian a ritualized form of dialogue with God: "Pinget could not find a more appropriate model for the union of daily ritual and intense confession, which constitute the natural result of his narrative style" (Bann, 53). Moreover, for Bann the division of *L'Apocryphe* into 168 sections numbered with roman numerals recalls the psalter made up of 150 poems to which is generally added the series of 18 biblical canticles (Bann, 53).

Through its very centrality, the shepherd motif connects the Christian influence to the pagan one. The effigy of "the Greek goatherd carrying a lamb on his shoulders" is a forerunner of the "statue of the sixteenth-century representing the good shepherd with a lamb in his arms" (*A*, 25). Just as Melibeus in Virgil's *Bucolics* chases after billy goats, so does the shepherd run after his flock and the dog after the adventurous nanny goat in Pinget's novel. This pursuit of the stray animal can be interpreted symbolically as a fight waged by a lucid consciousness against the chimeras welling up from the irrational part of the being. As the master watches the shepherd through his field glasses bringing the stray beasts back into the fold, he begins a meditation on the passage from the Gospel according to St. Luke, which bears a strange similarity to this episode: "Who is the one who if he lost one. . . . He reconstructs the context by memory then he consults the other book, opens it at the page where the shepherd appears and dreams about symbols, allusions, chimeras" (*A*, 50).

The return of the sheep to the fold (*"ite domum"*) reappears at the end of each cycle of *L'Apocryphe*, where it encounters the psalm motives (*A*, 78–167). The home is the sanctuary of the oppressed, the dream of the exiled; it is the house of the father where the dying person is welcomed by the angels, in accordance with the prayer of absolution quoted two times in the novel: "In Paradisum." As a sardonic counterpoint to this utterance, the narrator recalls a human parody of paradise, the retirement home where the so-called elect languish away in semi-senile solitude, where the institution bell rings to remind them to come for their soup at the same time that the nearby church bells comfort them with the message of salvation.

This example of self-mockery so prevalent in Pinget's works serves as a warning against any temptation to jump to overly optimistic conclusions. Certainly, the central shepherd motive linking Virgil to various biblical texts seems to indicate that for the writer at least, spiritual wholeness and redemption could conceivably come from the creative act. But as Jean Roudaut astutely points out, "[Literature]" does nothing more than imitate. Even if it borrows from religion the hopes which it carries forward . . . and the sacrifices which it inspires. It remains a parody."[10] Being circular in structure and based on permutations, literature can only produce contradictions, not resolve them. Roudaut goes on to observe that there may indeed be a hidden god somewhere in Pinget's text, but such a deity remains diffuse (Roudaut, 44).

And so a novel like *L'Apocryphe* can reveal only this yearning for a fullness of being that may never be attained. Pinget himself compares the author-narrator to a block gnawed at by the sandstorms in the middle of the desert (*A*, 141). Besides, words can only suggest the unspeakable, not formulate it, because "the unspeakable accompanies any formulation like its shadow." Death alone would perhaps enable the writer to reach the Absolute, since it abolishes words, which stand as a barrier between him and the truth he is seeking. Herein lies perhaps the meaning of the intriguing passage where the narrator, evoking the distress of the aging uncle, refers to "this voice which breaks your eardrum, ravages of the imaginary in a mind adrift, thunderclap of the death throes, breakdown, dizziness, collapse" (*A*, 55).

And yet despite the necessary caution irony provides and the equally necessary awareness of his limitations as an artist, Robert Pinget is loath to renounce his belief that poetry will indeed ultimately triumph over our failures. "Poetry has no age," he exclaims, "it has been here from the very beginning" (*A*, 153). By seeking to approximate through words that which is inexpressible, poetry plugs into the recesses of our being from which arise our deepest aspirations. For this reason a poet like Virgil remains immortal. He, like others past and present, has received "the gift of languages," and as a result he is "understood in the whole universe and perhaps even in the stars." Individual poets will pass from this earth without having resolved the enigmas of our human condition, but because they have evoked them in an arrestingly original way, their texts will always find admirers to bring them alive again: "Things retold which will be told yet again by our nephews, fresh voices, new eyes, innocent ears" (*A*, 176). Thus the writer will have justified his existence on earth.

L'Ennemi (*The Enemy*)

Seven years elapsed between the publication of *L'Apocryphe* and Robert Pinget's last full-scale novel, *L'Ennemi* (1987).[11] During that period critics and the public alike had become much more familiar with the author's books. Since he now enjoyed a certain notoriety, Pinget could challenge his readers, as did Balzac, by evoking characters and plots from previous works without identifying them. It would be up to his more attentive readers to place these in the appropriate contexts. Like most French literary journalists, Mariane Alphant had no trouble picking them out.[12] In Pinget's latest work, she zeroed in on the murdered child from *Le Libera*, the sinister dealings from *L'Inquisitoire*, the malicious gossip from *Le Fiston*, the ambiguous mysticism of *Baga*, and the repetitions of *Passacaille*. It would be wrong, however, to imagine that Pinget was trying to set up some kind of complicity with his readers by reminiscing with them. On the contrary, he is out to nonplus them. Twenty-five years after composing his first novel, *Mahu*, he again denigrates the "realistic" conception of literature based on plausibility and logic in favor of the imaginary, the irrational, and poetry. If the book seems destructive it is because the author is aiming for nothing less than the transformation of his reader's way of approaching fiction.

As though to prove that Pinget's works could still provoke animated discussions, the book's title, borrowed from a poem in Charles Baudelaire's collection, *Les Fleurs du mal*, gave rise to the most divergent commentaries. According to Alphant, the enemy is the "interior obstacle" that prevents the writer from delivering his secret and derives a sadistic pleasure in destroying him, much like Baudelaire's "Héautontimorouménos," the self-torturer. For Claude Prévost, this same enemy is Time, which sounds the death knell for the stubborn, pitiable old man. For many critics imbued with the theories for the New Novel, the enemy is the insistence on logical meaning or anything that prevents the reader from transforming himself. Perhaps Michèle Gazier came closest to understanding the book's title by observing that there exists in the narrator an enemy of order, which resists the temptation of the smooth and linear novel in favor of fragmentation and incompletion.

L'Ennemi does seem to be haunted by the awareness that for every possible series of events that takes place there are myriads of others that could just as easily have occurred instead. The same conviction, evident in many of Pinget's earlier works, that our human adventures have no essential justification for being returns here with a vengeance. At any given moment the flow of action can be reversed and replaced by an entirely dissimilar one, creating in the long run an inextricable tangle of contradictions. Needless to say, the more the novel teems with contradictory possibilities, the less credible the narrative appears. Thus, the judge is felled by an attack of apoplexy in the first version but suffers only a sprain in the second, which gets confused with the master's fractured ankle and the feeling of faintness that the wife of the American buyer experiences. Undermined by doubt, the novel advances through successive denials. But, as the narrator himself asks, "Up till what point can a given affirmation make one forget what it contradicts?"[13] At times the narrative seems to want to do away with any ambiguity.

Describing two paintings, the master takes great pains to distinguish between them. The first portrait, hanging in the former kitchen, is a profile of a bearded old man, balding, with a crown of salt-and-pepper hair. The second is the family portrait of the great-great-grandfather displayed in the smoking room, "with grey hair, hooked nose, thin lips, and a severe attitude," wearing the uniform of a Sardinian officer. He insists that the two personages have nothing in common, yet at the end of the novel we catch him in the process of altering all the passages in his manuscripts relating to the paintings so that the portraits of the ancestor and the old man get mixed up in the reader's mind (*E*, 189). The end result is that the ancestor's portrait cannot be located anywhere. It acquires a mythical status, that of a forbidding judge who scrutinizes the soul of his taciturn descendant with his inquisitorial gaze.

Another example of this deceptive attempt to dispel confusion is the "affaire X," which perhaps occupies an inordinately prominent place in the novel's structure. At first the two different versions of a child's disappearance are sharply contrasted. In section 19 we learn that the 11-year-old son of farmer X disappears in the forest on the second of June at noon while out picking heather. In section 48 we are informed that the six-year-old son of a married couple, who had come to visit friends for

Christmas, is kidnapped on 24 December during the midnight Mass. The drowned body of the farmer's son is discovered in a pond after a 23-hour search. The episode of the kidnapping, which begins at four o'clock in the afternoon, is interrupted at the moment when the child's disappearance is noticed. The first story concludes with a charge of rape and murder. The second is never completed. In section 77 the two anecdotes are again brought to the foreground. This time around it appears that the little boy—now a 12-year-old—was never kidnapped but simply ran away. Moreover, this incident greatly troubled the community, whereas the murder of the farmer's child was met with general indifference. In section 101 we are treated to yet a third version, which changes the hour and date when the farmer's boy disappeared. We are now assured that the crime took place on 21 June at midnight, the night of Summer Solstice, no doubt transposed by the master for far greater dramatic effect. We also find out that the master has reconstructed this third version of the drama by drawing on a newspaper article about the son of the mayor—a 12-year-old—who was discovered horribly mutilated in an abandoned trailer (*E*, 189). As a result, suspicion focuses on the gypsy Sirocco, whose annual visit coincides with the feast of St. John. But did Sirocco really commit the murder? For the townspeople, it does not matter. Since they are unsure of the murderer's identity, they will settle for a scapegoat.

What is the reader to make of these divergent versions? Is the master a mythomaniac and his work "an enterprise of mystification"? (*E*, 157). Is his mind confused? The press release written by Pinget himself for the novel's launching goes a long way in explaining the master's seemingly irrational conduct:

> The book could be considered, according to Pinget, as the deliberately deceptive Mémoires of a doddering old man who also takes pleasure in contradicting himself, for a reason which is difficult to know. At first glance, he does not seem to have any memory, but in the long run one suspects first his bad faith, then his uneasiness, his anguish and a kind of psychic unbalance. Now he is perfectly aware of this himself. The reason for his roundabout ways and trickery remains incomprehensible to the superficial reader.[14]

The author is emphasizing here the importance of the enlightened reader in giving coherence to a literary work. *L'Ennemi* does indeed appeal to a "providential third party" deemed indispensable for the realization of the text: "Through him will come the final synthesis," proclaims the narrator (*E*, 193). Now to effect this "final synthesis," the

ideal reader, according to Pinget, must not envisage a piece of literature
as a completed entity containing a moral or philosophical conclusion at
the end of its development. He should break the textual mold to apprehend the writer's intentions. Hence the cryptical statement that appears
during the course of the novel: "dismember disarticulate psychosis master." Rather than interpret a work from the point of view of the traditional critic, the reader should adopt the methods of the hermeneutic
scholar. Reading a text is therefore a spiritual project for which the reader's active collaboration is solicited. An alchemical metaphor underscores
the importance of such an enterprise: "The initial black must reach the
white stage. Cure synonymous with conscience. Seek out inspiration
from great lessons" (E, 51).

Much later in the novel we find another orchestration of this same
theme of the reader entrusted with synthesizing the scattered elements
of the text. It occurs in the descriptions of two mandalas (E, 117 and
185) inspired by traditional imagery and each followed by a white page,
which symbolizes its virtual or mental state. The first depicts the
alchemist's work and is embellished with ritual symbols and terms evoking the successive stages of the composition. The second designates the
alienated creature in the process of conquering his freedom. Both illustrate Pinget's belief that it is up to the reader, in active collaboration
with the author, to reconcile opposites and resolve contradictions, or at
least to attempt to do so: "The work will have as its raw material the
confused magma of the words of others, contradictory. Bring them
together by directing the operation according to the rules. Uncover the
succession of phrases of the ingenious device" (E, 102).[15]

Pinget is exhorting his reader to go beyond appearances and seek
beyond the ordinary anecdote the novel is relating, "a transcendent
image deliberately disguised" (E, 192). It matters not at all that the
reader's "transcendent image" may differ from the author's, or from the
one that yet another reader might discover. The master can proclaim his
sovereignty over his manuscript as much as he likes. He can dismiss his
collaborators. He can rant and rave, insisting that "there is only one version, only one, mine, you understand." Even he is forced to admit failure:
"Present situation irreversible. Definitive fissure profound aspirations
and surface discourse" (E, 191). It is obvious to the author as well as to
his enlightened reader that there can be no dogmatic approach to literature, since it must deal in ambiguities to retain its power of attraction for
future generations. The novelist suggests this indirectly when he uses

parody to express the so-called ideal truth of his book in the short, tele-graphic passages that are supposed to reveal it but never do.

Despite his dogmatic utterances, the master knows full well that if the novel is to endure it must propound unsolvable riddles. He demon-strates it by outwitting his secretary and reader. He constructs a textual labyrinth from which they will never quite emerge once they've pene-trated into it. He advocates incompleteness as his "distinctive trade-mark" (*E*, 54). Even if he has the occasional vague impulse to finish the task at hand, he will always postpone it indefinitely. The fascination his text exerts on this reader depends on the sense of mystery it generates, and this sense of mystery in turn depends on the work never being fin-ished. This is why patience is the very leitmotiv of the novel: "We have all the time / You have all the time."

Obviously the danger lying in wait for any writer aspiring to express through words that which goes beyond words is silence. Although Pinget may pretend to admire it, he knows that silence leads to a dead end. For a writer, to stop creating is to accept a form of spiritual death. Pinget is haunted, as was his close friend and colleague Samuel Beckett, by the fear of becoming walled into a kind of artistic muteness as a result of his obsessive desire to reveal the unrevealable. In his pursuit of this wordless reality he risks losing his reader.

And so the writer must continue creating networks of words which reverberate against one another, tempting the reader with the prospect of elucidating mysteries, withholding solutions in order to goad his col-laborator onward. The reader may destroy the text in his dogged deter-mination to grasp its meaning, but at the same time he is destroying it he is also regenerating it in his own way. "The transfiguration of the black text," insists Pinget, "is achieved neither through trial and error, nor through science, but through the thrust of a devouring flame" (*E*, 15). Thus, the fireplace can be interpreted as a metaphor of possible sal-vation. Those who survive the deceased poet will assume the responsibil-ity of lighting up his texts with their intelligence and making them glow again.

Chapter Six
Words with a Life of Their Own: The Theater of Robert Pinget

The reader who has followed Robert Pinget on his voyage of self-discovery through his successive novels will feel very much at home in the world of his theater.[1] He is by now used to finding his way through the intricacies of the Pingetian labyrinth without the reassuring traditional signposts of linear progression, character development, and logical sequence. Consequently, he will not be bewildered when confronted with contradictory events, structural breakdowns, unraveling characters, and snowballing verbal delirium in the plays. He will no doubt even be happy to renew his acquaintance with the same kinds of people he encountered in the novels, most of whom have simply made the transition from one literary genre to another. They all bear the same family resemblance. They are all dispossessed: M. Levert is searching for his son (*Lettre Morte*);[2] Pommard and Toupin are looking for memories of their past (*La Manivelle*);[3] the so-called writer Mortin (*L'Hypothèse*),[4] just like the self-styled playwrights Abel and Bela, struggles with an imaginary text.

All these characters yearn for a fulfillment that remains elusive, and their only hope of filling this inner void is to put on a show for themselves. M. Levert imagines the return of his son, and the two half-senile old men watch shadows flicker across the screen of their memory; Mortin presents a pseudo-public lecture, while Abel and Bella imagine that they are staging a play. This theatrical illusion or the play-within-the-play, so often used by Shakespeare, leaves them even more helpless, however. The object of their yearning is forever lost. They have recourse to words to help them elucidate their enigmas. But words have a perverse tendency to acquire a life of their own. Indeed, in Pinget's theater they seem also to have a mind of their own. And they give the process of dispossession a dizzying momentum that one does not find in the novels.

An audience witnessing just about any of Pinget's plays has the impression of a machine hurtling toward self-destruction. His plays are all based on the principle of an unraveling or breaking down of the action. To appreciate the novelty of this approach to drama, it suffices to compare it with the aesthetic that underpins the traditional theater. Conventionally a play can be defined as a scenic representation of a protagonist's search for answers to a specific dilemma and of his actions that result from this search. The plot unfolds from beginning to end according to a process of progressive revelation and affirmation. When the play ends the crisis is resolved one way or another. We are led from an initially confused situation to its clear and satisfying conclusion. Pinget, however, plots the exact opposite course. He deludes us into believing that we understand the problem at the outset. But just as we are settling back comfortably, what we *think* we know slips away from us—what seemed to be developing normally all of a sudden starts falling apart. In the end everything collapses.

That being the case, we move from clarity to obscurity. The image of reality, which we thought we had easily grasped, becomes all scrambled and eludes our comprehension. Just like the actors in *Lettre morte* performing the play-within-the-play *The Prodigal Son* to entertain M. Levert, Pinget puts his dramatic machine out of order. As Arnaud Rykner aptly stated, "The Pingetian act thus closely resembles that of the child who builds for himself a castle of cards for the pleasure of laughingly blowing it down."[5] Here is a theater, then, that functions by deconstructing itself, that entices the spectator with the illusion of recognizable surroundings, then leaves him suspended over the void.

The playwright begins constructing his disquieting dramatic world by conjuring up an atmosphere of daily life that seems both plausible and reassuring—an atmosphere with which many of us have been familiar at one time or another. In the words of Olivier de Magny,

> These slightly senile people with independent incomes, this sorrowing father, this interchangeable café waiter and postal clerk, this gossipy female newspaper vendor, this tippling tramp and this very improvised fortune-teller, this slightly zany literary figure (which literary figures are not?), do we not have here a very familiar little world and seemingly straight out of the most ordinary gallery of characters, if not out of the most inoffensively naturalistic of repertoires? They have something narrow, neutral and small-townish about them, the quavering obstinacy of the already seen and already heard.[6]

We can feel at home here, for here are people we have met before; this is everyday reality. In *Lettre morte* numerous references are made to commonplace objects, and their abundance convinces us that we are viewing a décor so solid that we could mistake it for something real. As though to reinforce this impression that we are looking at the reproduction of a place we could have frequented ourselves, Pinget has M. Levert rattle on for several pages about the glass he is holding, the counter against which he is leaning, the green plant nearby, and the bottle from which the bartender is pouring him drinks. Pinget persists in wanting to make us believe in the surroundings he is evoking for us. As a result, we absorb them and relate to them. But just when we have settled into a comfortable relationship with them, they are removed.

Generally speaking, each play in Pinget's theater creates an ambience with multiple, concrete references to reality. Relationships are drawn up, either between father and son (*Lettre morte, Architruc*), or master and servant (*Architruc, Paralchimie, Identité*). Trades, professions, and social status are clearly defined: the waiter and the actors in *Lettre morte*, the king and his minister in *Architruc*, the doctor in *Identité*, the maid in *Identité* and *Autour de Mortin*, the valet in *Paralchimie*. In addition, characters are assigned certain dramatic functions, which we come to take for granted. M. Levert, Mortin, and Clope are principal protagonists, whereas the waiter and the post office clerk are doubles or reflections. In any other dramatic system, these elements would ensure stability from beginning to end, giving the audience a feeling of security even when it waits with bated breath for the crisis to be resolved.

But no sooner does Pinget lull us with a false sense of security than he takes delight—indeed, he goes out of his way—to pull the rug from under our feet. He makes sure that we pay for our gullibility. Relationships get scrambled, statuses get confused, functions lose their viability, and the audience loses its bearings. The waiter in the first act of *Lettre morte* is transformed into the post office clerk in the second. The king in Architruc turns himself into a father figure, and his minister pretends to be a child. Servants become masters, and principal protagonists fade into mere reflections. Dialogue teeters on the brink of poetic madness before degenerating into gobbledygook. The whole dramatic machine revs itself up, tearing away at a breakneck pace, sweeping everything with it along its insane course. As Erard exclaims in *Paralchimie*, "I'm being carried away by the irreversible action" (*P*, 74).

Obviously it is the author's determination to destroy what he has created that propels Erard, as well as the other characters, along this reckless trajectory. One is almost tempted to use the term "perverse" to describe this determination to take away what the spectators were led to believe was given to them once and for all. They believed in the lonely, heartbroken father who was pouring out his heart to the waiter in *Lettre morte*. They believed in the café as the place where the action was supposed to unfold. Then, suddenly, the curtain comes down and when it rises again, the theatrical illusion is in ruins. The café is transformed into a post office, and the waiter is metamorphosized into a postal clerk. Levert has no recollection of the actors he met in the café during the first act. The author had set a trap for us all along, and now we are caught. Joyce O. Lowrie makes a very insightful comment on this double movement of construction and destruction: "Each work creates itself, as it were, and then proceeds on a self-destructing cycle that annihilates all that has gone before."[7] Because Pinget's plays careen toward self-negation, they lead to a dead end. It is useless and even impossible to go on when one knows that further down the road one will come upon nothing. Clope explains this sense of futility to Mme Tronc:

CLOPE: Let's avoid the last replies.
TRONC: What do you mean?
CLOPE: I say let's avoid the last replies. Let's stop this game for the morning [he has just drawn the cards].
TRONC: You're afraid of the last replies?
CLOPE: No, but they could not bring anything new.[8]

Four other plays suggest almost tangibly that the action has been permanently stalled by having one of the main protagonists repeat the same phrase or half-phrase several times in a row like a broken record:

Abel et Bela: "I descend within myself and what do I find? What do I find?"

Lettre morte: "What counts is . . . What counts . . . What counts . . ."

La Manivelle: "When you think, when you think . . ."

L'Hypothèse: "The lost opportunities to remain silent . . . (A pause) The lost opportunities to remain silent . . . (A pause) The lost opportunities . . ."

What are we to make of these inconclusive endings? Is there a meaning, beyond a method, to this madness? By having his plays self-destruct in the presence of his spectators, Pinget is perhaps drawing our attention to the fact that our ways of perceiving and interpreting the reality around us rest on very fragile foundations. We expect events to unfold in logical succession. We count on finding our everyday surroundings exactly as we had left them. We depend on language to structure our experience in rational patterns. But what if the whole underpinning of our understanding of existence suddenly disintegrated? What if predictability, sequential logic, familiar objects and people vanished overnight? How would we cope? Could we cope? This very fragility of a world we so often like to imagine as unshakably solid is what emerges from the debris.

In Pinget's theater truth is not something immutable. It is, rather, a yearning, or an expectation that never comes to fruition. M. Levert waits in vain for a reply from a son to whom he writes letters without ever mailing. Mortin in *L'Hypothèse* tries unsuccessfully to find a solution to an unverifiable hypothesis and in the process loses his sense of reality. The audience in *Autour de Mortin* is anxious to hit upon the explanation of an enigmatic existence, but such an answer remains elusive till the very end. Whereas the traditional theater offers us a coherent vision of our condition, Pinget leaves us with nothing but scattered fragments of a puzzle. Unlike a "normal" puzzle, however, these pieces cannot be matched or made to fit together.

The dramas in Pinget's theater may unravel in different ways, but the unraveling itself depends essentially on the process of repetition. When events repeat themselves within a given play, they cause it to destructure itself. *Lettre morte* provides a striking example of this. The second act is a contradictory rerun of the first. The funeral procession of the shoemaker's daughter passes by in act 2, even though she was supposed to have been dead and buried in act 1. Such a scrambling of time sequences is all the more surprising because the two acts often suggest a logical succession: events having taken place in the first part of the drama are recalled in the second. No wonder M. Levert is astounded. In the second act he questions the postal employee about the young woman's burial and gets an unexpected answer:

> LEVERT: And the burial takes place today?
> EMPLOYEE: Right now.
> LEVERT: Louis told me that it had taken place yesterday.
> EMPLOYEE: Why yesterday? This morning I tell you. (*LM*, 133)

This symmetrical inversion places the audience in an untenable position. Both the waiter and postal employee, played by the same actor, have similar lines to speak. But the differences are sufficient for the spectator to hesitate between believing the first or the second. He cannot

be sure whether he is witnessing a repeat of the same episode or participating in a new one. In this respect the very hostility of the criticism leveled by Jean-Jacques Gautier of *Le Figaro* in 1960 against the play's
self-destructive process is illuminating: "This play has two acts. A first
act marvelously composed, which fully satisfies our sensibility and is psy-
chologically, emotionally and dramatically unassailable. And then a second act, which tries to be demonstrative and sounds contrived."[9] The
French journalist and member of the French Academy in his day admires
the first act for its psychological soundness and linear structure, but
rejects the second act for sabotaging the first. In an indirect, critical way,
he shows remarkable insight into Pinget's aesthetics of destabilization. It
is very possible, if not probable, that the intensity of his adverse reaction
results from having experienced the play as a spectator. Unlike reading a
novel, attending a play challenges not simply the written word but the
audience as well. The playgoer has trouble either accepting or denying
the two contradictory episodes inasmuch as this contradiction is part of
an experience shared with the actors.

Similar contradictions weave and tear apart simultaneously the dramatic fabric of *Abel et Bela, L'Hypothèse*, and *Paralchimie*. The spectator
who participates in their unraveling senses that each succeeding moment
of his existence is being canceled out by the preceding one. In *Autour de
Mortin* (commissioned by the BBC) this cycle of construction and
destruction through inverted repetition reaches its climax. The play's
powerful impact on the spectator depends on its conveyed impression
that the interviews recorded on the subject of the writer, Alexandre
Mortin, were real, and that such a person did in fact exist. But as the discrepancies between the various interviews become more and more obvious, the spectator's feeling of disquiet intensifies. Just when we are
prepared to trust a person's judgment, another one, who appears equally
sincere, trustworthy, and well informed, gives a somewhat different
account of Mortin, which undermines our confidence. By the end of the
play we are completely bewildered. Contradictory repetition has led to
negation. No choice is possible in a reality that repeats itself only to
negate its very foundation.

Negation through repetition takes on a particularly frightening form
when a person enters into a relationship with his reflection or double.
Pinget would not at all concur with Gérard Genette's statement that the
reflection of a given person, being a double, is "both an other and a
self."[10] In Pinget's theater the Self does not manifest itself in the guise of
the Other but is negated by the Other. As Anne C. Murch observed very

perceptively, M. Levert's unceasing attempts in *Lettre Morte* to project onto the Other his own plight of a father deserted by his son brings on disaster: "[He] is soon reduced himself to the state of reflection, putting on grotesque disguises. Because the father identifies, despite himself, with the unworthy father of the waiter, with the ridiculed father of the vaudeville number, with the father of the postal employee, with the old man who sent letters to paradise, and so on. And to each new avatar of the father corresponds a similar image of the son."[11]

As the reflections multiply, M. Levert loses his identity. In fact, he gets dispossessed. We notice a similar occurrence in La *Manivelle*. Memories of past events cancel each other out as they are evoked in contradictory succession. As a result, the recollections of the two babbling old men, Toupin and Pommard, are reduced to empty words:

> TOUPIN: [. . .] you were in the class of 1900, 1900, 1902, right?
>
> POMMARD: 1903, 1903, and for you, then it was 1906?
>
> TOUPIN: 1906 yes, in Clermond-Ferrand.
>
> POMMARD: You were in the cavalry?
>
> TOUPIN: In the infantry, in the infantry.
>
> POMMARD: But the infantry was not in Clermond, remember, it was the cavalry, you must have been in Toulouse, in Toulouse the infantry.
>
> TOUPIN: I tell you in Clermond-Ferrand, go on, I remember well, the Café du Marronnier at the corner.
>
> POMMARD: Charbonnier, the Café Charbonnier. (*M*, 26–28)

In *Architruc* the dissolving power of the reflection appears in the form of a disguise. To dispel his boredom and fear of death, King Architruc asks his minister, Baga, to improvise different identities. But this game of illusions heats up into tragedy when Architruc mistakes Death, which enters carrying a scythe, for yet another one of the roles Baga has been incarnating.

L'Hypothèse is perhaps the play where Pinget has expressed most grippingly the ease with which the reflection swallows up the reality it is supposed to merely present. The protagonist, the ever-tormented writer Mortin, is rehearsing a lecture he is going to deliver before a public during which he will try to explain the disappearance of a manuscript. Although the idea is never explicitly stated, it is very possible that Mortin destroyed the text himself for fear that his literary ability was unequal to his lofty artistic aspirations. In any event, while he is speaking about his activity as a writer, a filmed image of the latter is projected on a screen behind him. It doubles in size as the action progresses. It even multiplies, overwhelming him physically. It challenges Mortin, contradicts him, and advances its own hypotheses until, utterly humiliated, the speaker withdraws into silence, repeating in a hesitating and broken voice the refrain that we have already quoted and that negates his existence: "The lost opportunities to remain silent."

The action here seems to underscore the unbridgeable gap between the ideal Self and the actual one. The ideal Self (Mortin the writer) may be only an illusion in the protagonist's mind. It may simply reflect his yearning for an unattainable perfection. But this reflection so terrifies Mortin the orator that he feels himself condemned from the start: "The author, where is the author," he keeps repeating, which is another way of saying, "Who am I?" and "Where am I?" He tries to flush out the author of the manuscript, but it is the author who ends up devouring him. The more panic-stricken Mortin becomes, the more his language, by its very incoherence, betrays his mental disintegration. The typography of the text suggests the whirlpool of madness into which the protagonist is being engulfed:

> why
> because why because why
> because why because why
> because why because why
> because why because why
> because (*H*, 184)

And so, Mortin's run-through of his lecture constitutes his swan song while at the same time illustrating the breakdown of language as a vehicle of communication.

In *L'Hypothèse* words break down when Mortin's self-confidence collapses. In *Abel et Bela, Identité,* and *Paralchimie* they acquire a disquieting yet fascinating will of their own. Like sorcerers' apprentices, protagonists in these plays unwittingly unleash a force they can no longer control. It takes over completely, sweeping them along in its wake. *Abel et Bela* focuses on two actors who entertain illusions about being playwrights. All the while that they endeavor to construct a truly significant drama, the poor misguided thespians wrack their brains to figure out the essence of the genre. During the course of their conversation (Abel provides the ideas, Bela assesses them), their text takes shape and unravels at the same time. To galvanize their potential audience, Abel hits upon the idea of staging a celebrity-studded party. Bela prefers an orgy. Gradually the dialogue they try to bring to life gets stalled. Protagonists and accessories decrease in number. Lines of dialogue follow one another yet have a strange sameness. What started as a light boulevard comedy threatens to skid into lurid melodrama. Styles criss-cross, blend into one another, as Abel and Bela fail in their attempts to breathe life into their ideal theater. To realize it, they set off in an entirely different direction. They deliver monologues on their lost youth, on love and death, thinking that here at last are subjects worthy of being evoked by drama. They soon come to the conclusion, however, that this raw material is insufficiently theatrical, so they again latch onto the idea of revving up the action.

The two actors may be bogged down in a quagmire of doubt. The audience, on the other hand, becomes increasingly aware as the play "progresses" that the real interest of the drama lies in the mysterious interrelationships of words. Abel and Bela may use them to evoke situations they feel are capable of exciting their public, but it is the complex, reverberating network of words that give this new conception of theater its raison d'être. Abel eventually shares the audience's awareness of what Pinget's theater is all about. When Bela reprimands him for repeating the same dialogue and action from one act to the next, Abel defends his conviction vigorously:

> ABEL: So you realize that the first act was purely gratuitous . . . and that it doesn't really start until the second act. In other words, that it's all a question of words, one word carrying along another after it.
> BELA: Well then it's not the second act, it's a replay of the first.
> ABEL: It's the second act. A question of words. (*AB*, 99)

Once the author has used his two "spokesmen" to express his views on the nature of theater, he puts an end to their interminable and futile discussion by materializing the much-discussed orgy before their astonished eyes: "The light becomes dazzling. A sumptuous set suddenly dresses up the stage. [. . .] Then arrival from the back of three elegant and smiling couples. Abel and Bela remain transfixed. The lighting dims as the couples begin to undress." This is a truly magical moment that can only be produced in the world of the imagination. After toying with a fanciful idea, the protagonists are subjugated by it when it takes on a concrete, living form.[12]

Identité and *Paralchimie* reincarnate the writer Mortin. This time, however, he is the subject rather than the object of the investigation. As the curtain rises on both plays Mortin is seated at his table, engrossed in his manuscripts. In both cases two other characters will intrude and disrupt his meditations: the Doctor and Noémi in *Identité* and Erard and Lucile in *Paralchimie*. In addition, the two plays conjure up a whimsical, almost baroque atmosphere. In *Identité* Mortin wears a dressing gown, whereas the doctor sports a morning coat and striped trousers, and the maid a long, sumptuous apartment dress. *Paralchimie* has a very simplified set, evoking in part an alchemist's study, in part that of a sound engineer of bygone times. In this particular play Mortin appears as "an old man with a disquieting and ridiculous bearing." Here Pinget is not so much deforming reality as he is distorting fantasy itself.

Identité revolves around Mortin's uncertainty as to whether or not he will dismiss the Doctor. At one moment he orders the latter out of his sight forever; at another, he clamors for the medical man's presence. Whether Mortin throws the Doctor out or recalls him urgently, the motive is always the same: the magnum opus on which he is at work. It gets sketched out under his direction and with the help of his two subordinates. But Mortin cannot count on them. They soon rebel against his tyranny by stealing his words, just as the images projected against the wall had done in *L'Hypothèse*. The author strives vainly to regain his power. The play ends as he is condemned once more to silence.

Obviously, then, *Identité* symbolizes the triumph of word over character. The writer who claimed superiority over language is compelled to submit to it or remain silent. Mortin's subjection to the discourse of which he thought he was the all-powerful master is thrown into striking relief when the roles played by the three protagonists are switched around. Far from deciding who will perform which function, Mortin is reduced, like the others, to being the mere instrument through which the verbal flow passes victoriously. He could easily cry out in despair, as he did in *L'Hypothèse*: "The author where is the author?" As I emphasized at the beginning of this study, one of the objectives of the New Novel was precisely to get rid of the omniscient author. For the novelist, the task is relatively easy to perform. All he need do is break up the omniscient authority into a multiplicity of narrators who thus fragment the vision to be presented. In the theater, however, the presence of different characters already ensures pluralistic viewpoints. Consequently, the playwright has several choices at his disposal. He can either suppress the omniscient author by using the different characters to express contradictions, as in *Autour de Mortin*, or he can arrange for one discourse, and one alone, to triumph. In the latter case (*Identité*) all of the protagonists fight to gain possession of the same spoken word.

In *Paralchimie* we meet with Mortin once more. He has aged but is still doggedly pursuing his ideal of art. This time he has come upon a new device: alchemy, or rather, as the play's title informs us, "paralchemy," a parallel form of alchemy for novices. As obsessed as ever by metaphysical considerations, the elderly author assigns to himself the awesome responsibility of deciphering our human nature: "Who are we," he asks. Perhaps it is the plumber who suggests alchemy as the supreme instrument of knowledge when he launches into his weird verbal chant: "(evacuation) [. . .] alimentation, fermentation, decoction, aeration, sublimation." Mortin's reaction shows both lucidity and naiveness. He senses that using paralchemic spells will unleash the infernal powers, yet he persists in thinking that he just might succeed in mastering them.

Having made his commitment to this occult science or pseudo-science, however, Mortin has thrown himself into the arms of Satan. The verbal machine he has set in motion will rattle on without him and even against him. His first failure is not long in coming. He tries in vain to produce an initial answer to his question based on answers that his niece Lucile has given him on the nature of the soul. Undiscouraged, he summons back his niece and valet, assigning them roles they are unwilling to play. Although dismayed, he tries nonetheless to reach his goal alone. But just then his two subordinates reappear, this time spouting words over which Mortin has absolutely no control:

LUCILE (Narrative tone):   That on the one hand the butcher was an ass and on the other the milliner was a goose, how can one expect under these conditions that anything sensible will emerge from this enterprise [. . .]

MORTIN: What's this story all about?

ERARD (Narrative tone):   Or that the butcher no more than the milliner had thought about the consequences of their initiative, it was all completely innocent, done spontaneously and without foreseeing an action of a duration superior to that needed to remedy the state we know about [. . .]

MORTIN   Could I get a word in? (*P*, 45–46)

Mortin furiously declares himself master of the discourse no matter what. But right off the bat, he carries on with the narrative, thereby demonstrating that he, too, has fallen victim to words. As the first act comes to an end, he finds an illusory reprieve in slumber. As soon as the curtain rises on the second act, Mortin's illusions are definitively dissipated. The verbal machine breaks down irreparably. He invokes, to no avail, alchemic powers such as the Ouroboros, Hermes psychopump, Sol and Luna. The process he had set in motion devours him in turn. The blindness that overcomes him at the end symbolizes the impossibility of grasping the ineffable through the approximate and refractory instrument that language provides.

The breakdown of the verbal machine and the moral collapse of those who believe they can make it bend to their will contains tragic overtones. To counteract them, Pinget introduces the element of humor. Its presence is ambiguous, however, because of its dual function. It both attenuates the impression of despair through laughter and intensifies it through exaggeration. It manifests itself first of all on the level of the play on words. In *Ici ou ailleurs* Mme Flan betrays her ignorance and vulgarity by piling bloopers one on top of another. She calls Watteau's famous painting *L'Embarquement pour Cythère* (*The Embarcation for Cythera*) *L'Embarquement pour clystère, clystère* meaning "enema." Later on her faulty pronunciation confuses the Old Testament with making money:

> FLAN: The day will come when no one will show an interest in you anymore. You will be like Job (she pronounces Djob) on his dung heap.
>
> CLOPE: There is not a shadow of Anglomania in this story!
>
> FLAN: What do you mean?
>
> CLOPE: You don't say Djob you say Job.
>
> FLAN: They all say Djob now. (*IA*, 130)

Another hilarious example of this brand of humor occurs in *La Manivelle*, based on the expression *pension alimentaire,* which normally means a living allowance. But here the half-deaf, half-senile old Toupin coins a bizarre connotation for the term, making it refer to meals in a boardingschool simply because the word *pension,* meaning boardinghouse or boardingschool, makes his mind go off on a tangent:

POMMARD: Did she have a living allowance [*pension alimentaire*]?

TOUPIN: What?

POMMARD: A living allowance after her divorce.

TOUPIN: Good gracious they put her in a boardingschool and she was malnourished there, a little girl of two years old isn't that sad (*M*, 36)

In addition to the delight he takes in perverting words, Pinget provokes merriment by unleashing verbal cascades. He does so by accumulating rather strange terms, enumerating heterogeneous elements, and revving up his narratives, all of which suggest an overheated machine racing toward a breakdown. The words snowball on and on, acquiring an irresistible momentum and volume, rendering the question of meaning irrelevant. The farcical duet between Noémi and the Doctor in *Identité* constitutes a superb illustration of this verbal overabundance or overkill. The two characters recite two different monologues at the same moment, creating utter chaos:

DOCTOR: A fat child with a protruding bum such as there sometimes are, not naughty for his age but spoiled by his mother, the father didn't like that always recalling his own childhood, the smacks, being deprived of dessert, took revenge on his kid but fortunately was not there during the week, only on Sundays. It was a Sunday, then. So the mother said darling really don't rough up our son like that, etc.

NOEMI: Before leaving I went to see my brother's widow, I have never been able to call her my sister-in-law, I had to forewarn her, so she could be on her guard, not so much for her although now I don't have it in for her anymore but for me, for the consequences all that was going to have. I found her in her kitchen peeling onions. She still is in mourning that's her business but in black like that and her eyes swollen she reminded me of the burial, etc.

In *Paralchimie* this verbal delirium is accompanied by the occasional scatological allusion that stands in sharp, even shocking, contrast to Mortin's lofty spiritual ambitions, suggesting the inevitable degradation of noble motives:

PLUMBER: By going up from the exterior canal works to the interior siphon, passing through the various twists and turns, curves, bends, loops, orbs and similar figures that the drainage pipe

> composes just like the emptying pipe let alone the supplying, fermentation, decoction, segmentation, ventilation, sublimation, copper, lead, enamel, tin, antinomy and company, coming up as I said from there to the cause of the blockage of materials situated at the lowest level of the bowl I notice that these were of a kind . . .

MORTIN: Get to the point, plumber, get to the point.

PLUMBER: Well sir, there is not just crap.

MORTIN: Gosh!

This torrential outpouring of terms relating to plumbing so exacerbates the relationship of the two protagonists that they end up hurling Latin quotations of a rather unusual nature at one another:

PLUMBER: *Primum cacare*

MORTIN: *Primum vivere* (P, 20, 22)[13]

The absurd situations into which Pinget's characters are dragged through the perversion of words and reality have led a certain number of well-meaning yet misguided commentators to compare the playwright's dramatic vision to that of his illustrious contemporary, Samuel Beckett. What is more unfortunate is that in the course of this comparison, Pinget has often come out a poor second. Yet it suffices to examine his plays carefully and impartially to realize how different they are in conception and outlook. In the first place, as I pointed out à propos of *Lettre morte*, Pinget's characters are rooted in the recognizable context of everyday reality. M. Levert, like Pommard and Toupin, is retired. Louis works in a café. Architruc is a king; Baga is his minister. Mortin is a writer, with Néomi as his maid and Erard his valet. None of Beckett's characters are so "situated." They are essentially divorced from life, wandering about in some abstract space. In short, they are symbols of a rudderless humanity. Second—and this is the more important difference—one does not discern any tendency of the action to unravel in Beckett's theater. Here, as in Ionesco's dramas, the absurd is a given from the very outset. The audience is plunged into it immediately. From then on his plays simply exploit this factor. In fact, one could maintain that the absurd in Beckett's plays is strangely reassuring inasmuch as it is *there* from the start and never disappears. It paradoxically signifies nonsignificance.

In Pinget's dramatic universe, conversely, we start with situations and relationships which "make sense" only to witness their disintegration into perplexity, confusion, or chaos, if not all three. The absurd is thus an end result that we see developing progressively until it engulfs everything in its wake. In this respect, it would be no exaggeration to affirm that Pinget's theatre carries the vision of his novels to their ultimate consequences. As we have observed, the latter debunk the classical conception of the well-constructed novel by showing that the so-called logical sequence of events and reactions are the result of arbitrary manipulations. In his plays Pinget goes one step further. He creates a stunning theatrical illusion to prove to us that a coherent vision of reality is in itself a monumental illusion. Yet far from giving us a lesson in despair, his dramatic works, liberated from the artificial constraints of psychological motivation and logic, invite us to join the author in the endlessly inventive games he so enjoys playing.

Conclusion: An Artistic Identity

Having followed Robert Pinget on his voyage of self-discovery through the novel and the theater, we can now appreciate just how resounding a confirmation it represents of the artistic credo he expressed in 1972 during the Cerisy Colloquium and 10 years later in "Propos de New York." His works *do* favor subjectivity, personal expression, and individual talent or "innateness" as he calls it. They also illustrate his conviction that literature is the means of finding his particular "voice" and imposing his distinctiveness. If he loses his identity in the mundane sense during the creative process, it is only to acquire, through invention, an original being whose particular tones cannot be confused with any others. The most perceptive commentators of Pinget's texts have noticed to what extent writing for him and the search for his innermost self are synonymous. Ana Otten, among others, has coined the term "autofictiography" to describe his literary production, and declares that he "writes to find out who he is and what he thinks."[1] Michèle Praeger goes even further, viewing Pinget's works as "a means of ridding himself of a burdensome weight, a cleansing exercise, a catharsis."[2]

This all-pervading presence of the author explains the powerful impression of unity that emerges from his works. As I have repeatedly emphasized, a certain number of themes keep recurring in Pinget's texts: the endless possibilities for the unfolding of events within an endlessly fluid reality; the exorcizing of death through a mixture of unflinching lucidity and humor; anamnesis, the hurtling of the being backwards through chronological time to its origins, enabling it to penetrate into the realm of atemporality; the myth of rejuvenation linked to that of the eternal recurrence; and the yearning for immortality through artistic creation. If we were to single out one person within the author's fictional universe who encompasses them all, it would undoubtedly be Mortin. He may sorely lack on many occasions his creator's impish sense of humor; nevertheless, he does embody the latter's deepest aspirations. From the novels *Quelqu'un* to *L'Ennemi*, from the plays *L'Hypothèse* to *Paralchimie*, he, like Robert Pinget, is embarked on an endless search for the magical formula—the essential truth or truths of his being that will make him whole again.

The author's statements, then, that I quoted in Chapter 1, about his being loath to bare his soul, are not entirely accurate. Granted, he remains adamant about revealing details concerning his intimate "daily" life, but through his literary production, he projects an identity that affords us stunning insights into his spiritual depths without ever informing us about the events making up his existence. Such is the fascinating paradox of art that his alter ego, Monsieur Songe, expounds: "when you write about yourself, you are conjuring up a character who is both authentic and unauthentic. He is a creation of your mind, so while being you, he is no longer you." Reflecting in his convoluted way on the nature of the diary he keeps to record the fluctuations in his mind, Monsieur Songe says,

> The great difficulty when one writes one's diary [. . .] is to forget that one is not writing it for others . . . or rather not to forget that one is not writing it for a time when one will have become another person . . . or rather not to forget that one is another person when writing it . . . or rather not to forget that it must be of interest only for oneself at the immediate moment, that is to say, for someone who does not exist since one is another person as soon as one starts writing. . . . In short not to forget that it is a genre all the more untrue because it aims for more authenticity, because to write is to opt for untruthfulness, whether one wants it or not, and that it is better to resign oneself to it in order to cultivate a true genre that is called literature and aims for anything except the truth.[3]

Having introduced Monsieur Songe indirectly, it is only fitting that we flesh out the portrait of a character whom Pinget created back in 1956 for his own relaxation and entertainment, and as a respite from the arduous pursuits of writing novels or plays. A somewhat pale literary clone of the author, this crotchety, aging retiree has allowed Pinget to express some of his most intimate thoughts on life and art while providing him with the protection of his privacy, which only fiction can afford. After publishing three fragments of his alter ego's diary between 1972 and 1980,[4] he produced the whole diary in 1982, followed by Monsieur Songe's notebooks or *carnets*, which appeared successively under the titles *Le Harnais* (1984), *Charrue* (1985), and *Du nerf* (1990). A perusal of these works reveals in the elderly, semi-idle gentleman the hero of intellectual hesitation, as Jean-Claude Liéber so appropriately described him.[5] Monsieur Songe seems congenitally unable to carry an argument forward to its logical conclusion. He skims over issues rather than getting to the bottom of them. He is an amateur poet with neither the complexity nor the artistic ambitions of his creator. Still, he reflects in a disarmingly naive manner the vague impulses, the moments of irresoluteness, the doubts, and the deep-seated anxieties of the man who brought him into existence. Most important of all, using this person as an alter ego enables Pinget to confide in his readers while maintaining a respectable distance from them, which often takes on the form of impish humor. The author can thus reveal his soul and protect his privacy at the same time.

This tendency is strikingly evident in the views on the whole business of writing Pinget has his literary "clone" expound on. Pinget's fascination with the virtually limitless possibilities of expression that the raw material of life offers the writer and the delight he takes in enticing his readers into inextricable mazes come out in Monsieur Songe's statement—a trifle exaggerated perhaps—about contradicting oneself. Far more than a writer's privilege, contradicting oneself "is the only source of joy that he has found in his work of sheer slavery to use the right term."[6] Pursuing his belief that the life of a writer implies a slavish commitment to his art, his alter ego asserts that "in order to give his notes the appearance of freshness, he must work on them with such tenacity that freshness has become synonymous for him with perspiration" (*N*, 51).

The crabby old gentleman reserves some of his funniest comments, however, for Variant II of the final chapter of *Monsieur Songe*, entitled "L'Hôtel des voyageurs." Here he lambastes certain theoreticians and practitioners of the New Novel who would view literature as nothing more than the product of an intellectual process that just happens to function in the body and mind of a particular individual called the writer—a rather expendable entity—and that consequently can be broken down into its components like any other. Also, by drawing up an exhaustive catalog of the techniques that, applied mechanically, would turn writing into a dehumanized and dehumanizing activity, he parodies the excesses of formalist criticism. The latter, according to Monsieur Songe, believe that the power a novel exerts on its readers depends on its obscurity. To be considered "modern," the intelligent writer must utterly confuse his reading public by suppressing all traces of plot, character, place, logical linkage, punctuation, and grammatical clues. One must not be able to guess who is speaking or what they are speaking about.

Through the devastating wit of his alter ego, Pinget proclaims the right of the writer not only to exist but to flourish, and he gives notice of his refusal to allow his texts to be analyzed simply as fields of signifiers where transformational processes occur. As for the coup de grace, the author has his clone administer it in the conclusion of *Monsieur Songe*, where he brings back for a final appearance the pretentious harridan Mlle Lorpailleur. Since we last saw her in *Le Libera*, she has recycled herself into a born-again new critic of the 1970s variety. She now spouts the jargon and extols the rather rancid theories that were the rage several decades ago. She has repudiated spontaneity and inspiration in favor of the "scientific" study of texts. With an enthusiasm equalled only by her ignorance and pretentiousness, she tears into a pseudo-scientific discourse where all kinds of undigested terms of the new critical methodology whirl around in utter confusion: "signifier, signified, referent, metaphor, metonymy, morpheme, phoneme, syntagma, algorithm, mise en abyme, metalanguage, connotation, structurality, semanticity, poeticity" (*MS*, 134). Is it any wonder, then, that the Sunday poet and no doubt his creator as well prefer the naive but heartfelt lyricism of the local poet, Mlle Louise Bottu?

Even funnier and more revealing are the descriptions of Monsieur Songe's hang-ups or dilemmas. Not that they are identical to the author's. The former fills up his empty existence by attributing an overriding importance to its trivialities, whereas the anguish and fears Pinget experiences are linked to lofty aspirations that can be threatened by failure. But by mocking Monsieur Songe's overblown nonproblems, his creator is indirectly poking fun at his own tendency to take himself too seriously. Each time he deflates his alter ego's vanity he proves to himself that the world is really not coming to an end and, as a result, that he need not feel overwhelmed by his own problems, however significant they may appear. Laughing at his literary clone has definite therapeutic value.

The main stumbling block in Monsieur Songe's relationships with others is his inability to be spontaneous and to let himself go. He tries to make up for his spiritual void by incessantly observing himself. His niece exhorts him to abandon this sterile activity and live for the moment. But the lady's epicurean philosophy gets in the way of her uncle's artistic principles. How can one savor the present moment and record it simultaneously? In order to rejuvenate himself, Monsieur Songe would have to abandon writing, which is his raison d'être. Yet as he discovers to his astonishment, it is his concern for and commitment to language that is having pernicious effects on his existence. The love of language is a very selfish pleasure. As his maid, Sosie, remarks with aphoristic concision:

"Love of phrases, dislike of people." A consequence of this love of language and of the self-surveillance that accompanies it is a chronic inability to take action of any kind. Monsieur Songe spends so much of his energy being conscious of himself, he wastes so much time recording the slightest fluctuations of his mind that he no longer enjoys being alive (*MS*, 99). Being walled up in his solitude, writing remains the only activity testifying to his presence on earth, the only function enabling him to anesthetize the anguish of nonbeing over which our human condition is hanging.

Hence Monsieur Songe's determination to pursue his literary exercises even if they are worth nothing. They consist essentially in noting the insignificant and manufactured little daily dramas and in blowing them up to colossal proportions as though they were earth-shattering, metaphysical issues. In Section V of the chapter "Le Retraité" he constructs a ponderous chain of reasoning to decide whether he will drink his coffee while it is hot or let it cool off so that he can devote himself to a futile meditation and/or take a nap. In Section XVII of the same chapter he records for posterity all the errands that he and his maid are supposed to do, were supposed to have done, did half-do, or were going to do. And in the chapter entitled "Une Fête chez Monsieur Songe" he relates the mind-boggling nightmare into which a large family reunion degenerates when, aided and abetted by his maid, the well-meaning yet totally unrealistic old man miscalculates the number of nephews, nieces, great-nephews, great-nieces, and their respective offsprings who would conceivably accept his invitation to converge upon his dwelling.

While hilarious in themselves, these episodes also betray a deeply rooted fear of old age and the decline of one's faculties. Monsieur Songe exorcizes this fear in the only way he knows: he writes about it. Since his creator has a marvellous sense of humor, his alter ego evokes this dreadful prospect of aging and growing senile without ever lapsing into maudlin sentimentality. For any self-respecting writer, the worst scenario imaginable is the drying up of his inspiration. With one foot already in the grave (or so he imagines) and having completed his *mémoires,* Monsieur Songe senses that he has reached the end of the line: "It seems to him suddenly that he has nothing more to do, nothing more to say, as though the completion of this work sounded the death knell of his very existence."[7]

The particular anguish afflicting the writer is, however, the knowledge that there is no such thing as retirement per se. Once bitten by literary madness, he will always be stricken. So whether his talent has dried up or not, he cannot free himself from this enslavement: "Take up the horrible harness again joyfully writes Monsieur Songe. And then he crosses out the horrible. And then he crosses out harness. What is left is take up again joyfully" (*H*, 15). He will continue scribbling in his notebook until the candle is snuffed out, even though he realizes that the act of writing for him is now only a form of evacuation in the medical sense of the term. He describes this phenomenon with a mixture of innocence and mischief in the chamber pot episode, which he sends off to the editorial board of a newspaper: "First empty, then full. Two paragraphs" (*C*, 29).

Behind this depiction of the Sunday poet's decline we can make out the contours of a myth, that of the fall from grace. Monsieur Songe walks about like the survivor of some Herculean struggle that has left him physically battered and traumatized forever: "You will see him in the street all misshapen, aching all over, limping and trembling making the rounds of the neighbourhood cafés" (*C*, 55). To emphasize the point, Pinget (or his alter ego) adds this ferocious comment: "It is the *vita nuova* of Monsieur Songe." As punishment for his misguided literary ambitions, the students get him drunk and carry the old jerk around in triumph. He has become the very symbol of madness. The old man fights this public contempt and self-loathing with the only weapon he has left: self-mockery. He draws from his very failure a source of entertainment. He makes of his powerlessness the theme of his writing: "There we go, there we go he's latched on to this little story to exercise his imagination. He gets out of bed, puts on his dressing gown, sits down at his table, takes a pen, a piece of paper and writes . . . that he gets out of bed, puts on his dressing gown, sits down . . ." (*C*, 12).

The old scribbler continues pretending that he's inspired even though nothing happens. He persists in hitching himself up to the same plough. Far from concealing the disaster, he jeers at it: "Just the idea that his notes will not make anyone laugh makes him laugh at the thought of continuing them." Through this ferocious self-derision, Monsieur Songe can resist the temptation of self-pity and so preserve some semblance of dignity.

Fortunately, Robert Pinget need not fear the jeers and oblivion that are the lot of his antihero. Whatever the artistic shortness of breath from which he may be suffering at present, his important production will ensure his survival. As though to serve notice to the world that he should not be confused with his alter ego, the author, at the age of 74, demonstrated that he could still perform little miracles. His latest novel, *Théo, ou le temps neuf*, has a marvellous freshness and gracefulness that one does not find in his previous works. It relates the tender relationship between an aging uncle (Mortin or Pinget himself?) and his young nephew. During the course of their dialogues it becomes obvious that the extremely inquisitive, perceptive, and winsome child embodies the future generations of readers who will guarantee the writer's triumph over the ravages of chronological time whenever they immerse themselves in his books. His literary identity, the only one worth remembering, will thus survive in the weightlessness of the forever new, atemporal time. Thus as Pinget enters the final, nocturnal period of his life, he can derive solace and joy from the two sentences that appear toward the end of this charming little book: "And may the words of the child resurrect those of the poets. Therein salvation."[8]

Notes and References

Chapter One

1. L.-A. Zbinden, "Robert Pinget: 'Je n'ai pas de vie autre que celle d'écrire,'" *Gazette de Lausanne*, 4 November 1965. This and all subsequent translations are my own.

2. Madeleine Renouard, "Entre sensibilité et intelligence," *Revue des Deux Mondes*, November 1990, 71.

3. For this biographical section as well as for the division of Pinget's literary production into cycles, I am indebted to Robert M. Henkels, Jr., whose *Robert Pinget: The Novel as Quest* (Tuscaloosa: University of Alabama Press, 1979) was a trailblazer for further studies on the French novelist in North America.

4. Jean Roudaut, "Monsieur Pinget" (interview with Pinget), *Magazine Littéraire*, no. 232 (July–August 1986): 90; hereafter cited in text.

5. Madeleine Renouard, *Robert Pinget à la lettre* (Paris: Belfond, 1993), 21–22.

6. The preceding remarks are a résumé of a portion of the same interview with Pinget in *Magazine Littéraire*, 93.

7. Seen in Réal Ouellet, *Les Critiques de notre temps et le Nouveau Roman* (Paris: Garnier Frères, 1972), 11.

8. For a detailed discussion of these two writers' views on the New Novel as expressed at the colloquium in 1982 at New York University, see *Three Decades of the French New Novel*, ed. Lois Oppenheim (Urbana and Chicago: University of Illinois Press, 1986), 179–94.

9. Laurent Le Sage, *The French New Novel: An Introduction and a Sampler* (University Park: Pennsylvania State University Press, 1962), 13.

10. Edmund Husserl (1859–1938) is the originator of phenomenology, which he tried to establish as a rigorous science and a theory of knowledge in the service of other sciences, notably in *Leading Ideas for a Phenomenology* (1913) and *Cartesian Meditations* (1931). He proposed a very fruitful critique of contemporary logic in his *Formal Logic and Transcendental Logic* (1929). In addition to Jean-Paul Sartre, he had a marked influence on another prominent French philosopher, Emmanuel Lévinas.

11. "Propos de New York," *Nouvelle Revue Française*, no. 368 (April 1983): 95–104.

Chapter Two

    1. See "Propos de New York," 104–105.
    2. *Entre Fantoine et Agapa* (Paris: Editions de Minuit, 1966), 9: hereafter cited in text as *EFA*.
    3. See "La Cassette de Robert Pinget," in *La Chouette*, special issue (1991): 5.
    4. *Mahu, ou le matériau* (Paris: Editions de Minuit, 1952), 212; hereafter cited in text as *M*.
    5. *Le Renard et la boussole* (Paris: Editions de Minuit, 1953), 92–93; hereafter cited in text as *LRB*.
    6. *Graal Flibuste* (Paris: Editions de Minuit, 1956), 7: hereafter cited in text as *GF*.
    7. *Baga* (Paris: Editions de Minuit, 1958), 66; hereafter cited in text as *B*.
    8. See Olivier de Magny, "*Baga* par Robert Pinget," *Les Lettres Nouvelles* (October 1959): 452–53.

Chapter Three

    1. *Le Fiston* (Paris: Editions de Minuit, 1959), 17–18; hereafter cited in text as *LF*.
    2. "Narre" obviously evokes the term *narrateur*. By using this name, Pinget may be poking fun at novelists who act like omniscient creators, sparing their readers no details about the characters in their works of fiction.
    3. *Clope au dossier* (Paris: Editions de Minuit, 1961), 19; hereafter cited in text as *CD*.
    4. Quoted in Jean-Claude Liéber's masterful article "Le Procès du réalisme," which appears at the end of the 1986 Editions de Minuit volume of Pinget's *L'Inquisitoire* (p. 496).
    5. In the same article Liéber states, "*L'Inquisitoire* is for me Robert Pinget's most remarkable novel. It recapitulates his imaginary universe and is at the same time an experimental work. The critique that begins with the cross-examination of the servant is both that of an archaic world and an outdated form. Reality is only an illusion, a construction of the mind, an artistic effect. Today's reader appreciates the work's science-fiction atmosphere even more than its documentary or 'Balzacian' aspect. The servant is treated like a laboratory animal, a rat in a labyrinth forced to answer instinctively questions of a digital type (yes or no), which makes it possible to classify information without taking the narrator's emotions or instincts into account" (494).
    6. *L'Inquisitoire* (Paris: Editions de Minuit, 1962), 115; hereafter cited in text as *I*.
    7. Michael Foucault, *La Volonté de savoir* (Paris: Gallimard, 1976), 119.
    8. *Quelqu'un* (Paris: Editions de Minuit, 1965), 9–10; hereafter cited in text as *Q*.
    9. Dominique Rollin, "Un rire de deux cent cinquante pages," *Nouvel Observateur*, 15–21 November 1965.

Chapter Four

    1. See pp. 226–46 in Jean-Claude Liéber's unpublished work, "Robert Pinget, ou Le Salut par l'écriture" (1986), based on his doctoral thesis, "Réalisme et fiction dans l'oeuvre de Robert Pinget," University of Paris, 1986.

    2. See Tony Duvert, "La Parole et la fiction," *Critique* (May 1968): 540–55.

    3. *Le Libera* (Paris: Editions de Minuit, 1969), 11; hereafter cited in text as *L*.

    4. The word *creux* means "hollow." Hence the allusion to a mold into which all future victims will be cast.

    5. Jane Davidson, "Pinget and Music," *Chouette*, special issue (1991): 64.

    6. *Passacaille* (Paris: Editions de Minuit, 1969), 8; hereafter cited in text as *P*.

Chapter Five

    1. Jan Baetens, *Aux frontiéres du récit: Fable de Robert Pinget comme nouveau nouveau roman* (Toronto: Paratexte, 1988).

    2. *Fable* (Paris: Editions de Minuit, 1971), 25; hereafter cited in text as *F*.

    3. Stephen Bann, "Extremities of Discourse: Walter Pater and Robert Pinget," *Signs of Change* (Summer 1986): 130–33.

    4. The legend of Narcissus is related by the Latin poet Ovid in his text entitled *Metamorphoses*, book 3, and by Conon in his *Narrationes*. Pinget borrows heavily from Ovid. He acknowledges his debt indirectly to the Roman poet by having his narrator exclaim on p. 54 of *Fable*: "Who is dictating these laments, which ham actor has made up his mind to do me in?"

    5. Robert Henkels and Esteban Egea, "Using a Computer-Generated Concordance in Stylistic Analysis of Pinget's *Fable*," *Computers in the Humanities* (Autumn 1978): 325–38.

    6. *Cette voix* (Paris: Editions de Minuit, 1975), 34; hereafter cited in text as *CV*.

    7. *L'Apocryphe* (Paris: Editions de Minuit, 1980), 147; hereafter cited in text as *A*.

    8. Stephen Bann, *"L'Apocryphe* ou la loi nouvelle," *Revue de Belles Lettres* 1 (1982): 52.

    9. The complete verse from which these two words are taken is *"Ite domum saturae, venit Hesperus, ite capellae"* ("Return home, you are glutted, little nanny goats, return home").

    10. Jean Roudaut, "Un beau livre," *Revue de Belles Lettres* (1982): 42.

    11. In 1991 Pinget published a very short work, *Théo, ou le temps neuf*, which can be considered a novel of sorts. I refer to it in the Conclusion.

    12. See Marianne Alphant, "L'Ennemi intime," *Libération*, 3 September 1987.

13. *L'Ennemi* (Paris: Editions de Minuit, 1987), 54; hereafter cited in text as *E*.

14. See "Note sur *L'Ennemi*," *Libération*, 3 September 1987.

15. To further suggest this striving to eliminate confusion and achieve clarity, Pinget quotes fragments from liturgical prayers in Latin, such as the ones taken from the hymn of St. Ambrose: *"Procul recedant somnia / Etnoctium phantasmata"* ("Drive away vain dreams; / the fantasies of the night") (185). Or the two passages from the "Veni creator" by Raban Maur: *"Accende lumen sensibus"* ("Light up your light in our senses") (170) and *"Hostem repellas longius"* ("Repulse the enemy") (185).

Chapter Six

1. Robert Pinget's plays were published as follows: *Paralchimie*, 1973; *Identité*, 1971; *Abel et Bela*, 1971; *Autour de Mortin*, 1965; *Hypothèse*, 1961; *Ici ou ailleurs*, 1961; *Architruc*, 1961; *La Manivelle*, 1960; *Lettre morte*, 1959. Space limitations do not permit discussion of the author's radio plays, despite their high quality. This discussion of the thematic material and techniques used in the stage plays, however, offers the reader a good idea of the preoccupations expressed in the radio plays.

2. *Lettre morte* (Paris: Editions de Minuit, 1959); hereafter cited in text as *LM*.

3. *La Manivelle* (Paris: Editions de Minuit, 1960); hereafter cited in text as *M*.

4. *Paralchimie*, with *Architruc*, *L'Hypothèse*, and *Nuit* (Paris: Editions de Minuit, 1973); hereafter cited in text as *P*, *AR*, *H*, and *N*, respectively.

5. Arnaud Rykner, *Théâtres du Nouveau Roman: Sarraute-Pinget-Duras* (Paris: José Corti, 1988), 87.

6. Olivier de Magny, "Le Théâtre de Robert Pinget," *Cahiers Renaud-Barrault* 53 (February 1966): 50.

7. Joyce O. Lowrie, "The Function of Repetition in Pinget's *Lettre morte*," *French Review* 49, no. 5 (April 1976): 687.

8. *Ici ou ailleurs* (Paris: Edition de Minuit, 1961), 53. Hereafter cited in text as 1A.

9. Jean-Jaques Gautier, *Deux fauteuils d'orchestre* (Paris: Flammarion, 1962), 331–32.

10. Gérard Genette, *Figures I* (Paris: Edition Points Seuil, 1982), 21.

11. Anne C. Murch, "Couples et reflets dans le théâtre de Robert Pinget," *Revue Romane* (October 1970): 164.

12. *Abel and Bela* has often been compared to Molière's one-act play *L'Impromptu de Versailles*. Like the seventeenth-century playwright, Pinget uses his characters to express his conception of the nature of theater and the pleasure it can bring his audience.

13. The two Latin lines can be translated as "First to crap" and "First to live."

Conclusion

1. Anna Otten, "The Search for Identity in the Work of Robert Pinget," *Review of Contemporary Fiction* (Summer 1983): 152.
2. Michèle Praeger, *Les Romans de Robert Pinget: Une écriture des possibles* (Lexington, Ky.: French Forum Publishers, 1987), 40.
3. *Monsieur Songe* (Paris: Editions de Minuit 1982), 93; hereafter cited in text as *MS*.
4. These three fragments appeared previously in literary magazines or in anthologies: *Le Retraité* (*The Retiree*) was published in Germany in a volume of children's stories under the title *Herr Traumer* (1972); the section "Le Mois d'août" ("The Month of August") was published in its much longer original version in the review *Minuit 13* in March 1975; the section "Une fête chez Monsieur Songe" ("A Celebration at Monsieur Songe's Home") was published in *Bas de casse* in the spring of 1980.
5. Jean-Claude Liéber, "Monsieur Songe," *La Chouette*, special issue (1991): 29.
6. *Du nerf* (Paris: Editions de Minuit, 1990), 28; hereafter cited in text as *N*.
7. *Charrue* (Paris: Editions de Minuit, 1985), 29; hereafter cited in text as *C*.
8. *Théo, ou le temps neuf* (Paris: Editions de Minuit, 1991), 85.

Selected Bibliography

PRIMARY WORKS

Books

Entre Fantoine et Agapa. Jarnac: Editions de Feu, 1951. New edition. Paris: Editions de Minuit, 1966.

Mahu, ou le matériau. Paris: R. Laffont, 1952. New edition. Paris: Editions de Minuit, 1956.

Le Renard et la boussole. Paris: Gallimard, 1953. New edition. Paris: Editions de Minuit, 1971.

Graal Flibuste. Paris: Editions de Minuit, 1956. Unabridged version. Paris: Editions de Minuit, 1966.

Baga. Paris: Editions de Minuit, 1958.

Le Fiston. Paris: Editions de Minuit, 1959.

Lettre morte. English text by Samuel Beckett. Paris: Editions de Minuit, 1960. With *La Manivelle*, a radio play.

Clope au dossier. Paris: Editions de Minuit, 1961.

Ici ou ailleurs. Paris: Editions de Minuit, 1961. With *Architruc* and *Abel et Bela*.

L'Inquisitoire. Paris: Editions de Minuit, 1962.

Autour de Mortin. Paris: Editions de Minuit, 1965.

Quelqu'un. Paris: Editions de Minuit, 1965.

Le Libera. Paris: Editions de Minuit, 1968. Accompanied by a reprinted preface by the author. New Edition. Paris: Editions de Minuit, 1984. Includes preface of the first edition.

Passacaille. Paris: Editions de Minuit, 1969.

Fable. Paris: Editions de Minuit, 1971.

Identité. Paris: Editions de Minuit, 1971. With *Abel et Bela*.

Paralchimie. Paris: Editions de Minuit, 1973. With *Architruc*, *L'Hypothèse*, and *Nuit*.

Cette voix. Paris: Editions de Minuit, 1975.

L'Apocryphe. Paris: Editions de Minuit, 1980.

Monsieur Songe. Paris: Editions de Minuit, 1982.

Le Harnais. Paris: Editions de Minuit, 1984.

Charrue. Paris: Editions de Minuit, 1985.

Un Testament bizarre. Paris: Editions de Minuit, 1986. With *Mortin pas mort, Dictée, Sophisme et Sadisme, Le Chrysanthème*, and *Lubie*.

L'Ennemi. Paris: Editions de Minuit, 1987.

Du nerf. Paris: Editions de Minuit, 1990.

Théo, ou le temps neuf. Paris: Editions de Minuit, 1991.

Theoretical Writings

"Le Nouveau Roman est-il mort?" *Nouvelles Littéraires*, 30 September–6 October 1976, 4.

"Propos de New York." Colloquium on the Nouveau Roman. City University of New York, October 1982. *Nouvelle Revue Française* 368 (1 September 1983): 95–104.

"Pseudo-principes d'esthétique." *Nouveau Roman: Hier, aujourd'hui*, 311–24. Paris: Union Générale d'Edition, 1972.

"Toute ma vie a passé dans mes livres." *Le Monde des Livres*, 5 December 1980, 18.

ENGLISH TRANSLATIONS

About Mortin. Translated by Barbara Bray. In *Plays*, vol. 2. London: Calder & Boyars, 1967. Includes *Architruc* and *The Hypothesis*.

The Apocrypha. Translated by Barbara Wright. New York: Red Dust, 1986.

Baga. Translated by J. Stevenson. London: John Calder, 1967.

Between Fantoine and Agapa. Translated by Barbara Wright. New York: Red Dust, 1982.

A Bizarre Will and Other Plays. Translated by Barbara Wright. Introduction by Madeleine Renouard. New York: Red Dust, 1989.

Clope. Translated by John Calder. London: John Calder, 1963.

The Enemy. Translated by Barbara Wright. New York: Red Dust, 1991.

The Inquisitory. Translated by Donald Watson. London: Calder & Boyars, 1966. New York: Grove Press, 1966.

The Libera Me. Translated by Barbara Wright. London: John Calder, 1972.

Mahu, or the Material. Translated by Alan Sheridan-Smith. London: John Calder, 1967.

Monsieur Levert. Translated by Richard Howard. New York: Grove Press, 1961.

Monsieur Songe. Translated by Barbara Wright. New York: Red Dust, 1987. With *The Harness* and *Plough*.

No Answer. Translated by Richard Coe. London: John Calder, 1976.

Passacaglia. Translated by Barbara Wright. New York: Red Dust, 1978.

Recurring Melody. Translated by Barbara Wright. London: John Calder, 1975.

Someone. Translated by Barbara Wright. London: John Calder, 1983.

That Voice. Translated by Barbara Wright. New York: Red Dust, 1982.

SECONDARY WORKS

Book-Length Studies

Baetens, Jan. *Aux frontières du récit: "Fable" de Robert Pinget comme nouveau Nouveau Roman*. Toronto: Editions Paratexte; Louvain: Université Pers

Leuven, 1987. A perceptive interpretation of one of Pinget's most haunting novels. According to Baetens, Pinget has taken the Nouveau Roman one step further by creating in this particular work a closed-circuit novel without any connection to external reality.

Baqué, Françoise. *Le Nouveau Roman*. Paris: Bordas, 1972. Concise, accurate appraisals of some of Pinget's earlier works.

Bothorel, Nicole, Francine Dugast, and Jean Thoraval. *Les Nouveau Romanciers*. Paris: Bordas, 1976. Solid assessment of Pinget's significance as a writer within the Nouveau Roman context.

Esslin, Martin. *Le Théâtre de l'absurde*. Paris: Buchet-Chastel, 1971. Stimulating views on Pinget's theater, even if one does not always agree.

Henkels, Robert. *Robert Pinget: The Novel as Quest*. Tuscaloosa: University of Alabama Press, 1979. A ground-breaking study in the English-speaking world of Pinget's works up till 1978. Includes a short biography, analyses of his novels and plays, as well as a comparison between his works and those of such other Nouveau Romanciers as Beckett and Robbe-Grillet.

Liéber, Jean-Claude. "Robert Pinget, ou le salut par l'écriture." Doctoral dissertation, University of Paris, 1986. An outstanding, very detailed study of all of Pinget's works up till 1986, tracing his evolution as a writer and the changes taking place in his artistic vision.

Mercier, Vivian. *The New Novel: From Queneau to Pinget*. New York: Farrar, Straus & Giroux, 1971. Although not unreservedly enthusiastic, the views presented are quite insightful in their way.

Praeger, Michèle. *Les Romans de Robert Pinget: Une écriture des possibles*. Lexington: French Forum Publishers, 1986. A very interesting analysis of the writing process as illustrated in Pinget's novels with keen insights into his art.

Renouard, Madeleine. *Robert Pinget à la lettre: Entretiens avec Madeleine Renouard*. Postscript by Jean-Michel Place. Paris: Belfond, 1983. Very probing and entertaining comments made by the author on his life and works.

Ricardou, Jean. *Pour une théorie du nouveau roman*. Paris: Seuil, 1971. Perceptive analysis of *Le Libera* using Ricardou's own theoretical approach to the Nouveau Roman. Emphasis placed on the destruction of the traditional character as illustrated in Pinget's novel.

———. *Le Nouveau Roman*. Paris: Seuil, 1990. Some very striking comments made on *Le Libera* to corroborate the notion of the "corrupted narrative" as well as an annotated bibliography of Pinget's novels.

Roudiez, Léon S. *French Fiction Today: A New Direction*. Rutgers: Rutgers University Press, 1972. An excellent assessment of Pinget's significance as a *Nouveau Romancier*.

Rykner, Arnaud. *Théâtres du Nouveau Roman*. Paris: José Corti, 1988. Very sound analysis of the relationship between Pinget's novels and his plays.

Vareille, Jean-Claude. *Fragments d'un imaginaire contemporain*. Paris: José Corti, 1989. A playful yet profound evocation of Pinget's imaginary world.

Special Issues of Journals

Bas de Casse. "Autour de Pinget." Edited by Nancy Blake, Philippe Jaworski, and Harry Blake. 2 (1980). The works of Pinget viewed from different angles in articles of high quality.

Revue de Belles Lettres. "Robert Pinget." Edited by Olivier Beetschen. 1 (1982). Well-balanced appraisals of Pinget's art in a variety of articles.

Etudes Littéraires. "Robert Pinget." Edited by Gaétan Brulotte and Robert Henkels. 19, no. 3 (Winter 1986–87). Many very high-caliber articles discussing the various facets of Pinget's art.

La Chouette. "Robert Pinget." Birbeck College, University of London. Edited by Madeleine Renouard (1991). Some outstanding contributions by Pinget specialists. Includes an interview with the writer as well as with the stage director Gabriel Cinque.

Articles

Bann, Stephen. "The Apocrypha or the New Law." *Review of Contemporary Fiction* (Summer 1983): 199–26. Emphasizes the tensions within Pinget's novel between the religious and calendar systems of measuring time. Very insightful.

Baumann, Su. "Passacaille, Passacaille? Etude sur un roman de Pinget." *Kentucky Romance Quarterly* 22, no. 1 (1975): 125–35. A perceptive analysis of the intricacies of *Passacaille.*

Duvert, Tony. "La Parole et la fiction." *Critique* (May 1968): 540–55. A masterful study of the expanding structure of *Le Libera* based on the opening pages of the novel.

Henkels, Robert, and Esteban Egea. "Using a Computer-Generated Concordance in Stylistic Analysis of Pinget's Fable." *Computers in the Humanities* (Autumn 1978): 325–38. This intelligent use of the computer to analyze the style of Pinget's *Fable* yields some very unusual results.

Lowrie, Joyce O. "The Function of Repetition in Pinget's *Lettre morte.*" *French Review* 49, no. 5 (April 1976): 676–88. Points out the double movement of construction and destruction in the play.

Magny, Olivier de. "Le Théâtre de Robert Pinget." *Cahiers Renaud-Barrault* 53 (February 1966): 49–54. A succinct yet probing appraisal of Pinget's theater.

Murch, Anne C. "Couples et reflets dans le théâtre de Robert Pinget." *Revue Romane* 2 (October 1970): 159–72. Focuses on the dilemma of loss of identity in Pinget's theater.

Otten, Anna. "The Search for Identity in the Work of Robert Pinget." *Review of Contemporary Fiction* (Summer 1983): 152–59. Puts forward the view that all of Pinget's work is an attempt at self-exploration.

Index

The Author

Léonard A. Rosmarin is a professor of French literature at Brock University, Ontario. He received his B.A. and M.A. from McGill University and his Ph.D. from Yale University. He has published studies on the seventeenth-century French moralist Saint-Evremond, *Saint-Evremond, artiste de l'euphorie*; on the French philosopher Emmanuel Lévinas, *Emmanuel Lévinas, humaniste de l'autre homme*; and on the Swiss novelist of Jewish origin Albert Cohen, *Albert Cohen, témoin d'un peuple*. In 1993 he was made Chevalier in the order of the Palmes Académiques by the government of France in recognition of his contribution to the cause of French letters.

acx -2630